THE REST IS PROPAGANDA

THE REST IS PROPAGANDA

STEVE IGNORANT

WITH

STEVE POTTINGER

SOUTHERN RECORDS
LONDON
2010

Published by Southern Records
P.O. BOX 59   LONDON   N22 1AR
www.southern.com
Cat No. 281659

1

ISBN: 978-0-9566746-0-9

Cover design by Paul Jackson at Othila

Set in Monotype Bembo Book
Typeset by Kes at Bracketpress

Printed and bound in England by the
MPG Books Group, Bodmin and King's Lynn

www.steveignorant.co.uk

Dedicated to Alan Sillitoe and Barry Hines

Preface

This is not a book about Crass, although there is a section about it; there's no exhaustive catalogue of Crass gigs or releases. This book is about me and the journey I made to become the lead vocalist in that band, and the journey I made (and am still travelling on) after that amazing band had finished. Photographs of Crass I kept to a minimum as there is so much documentation on the internet and in peoples' personal collections. Unfortunately, believe it or not, I've got very few photos of Schwartzeneggar or the Stratford Mercenaries; the ones I do have are mostly close-ups of me, so the lack of images from those bands isn't because of dislike or seeing them as less important. As for Conflict, I have no photographs at all.

The language used in the book is how I spoke at the time and certain terms aren't what I'd use today, so the P.C. police can stop writing those letters of disgust right now; also for obvious reasons some names had to be changed.

So here it is, the skeleton in my cupboard rattling for all to see.

Steve Ignorant, 2010.

I could be here all week thanking people, so I'll try and keep it brief. Steve, you've been a pleasure to work with, and a massive thanks to you and Jona for your hospitality, banana bread, and the odd pint down the pub. Thanks to friends for their encouragement, and the occasional kick up the proverbial when it was needed. Special thanks to Ness for her patience when I've spent day after day working on the laptop, lost to the world.

And above all, thanks to my parents, for their love and understanding.

– Steve Pottinger

Thanks must go to so many people, most of whom don't even know I exist, people whose work moved me to tears by showing me I wasn't alone.

Firstly, to Alan Sillitoe and Barry Hines for *Saturday Night and Sunday Morning* and *Kes* respectively. To Stan Barstow, Shelagh Delaney, Bill Naughton and Graham Greene. To Nell Dunn for *Up the Junction*. To Tony Richardson, Ken Loach, Karel Reisz and all the other film-makers who brought the above authors' books to the screen so brilliantly. To David Bradley for his heart-rending portrayal of Billy Casper – thanks so much mate – and to Albert Finney and Tom Courteney for their respective roles as Arthur Seaton and Billy Liar. To David Bowie, Toots and the Maytals, Joni Mitchell, Miles Davis and Ralph Vaughan Williams for the words and music. To my sister Carol for sharing her memories and some great nights down the 'arrer'. To Alan and Dee for their recollections and for their love and kindness. To Penny and Gee with love. To Bron also. To John Loder and Vic Short, my dear, dear friends – you went too soon and I still miss you. To Allison, Damon and all at Southern for your continual support no matter what, and to all the various people I've had the good fortune to get on stage with, it's been a privilege. To all the people who came to gigs, wrote letters, and to this day still show support, a massive Thank You. To Gordon, Nicky and Alice for being there with a lager and a shoulder to lean on.

A special thanks must go to Spot for his wonderful help with this book, I really couldn't have done it without you mate, thank you, and to Christian at Bracketpress for the typesetting.

And last but not least, thank you to Jona for the years of love and support in everything I do, even through my tantrums of self-pity and indulgence. A hundred thousand tons of love to you.

And to Oscar, thanks for the years of a wet snout in my earhole. Love you.

– Steve Ignorant

B C

D C

A C

BEFORE CRASS

Stoke

When I was two we moved back to Dagenham, and suddenly everything was in colour.

That's genuinely how I remember it. We were living at Nan and Granddad's, there was a sweet shop across the road, there was food and a garden we could play in. There was a cat and a dog and a TV. And life was in colour.

The contrast with Stoke couldn't have been greater.

For my mum, Dagenham was home, and my sister had been born in Barking, but although I'd been conceived in a field behind the Ford factory not far from where Nan and Granddad lived, by the time I arrived on the scene Mum and Dad had moved up to Stoke to be with his family. Or maybe simply to be away from hers. Either way, I was born in Newcastle-under-Lyme Infirmary at 11.45pm on 31st December 1957. Stephen Alan Williams, son to Bert and Patricia. I've never liked my name, but I'm really lucky Grandpa Williams – who was very proud of being Welsh – never got his way, otherwise I'd have been called William William Williams. Mind you, imagine the copyright I could be collecting now with those initials!

My parents had met and married down in Dagenham just after the war, when my dad was in the Army, serving in the King's Own Scottish Borderers, and my mum was a fresh-faced nineteen. My Granddad didn't approve at all – not only was my father a soldier, he was from the dirty North, and the St. Piers were better than *that* – and when my mum nearly died giving birth to Carol he went and found Bert, grabbed him by the throat and told him that if he ever got his daughter pregnant again he'd knock his block off.

So after the night in the field by Ford's, when my mum found out she was expecting me, she spent her shifts at the cinema where she was working as an usherette running up and down the stairs, hoping her little problem would be bounced away. It wasn't, and so, late in the summer of '57, twelve years into her marriage, with me on the way and no sympathy from her parents, my mum and my dad and my sister travelled back to Stoke to make a go of things there.

It's easy now, in a world where we take communication for granted, where everyone has a mobile phone and most people have cars, to forget what a big deal it was for my mum to leave Dagenham, the town she'd been born and bred in and a place she'd never left, and take the train up North with one small child and another one due. It meant severing all the ties with her own family, whose view was that she'd made her bed so she'd bloody well lie in it, and starting out again in the great, frightening unknown. Maybe my dad told her things would be fine there, maybe he told her the streets were paved with gold, who knows?

They weren't. Dad didn't find life out of uniform easy. He worked in the mines for a while, but it didn't last. Nothing did. Pretty quickly his life fell apart. He couldn't settle to anything but alcohol and petty theft, and he spent more time locked up than he spent with us. Mum said later he used to knock her about, but I was too young to remember that.

We wouldn't have got by without Granddad. Every week he'd send up a *Dagenham Post* for Mum, and hidden inside it would be a ten-bob note. Mum was drinking too now, so it didn't always get us through the week, and sometimes she'd spend the evening playing piano in pubs to bring in a few extra shillings.

One of my earliest memories is of lying in a big, cold bed with my sister in our old miner's house on the top of a hill, waiting for mum to come home. The room was empty, the walls and floorboards were bare, and we were too terrified of what might lurk on the cavernous unlit stairs to go outside and use the privy, so we tiddled in an old saucepan. We'd watch the bugs crawl across the ceiling in the flickering candlelight, or kneel on the bed and look down the hill to Etruria station, all yellow lights and smoke, waiting for mum to bring home a jamboree bag or a packet of crisps for our supper. Waiting to feel safe.

I don't know if it's because I was so young, or because life was so bleak, but my memories of Stoke ... it's as if they're all in black and white, and I can only see them out of the corner of my eye. If I look at them directly they dissolve into smoke, and are gone. What do I remember? Not much. Holding hands with Carol as we hurried home through long grass by a canal. An old lady called Granma Williams who smoked a clay pipe and had a broken mangle in her garden. Dad drowning our dog's pups in an old boiler in the garden. Crying because I knew Sugarplum, my favourite, couldn't be cuddled anymore. I remember the smell of tar on the roads. Riding on my dad's shoulders on a dusty, sunny street – I can still feel his hands on my ankles – and making him laugh by saying *It's not a duck, it's a dook*. And I remember one morning, my mum holding me in her arms saying *Look what your father's done* and showing me holes in all the walls where he'd taken a hammer to them, and all the windows put through. And later that night I remember standing at the top of the stairs with Carol, watching the coppers take him out in handcuffs, frothing at the mouth.

This was the last straw for Mum. There was no better, just worse; no richer, just poorer. Next morning she did the flit. She marched us out of the house and down to the train station.

She charmed the money for our tickets from a man she got talking to, and we took the train to London. I remember the pattern of the fabric on the seats, and the smell of the steam, and then we were in Dagenham and everything was in colour.

It wasn't exactly a happy homecoming – we arrived with nothing but the clothes on our back. And when we got down there Nan grabbed me and my sister and told my mum *They can stay, but you can bugger off.* It took Granddad speaking up for her to change Nan's mind – eventually she was persuaded family was family, and that was what mattered, and so we all moved in with Nan and Granddad in their council house at 3 Whitebarn Lane.

I only saw my dad once more. He came to visit, but had to stand at the back door. Mum told him she wanted a divorce, and then she said to me *Say goodbye to your father.* He held me to him and kissed me, pressed me into the herring-bone pattern in his brown overcoat, gave me back to Mum, and turned and walked away. I was two and a half years old.

And it was here, in Dagenham, that life really started. This was where I grew up, learned who I was, and what I was, and became myself. It's in Dagenham that I set out on the road to Dial House and Crass, to life as Steve Ignorant, to Conflict and Schwartzeneggar, and all the rest of it. But that was all way off in the future. For now there was a cat and a dog and a sweet shop. There was Nan, and there was Granddad, and a new, colour-filled, beginning.

Dagenham

After the slum we'd lived in in Stoke, Nan and Granddad's house was like a palace. It had a little patch of garden out front and a bigger one round the back full of cabbages and peas and potatoes, like a mini-allotment. You walked in through the front door and the pantry was on your right, maybe with a rabbit someone had trapped and brought round hanging up there, waiting for Nan to skin it later. Straight ahead was the kitchen, which was Nan's domain, with an Ascot water boiler and a sink with a draining board, and a formica top table with three chairs, and beyond that was the toilet and a poky little bathroom. Upstairs there were three bedrooms, front, middle, and rear, and back downstairs at the front of the house was the living-room, and in there was a drop-leaf table with a velvety cover and a pot of chrysanthemums which was always full of earwigs, a carpet in the middle of the room with lino round the edge, Granddad's chair with a rag rug in front of it, a sofa, Nan's armchair and a tiny black and white telly in the corner of the room.

It was just a bog-standard post-war semi, like very other house in the street, and every other street in Dagenham. But for me it was like heaven. After the unpredictability and poverty of life in Stoke, Nan and Granddad's house offered certainty and routine, and while I'd rebel against all of that as a teenager, for now I couldn't dream of anything better. It was life in the suburbs, where nothing exciting happened but you knew everybody in the street, you knew all the people who worked in the local shops. It was a little community, with a park and a playground; slides and swings and a council swimming pool. The kind of place where a whole generation of kids grew up, and I was one of them.

Nan and Granddad had been childhood sweethearts. She was from Chadwell Heath, which is the next borough up from Dagenham, and Granddad used to go past her house on his horse and cart, taking goods from Romford to London. So every day he'd see her, and she must have stuck in his mind, because in 1918, when he came back from the war he went down the Cross Keys, where she was working as a chambermaid, and proposed to her. Before long they were living down by Dagenham docks in a place called Piano Row, just off Chequers Lane. The cottages there got their name because the front room was just large enough to squeeze a piano in, which you couldn't do if you lived anywhere else on the lane. Affording a piano was another matter entirely, but at least you had the room. They lived there for just over 20 years, and during that time my mum and Uncle Alan were born, in the maternity hospital along to the west in Barking. At some point, too, Granddad carved his and Nan's initials into a brick somewhere in the road. Many years later, when it was their golden wedding anniversary, I went down there looking for it, to give it them as a present, but I couldn't find it, and the place was knocked down not long after, gone forever.

But when I came to Dagenham they were living at Whitebarn Lane and the stability they offered was in stark contrast to how life had been before. Right from very early on I just felt like I belonged, and that made all the difference in the world. The difference between a world in black and white, and one in colour, and you can't ask for much more than that. The estate they lived on, like so much of Dagenham, had been built after the war specifically to house workers for the Ford plant, and this gave the whole town a sense of something common and shared in their lives, as most people either worked for Ford's or for companies that supplied them. During the week you could tell the time by the factory hooter at Ford's announcing the change of shift, and the streets would fill with cars and people, then go quiet again till the next shift ended. Only on Sundays did the hooter fall quiet and the whole town made itself comfortable and relaxed in the silence. In the evening people went visiting. Friends and relatives would drop in on Nan and Granddad, and sit supping bottles of ale, eating winkles and salad, everyone picking the winkles out of their shells with a needle. Once the bowl was empty – and it was a big bowl – then we kids could leave the table and the adults would pull out the little card table and play whist, with money in a kitty for the winner. Then on Monday morning the hooter would sound and the working week began again.

It was all as regular as clockwork. And just as the hooter marked time for the town, so Nan's cooking marked off the days of the week. Sundays would be a roast: pork because it was cheap, or maybe lamb, then the salad and winkles later. Mondays was cold meat leftovers from the roast the day before, usually with pickles, then on Tuesday the bones from Sunday's roast went into a soup with pearl barley and carrots. By the middle of the week Nan would be skinning a rabbit – with Dagenham being such a new town there were still rabbits every-where – while a day or so later you had every chance of finding a pig's head in a saucepan when you went to the bathroom, because Nan would be making brawn. Then on Saturday after-noon we'd have banana sandwiches in front of the TV while Granddad ate his kippers and checked his football pools and we waited to watch *Doctor Who*. The next day was Sunday, and roast again.

With the veg garden outside there were always cabbages and greens, so we ate well enough. Good solid food, with nothing going to waste. Like everyone of their generation, Nan and Granddad had lived through the Second World War and then through rationing, and in their house you ate what you were given and you ate the lot. They taught me a lot about food, about how to make it filling and cheap. Pearl barley in soup, or currants in rice pudding will swell and bulk it up. That kind of thing. Even now I won't waste food and I hate to see it happen. That's one of the things they taught me, and they taught me well.

Luckily I'm a quick learner. And while I learnt about pearl barley I also learnt very quickly, very very quickly, that what Granddad said went, that you kept your head down else you'd feel the back of his hand. It wasn't a difficult lesson, but it was one my brother never, ever learned. He and my Granddad were at loggerheads from the moment I knew them. And I think, in many ways, that I got all the luck for both of us, for me and my brother, and how different things could easily have been.

David

As kids we take so much in our stride and accept it as normal. Everything's new and we've nothing to judge it against, so as long as it's not hurting us or causing pain, well, we're pretty resilient. I'm not saying it doesn't affect us, because it can and it does, and pretty much all of us know someone who's been royally screwed up by how they were treated when they were young, but at the same time some stuff will just wash over us simply because our attention is elsewhere and our minds are kids' minds, with a whole different set of priorities.

So where an adult might have seen that my mum had to leave Stoke because her marriage to a violent drunk had finally broken down, and she couldn't handle bringing two kids up in poverty on her own, and where an adult might have thought that was dreadful, for me the move to Dagenham was great. Simple as. I don't remember being disturbed by it at all. I didn't really know who my biological dad was, so him not being there didn't fuck me up, it was just the way it was. Other kids had a dad, I didn't. Most kids didn't get a brand-new older brother, and I did.

We turned up in Dagenham and David was there. All the time my mum and my sister and me had been living in Stoke, he'd been back in Essex with my Granddad and Nan. Writing about it now, it seems a bizarre thing for my mum and dad to have done, to have left their eldest child down South while they set up a new life in the Midlands, but I never knew whether they'd meant for him to join them once they'd established themselves (they never did, of course), or whether they'd simply abandoned him. At the time, these questions never occurred to me. I was just made up to have a big brother of my own, and I tagged along after him wherever he went. Even better, we shared the bedroom at the front of the house, with my mum and sister in the middle one, and my grandparents sleeping in the back, and I remember how my brother and I would lie there at night in the same bed, and he'd ask me what I could hear, and I'd listen, and I'd hear the ships at Dagenham Dock, a dog barking, trains at Dagenham Heathway, and the constant hum of Ford's factory.

He was bright – very bright – and artistic, and he had a vivid imagination, and I idolised him. I'd follow him round, traipse after him down the street. Sometimes I think if he was going out he was told *Take Stephen with you*. And he did. He shared all his knowledge of Dagenham with me, from the ants' nest under the stopcock in the front path to the old air raid shelters behind the Ford factory. He'd take me for walks and show me all the secret places where you'd find newts, he taught me what frogspawn was, or the best place to find a slow-worm, or he'd tell me *Just sit still* and we'd sit there for what felt like hours then – suddenly – *Look! A lizard!* He really taught me that if you want to see nature, you just sit there quietly and wait for it to come along, and I loved him for that.

One time he took me up Green Hill, which was a big old slag heap built of rubbish and furnace clinker from the Ford factory. Children used to scare each other with stories of kids who'd fallen through the soft bits of the hill and burnt to death because it was still alight inside, and even though you knew it couldn't have really happened, it was a big deal when my brother took me up there, telling me to be careful and only tread where he trod, else I might slide down a hole into the middle of the hill and never be seen again. And even though I knew he was winding me up I was still scared, but excited to be up there with him, and we got to the top and it was incredible. There was this wonderful vista of the River Thames from east to west, a great long reach of it. You could see down into Kent, northwards to Essex, look out over all of Dagenham. In London you could see St. Paul's, and the Monument and the City stretching out beyond it. It was sunset that first time we went up there, and my brother said *Look at it. Isn't it great? Shhh ... just watch* and our shadows grew longer and longer and disappeared, and it was a wonderful magical time.

I loved him to death, with all my heart, like kids do, and I could never understand why he beat the shit out of me. Because he did. At the time – as any kid would be – I was bewildered and confused; as an adult, thinking about how things were for him, I'm amazed he had any love to give at all, because he really had it rough.

Granddad was a disciplinarian, and David took the brunt of that. It's hard to say why he did, and I didn't, because none of the people involved are there to ask, and so anything I say is nothing more than an educated guess, the result of chatting with people like my sister, or Uncle Alan and Auntie Dee, who saw it all at second-hand, and of sitting on my own in the pub with a pint, mulling it over and wondering just why things turned out the way they did. And even after all that, I'm not sure there's really anything that comes up as an explanation, just theories, and possibilities, and the conviction that sometimes people are lucky. And sometimes, again, they're not.

Very early on, not long after we'd moved down to Dagenham, I was out with David and he said *Look at this* and pulled up his shirt, showing me a mass of bruises where Granddad had taken a cricket bat to him because he and my sister had gone walking through long grass and got their new sandals wet. My brother's body was black and blue. I remember it put the fear of God into me and that I decided there and then that whatever Granddad or Nan said went, and that I wasn't going to get into trouble with them. Ever.

For my brother, I don't think things were anything like as simple. Mum had gone to Stoke with Bert, and she'd left him behind. And so sometimes I think my brother got it in the neck because of who his dad was, rather than for anything he'd done himself, because he was a constant reminder of a bloke my Granddad didn't approve of in the slightest. In some respects I think he paid for the sins of the father, so to speak, and caught the full force of Granddad's anger that my mum had left him and Nan, left them for my feckless father, and left them to bring up their eldest son.

Many years later, when I was grown up myself, and the relationship between myself and my brother had finally broken down, I found out that Mum had had hundreds of injections over several years to help her conceive before she and Bert had finally had David. I was stunned. I still don't really understand how she could go through all that, and then leave him behind when she moved to Stoke, because that really messed my brother up.

Brought up by people who didn't spare the rod, or miss an opportunity to tell him what a waster his dad was, David rebelled. I know I wasn't allowed to mention Bert's name, but David would, because the first present he'd ever had was an ammonite, and Bert gave it to him, so he'd stick up for him. And because of that he was jumped on every time he stepped out of line and told *You'll end up like your father* and I think he went *Fucking good then* and so the battle lines were drawn.

And I think he built up this fantasy, as kids do when they need to hope for something, that his dad would come back one day, and love David just like David loved him. And then we came back, and Bert didn't, and David realised he was all on his own, and I don't think any kid can deal with that without getting twisted up inside to some extent or other. Sure, I was David's kid brother, and he loved me, but he resented me too. He turned me on to the natural world, and it was him that introduced me to Dial House when I was older, but sometimes the sense that life was unfair and that he was getting a raw deal would break through and he'd kick the shit out of me. And there was always this swing between love and hate with the two of us, till – finally – years later he turned up at a party one New Year's Eve, very drunk, and gave me a proper kicking, breaking one of my ribs.

And all I know is I was lucky, because broken ribs will mend. And my brother, poor sod, got all the bad luck, because being passed from one person to another like a parcel, and the hurt that causes – that doesn't heal as easy, or as clean.

Granddad

What didn't help was that Granddad and I got on. And I reckon that must have added insult to injury as far as my brother was concerned. At school he was the freak who got the shit kicked out of him, who had a big nose and sticky out ears. At home he couldn't do right for doing wrong. And then I turned up, the newcomer down from Stoke, and fitted in like he just wasn't allowed to.

A big part of it was that where David fought back and got into trouble, I kept the rules and kept my head down, but I think there was pure blind luck involved too – I was there because Mum was back home and Bert was no longer on the scene, and so Granddad had mellowed. He had no reason to give me a hard time, and I was bloody sure not to give him one. And so where David's life was hard, mine was easy, because Grand-dad took to me like he never took to him.

At first I didn't trust that. I knew Granddad was keen on discipline because I'd seen the bruises he left on David, and I expected it was only a matter of time till he gave me a good hiding too. So even when he was trying to be nice I was cagey. For my birthday one year he bought me a cap gun. It had a black handle and a silver barrel and a paper roll of caps you put in. Rather than giving it me all wrapped up, or in a box, Granddad pulled it out, pointed at me, and fired. I really thought I was being shot, that I'd done something wrong and Granddad had decided to kill me. Mum had to come through and calm me down, because I was crying and screaming and trying to hide behind the sofa. Even when Granddad gave me the gun, handle first, and told me *It's all right. It's only a toy!* I wasn't convinced. The handle was warm from his grasp, and I somehow connected that heat with being shot.

But I learned to love the cap gun, and I learned to love Granddad too. Every day, after he'd come back from his shift down the Cables and had his dinner, he'd sit me on his knee and read me some of Reverend Awdry's *Railway Series* books while I looked at the pictures. Sometimes he'd cough and I'd ask *Why are you coughing, Granddad?* He'd tell me *It's the pictures of the smoke making me cough.* Nothing to do with the roll-up permanently stuck to his bottom lip. We both looked forward to this time spent together reading, and little by little my relationship with my Granddad grew.

Back then there was a ticket called a Red Rover which let you on any bus all day and cost five shillings, and one day Granddad decided me and him were going to have a day out. So we walked round the corner to Chequers and caught a No.87 bus down the A13 to Barking and another bus to Woolwich, sitting upstairs at the back because the seats there had armrests and Granddad could make himself comfortable and roll himself a fag. It was my first trip out of Dagenham since we'd moved down from Stoke, so it was a massive adventure, and everything was new and exciting, even Woolwich, which was a wasteland of bombed-out buildings and slums, and had been really heavily targeted in the Second World War because of the docks and the gas works. It was a very different world from Dagenham. And now it's a very different world again, of course, become the desirable Docklands, with the heart ripped out of it, and people living there who wouldn't have dreamed of doing it then.

At the end of the line we got off and had a cup of tea in a cafe while we waited for the ferry, then when it came in we walked on and took the five minute journey across the river to Woolwich Arsenal. You used to be able to climb down to the engine room on the ferry and look through the glass of the engine room door to see the engines working, so Granddad took me down there to the noise and the heat and the smell of oil and the blur of moving brass.

When we docked on the south side of the Thames we took another bus through Greenwich to Surrey Docks, this time sitting upstairs at the front so we could see over the dock walls where the ships were being loaded and unloaded, bringing cargo from all round the world, though already the decline was setting in and they were nothing like they'd been when Granddad was a boy. When we crossed the river again it was as if we burst out from the dark, narrow, walled streets south of the river to an entirely different world – to the magic of Tower Bridge, looking like something from a kid's fairytale. On through the City, along Fleet Street and The Strand to Trafalgar Square, where we stood feeding the pigeons while the traffic roared round us, before catching a bus back home, Granddad smoking rollies the whole way, and me with my nose pressed against the window, drinking it all in.

Another time – and this was either before I ever went to school or in the school holidays – Granddad decided the front garden, which wasn't anything much, was going to be a lawn. So he picked up an old hessian sack, took me by the hand, said *Come on* and we went off to the back of Ley swimming pool, where there was an area of waste ground, all long grass and nettles, butterflies and hidden worlds. And the two of us spent all day there, collecting grass seed and putting it in the sack. Then when we got back home Granddad dug the front garden over, scattered the grass seed on top of the freshly turned soil, and –

I must have been at school, come to think of it – said *Right. Go and get all your mates, run about on that for me. Tread it all in.* And we had great fun, racing round on it, helping Granddad grow his lawn. It was kid heaven.

So when, a few weeks later, I came back from school and saw that Mr. Todd had dug his front garden over, I thought I'd help him out too. I ran around on it, kicking dirt every which way, jumping and stamping it down – and then Mr. Todd flew out of his front door, shaking his fist and yelling at me. How was I to know I'd kicked his neat rows of vegetable seeds into an unholy mess?! He was furious! Now if David had done that, Granddad would have knocked him into the middle of next week, but I got away with nothing much more than a ticking-off.

And that kind of sums up the difference between how Granddad treated me, and how he was with David. He was hard on my brother, just like he'd been on his own son, Alan. It was his nature. When my parents had gone to Stoke, Granddad had kept David down in Dagenham because he didn't approve of Bert, of the drinking, of the rows between my mum and him. He pretty much took David off my parents to give him a better chance, and said *You're not taking him with you.* And while we were in Stoke he brought David up as if he was his own son. And he sent my mum that ten-bob note hidden in the newspaper every week, helping her out even though she was hundreds of miles away. Even though he thought she'd made a bad choice in Bert.

Because for my Granddad, family was family, and blood was thicker than water, and I really respected him for that. He showed me affection, and he showed me the world of men too, just like my brother showed me the natural wonders of Dagenham, and I was lucky enough to have both of them in my life.

School

At some point before I went to school I'd sat with my brother and sister while they watched *Tom Brown's Schooldays* on the telly. As far as I was concerned, that was what school was going to be like: terrifying teachers in vampire cloaks with mortarboards, evil prefects who'd hold you in front of a fire and burn you, and every day a battle just to survive. Unsurprisingly, on my first day I was terrified, and when Granddad left me there and walked away I screamed the place down, and wet my pants. Nice one, Steve. Great first impression.

In fact my time at Marsh Green Infants, down on the A13 by Ford's, was as cosy and comfortable as you can imagine. The headmistress, Mrs. Brownsil, might have looked stern in her brown two-piece suit, but she ran a school where I got to play with plasticine and crayons all day long, where I learned to write before going back home at 3.30 to sit in the front room eating banana sandwiches and watching cartoons on the TV. I'd started writing before I ever got to Infants actually. I remember writing the word *phone* and being really proud that I knew the letters *ph* made an 'f' sound, like in Stephen. Mind you, I wasn't always so bright – for years I wouldn't have it that *fuck* wasn't spelt with a *ph* too. *For phuck's sake, Williams!*

Life was pretty much perfect, really. A cosy little time. Then, when I was eight, I moved up to junior school with everybody else, which held no fears for me because my brother and sister had told me exactly what to expect, and anyway, I was eight now, not four, and Marsh Green Juniors was right next door so I knew the school would smell of soap and school dinners and strangers, just like the Infants.

And like all the other kids, I was growing up, becoming more aware of what went on around me. Putting two and two together and making four, or something close enough to it. Learning about the world outside my grandparents' house and finding out what was right and what was wrong. One day at Juniors – I was still only eight – I went to school and there was a very strange sight: a black kid all on his own lying on the ground in the playground, crying. And a crowd of kids going *Whatsamatter? Whatsamatter?* And I felt this real mix of emotions: on the one hand, curiosity, because this was the first real live black person I'd ever seen, and just like everybody else I was really intrigued, especially by his hands, that he could have brown hands but pink palms; and on the other hand, I felt really sorry for him, the poor little sod, all on his own in the school, a different colour from everyone else. And we called him *chocolate drop* because we were just kids and didn't know any better, and we never thought of this as bullying him, it was just a way of describing him, but the truth is that even now I can't remember what his name was. And I imagine what it must have been like, to be eight years old and have everyone stare at you like you're from another planet so that you end up lying in the playground, crying, and it still makes my toes curl, to this day.

Because I was growing to hate bullies. And there was another little realisation from that time, which stays with me to this day, and really changed the way I looked at the world and how I behaved. My sister Carol used to knock around with a Catholic girl, Christine Noonan, and her family was Irish. That wasn't unusual in Dagenham, as much of the Ford factory was built with Irish labour and a lot of Irish worked in and around the plant. In fact there was a whole estate, Rylands, which was predominantly Irish, and had several Catholic schools on it. Sometimes as kids this would feed into a Catholic vs. Protestant thing, where we'd pick fights with kids from the Catholic school as they walked home to Rylands but it was a load of bollocks and just an excuse for a fight with kids we didn't know. I had no idea what 'Catholic' was, or 'Protestant' for that matter or what any of it meant ...

Anyway, Carol used to hang around with Christine, and the Noonans lived round the corner. There was a knackered old car in the front garden, and they never cut the grass or trimmed the privet hedge – so as far as my grandparents were concerned they were one step up from tinkers, and at risk of being evicted, because in those days the council used to send you written warnings if you didn't keep the garden nice and tidy – and they had a huge family, and one of them was Christine's little brother Jimmy.

Jimmy was in the year below me at Juniors, and I used to terrorise him something awful. I'd get other kids to chase him, I'd thump him, I'd bully him. I guess it was what I'd learned, what I'd seen, and now I had a chance to do the same. Then one day Christine and my sister went to the swimming baths, and Jimmy and I tagged along. The girls were off chatting and Jimmy and me were hanging onto the side of the pool, and – in the way kids do – I thought how the Noonans had an apple tree and a pear tree in their back garden, and it would be great to play pirates and then the trees could be the masts of the ship. So I said to Jimmy, *Let's go and play pirates in your garden* and I remember really clearly how he got up on one elbow and said *Promise not to chase me again?* and I said *Yeah, I promise*. And from that point on I never bullied anyone ever again in my life, because just the way he said it, and the expression on his face, was a real turning point for me. I realised what a little shit I'd been, how I'd hurt him. And I've never been able to stand bullies since.

So that day Jimmy and I went and played pirates in his back garden, and from then on I went round to the Noonans' quite a lot. It was really scruffy, but very friendly, and it was the first time I'd ever got to see how other people lived. And it was a whole new world. Firstly, and most importantly, as soon as I was through the door Mrs. Noonan would ask if I wanted something to eat, and fix something up. If I was lucky it'd be fish finger sandwiches, which were just the best and most exotic thing I'd ever had, and my all-time favourite Noonan food. I don't think I ever got bored of them. Secondly, you could put your feet up on the sofa when you sat on it and it was fine. If you did it at ours you'd get a clip round the ear. And above all I remember being really amazed that Jimmy was allowed to pour the hot water from the kettle to make the tea, because in our house that was something Nan would always do, but here was Jimmy Noonan doing this very grown-up thing, and he was a whole year younger than me! If my jaw didn't actually hit the floor it wasn't far off. Here I was in a Catholic house, which I'd expected to be really different – I don't know how, maybe they'd walk on the ceiling or have revolving heads or bite the heads off chickens – and it was really normal, and it was enjoyable, and it was free.

Back home with my grandparents, it all felt very different. Very different. A pair of shoes lasted a year, and Granddad chose them. This meant they'd be clumpy, shapeless, hard-wearing, and cheap. But Granddad set the rules, because it was his house, and what he said went. So we had no birthday parties, because he said we couldn't afford it, and when it came to bath time my brother had a bath, then my sister, then me, one after another in the same water, which wasn't anything like as warm or clean by the time I got in it! I guess it was all a legacy of having lived through times when he and Nan really did have to make use of everything and watch every single penny, and it stood me in good stead in later years, but now that I'd been to the Noonans' and seen that not everybody was ruled with a rod of iron, I wished it was like that for us too. Don't get me wrong, my grandparents looked after us just fine: the back garden was a mass of vegetables, they were very self-sufficient, and we were always clothed and fed. And they'd taken us all in, and not left us abandoned in Stoke, but it was very regimented, as if we were still digging for victory and fighting the war, and now I had something to compare it to, it was coming up short.

And it was really really strict. Very quickly I learned to keep my mouth shut and my eyes open so that I didn't end up with bruises up and down my body like my brother and sister. Quite regularly they'd get thrashed for something, like wearing their Sunday clothes on a weekday, but I managed to avoid it. I got the occasional clip round the ear but that was about it. My punishment came at secondary school, where I was always getting slippered and caned, but that's for later in our story. Now I could see the mistakes my brother and sister were making and I knew I had to fall in line with how Granddad wanted things to be because, basically, I didn't want to get beaten up. At that age you're too young to realise there are ways you can rebel, you're too young to rebel at all. Things are just the way they are and you've got to get on with it.

So I kept schtum, and kept my nose clean, and I think because I was the youngest they were more lenient with me, in the way parents and grandparents often are, and that helped me too. One day I was playing outside and I went round the corner, and there was Jimmy Noonan sitting on top of a white Morris Minor, playing around on the roof. And I asked if it was his car and he said yes. And I asked if I could play on it too, and he said *Come on up*. So I did. And we were up on this car, mucking around, when this woman appears. Mrs. Kemp from down the road. And she's screaming at us, asking what the hell we think we're doing, yelling that we've broken her windscreen wipers, smashed her wing mirror. And I'm looking at Jimmy, wondering what's going on, because I thought it was his car. And at the same time, in the back of my mind as Mrs. Kemp marches me back to Granddad's, I know that really won't work as an excuse, and I just know I'm about to get a good hiding.

And all that happened was I was sent to bed for the day, which was a relief, and a lucky escape, and something I really can't explain. All I know is that I never ever played on the roof of a Morris Minor again! And I can't help wondering if, when he went to bed that night, little Jimmy Noonan was chuckling to think he'd got me back for all those days I'd bullied him ...

Nan

When I wasn't at school, or hanging out with my brother or the Noonans, chances are Nan would have me helping her. Granddad still had a part-time job for a haulage firm (which supplied Ford's, like everything else in Dagenham), and Nan looked after the house. She was a typical traditional housewife of her time: she'd look after the week's housekeeping money and stretch it out as far as possible with cheap, filling food; she'd clean the doorstep, and sharpen the kitchen knives on it; and she'd have me running errands.

All the kids did. If I was taking Granddad's copy of the *Dagenham Post* round the corner to Auntie Florrie's so she could read it, chances were I'd bump into someone I knew from school lugging a shopping bag back home for their mum. And if Nan had sent me down the shops, 10–1 one of the neighbours would see me going past, and it would be *You going down Sturges? Get us half a pound of bacon. Tell Maud I'll see her right and I'll stick it on the note.*

Because in those days the street that led on from Whitebarn Lane and down to the Heathway was a long parade of shops, with pretty much everything you'd need. There were a couple of little mini-markets, and a butcher's, baker's and greengrocer's, a wool shop, a place selling and renting TVs, even one selling car tyres. There was Butler's the funeral directors, and there was the chemists where Uncle Alan first went to work and met Auntie Dee. There was The Admiral Vernon pub, which was my local when I was older. But for us kids the two most important shops were the bike shop – which also sold Airfix kits and Dinky toys – and the sweet shop, Candys, which was my first port of call if Nan had given me a penny to spend, and where I could spend mouth-watering minutes choosing between blackjacks or fruit salads.

Further on were the covered stalls of Broad Street market. That was a ten minute walk from home, and about as far as we ever needed to go. There was another parade of shops way up at the Heathway, where the station was, but that was over a mile away and a special day out, and had nothing we couldn't get nearer to home.

And shopping was a social exercise. If Nan took me with her when she went to the shops, that ten minute walk to Broad Street market would take about an hour, because she'd be meeting people the whole way. My memory is of standing holding that flippin' shopping bag with the dust from the potatoes in the bottom of it, standing in the street waiting because every two minutes someone would bump into Nan and talk and natter, and it'd take for ever. Now, it's totally dead. Just waste paper and kebab cartons blowing along down the street, because they built a supermarket out at the Heathway, and pretty soon all those little shops round Broad Street were closed and gone. Shopping now would be a five minute drive past the houses built on the old market site and on to the Heathway, without ever meeting anyone you know, the same in Dagenham as anywhere else, and Maud would hate it.

She was a strong person, my Nan. Wasn't afraid to voice her opinion about my mum when she came back from Stoke, and while Granddad made the rules, it was Nan who ruled the house and put food on the table. Good solid food, home-made steak and kidney pie and the like. She was also a demon with the tea towel if you were messing around. It's a dying art, but I swear the tip of the tea towel was going through the sound barrier when she flicked it at you. Nan was no more of a soft touch than Granddad. Her view was that, whatever life threw at you, you dusted yourself down and got on with it. She'd dealt with having a hysterectomy after Alan was born, and I've a feeling that if some local girl found herself in trouble, Nan was the one she'd come to see, who'd help her resolve her little problem. Because life for unmarried mothers was hard, and there was definitely a stigma attached, so often a wedding would be rushed through if the woman was pregnant. I remember one girl crying because her parents wouldn't pay for anything to do with the wedding because of the shame, so all the neighbours clubbed in to help her, making sandwiches and the like so there could be some kind of reception, and her start to married life wouldn't be totally unmarked and unnoticed. It was a no-nonsense kind of help – everyone pitched in, yet at the same time the attitude was that once you'd made your bed you'd bloody well lie in it.

Above all, Nan loved a good funeral, so if someone died she'd be the first round to lay the body out, tie the cord round the jaw, and get it ready for the undertaker. Death was just part of life, and Nan wasn't squeamish about it in the least. When Aunty Reenie gassed herself in the oven and Uncle Fred came round in bits, Aunty Reenie ended up in Butler's Chapel of Rest, and I wanted to go, because I'd never seen a dead body. So I pestered mum and Nan. *I want to see one I want to see one I want to see one.* And so when they went to pay their respects they took me and my sister along. I remember being in this little room with a funny smell, and standing on tiptoes trying to look in the coffin. Then Nan comes bustling in, and grabs Reenie's head, rolling it from side to side *Oh Reenie, they had to break your neck to get you out of that oven, didn't they, gel?* My sister screamed, I felt sick, and my mum went *You've got to kiss her else it'll haunt you the rest of your life.* Nan's plan worked – I never asked to go with her again, and I learned to be really, really careful what I wished for!

Skinhead

It was the summer holidays, and I'd just finished junior school. So there was a couple of long months coming up, with nothing much happening, nothing to do and no money to do it with. Kids all over Dagenham hanging around, watching the world go by. Bored. Stuck in the doldrums.

Then, suddenly – and I remember this very clearly – I was woken up out of this sterile drifting along. I was round at a mate's house, Malcolm Roberts it was, the two of us sitting on his mum's doorstep in the back garden waiting for something to happen. And something did. This guy came walking down the garden path of the house next door. He had a shaven head with two partings shaved in, a black-and-white gingham button-down shirt under a two-tone suit which shimmered mauve and yellow in the light, red socks, highly polished brogues, and a pair of bright red braces. And he strode – no – he *floated* down the garden path, and Malcolm and myself sat there open-mouthed, thinking *Cor!*

He nodded and went inside, and then he put on this incredible music. Ska. The original Prince Buster 'Al Capone's guns – don't argue!'

And just like that, life changed.

He was the first skinhead I'd ever seen, and right there, right then I went *I wanna be like that!* In a complete rush, I knew I wanted to be a skinhead, because it was all rebellion and two's up, and having your own identity. I wanted it. I wanted it so much I could taste it.

That afternoon was the first time I realised there was this thing called fashion, that you could look good, and look smart. That you could say *I am a skinhead* and people would look at you with respect. And for the next two years it seemed like every kid in Britain was thinking the same – I know every kid in Dagenham was, and everyone I've spoken to, wherever they grew up, seems to have shared that experience. It was like a whole generation went *I'll have some of that!*

And I started plotting and dreaming, wanting to get that look, to feel the buzz of the clippers when I'd get a number two cut, imagining myself putting the turn-ups on a pair of jeans, and listening to that wonderful sharp, crisp music. Dancing to it.

And it would take me years, but one day I put Toots and the Maytals '54–46' on the old radiogram at my grandparents when they were out, and it was the most perfect thing I'd ever heard. It makes the hair stand up on my neck to this day.

Stan

A little while before this whole skinhead thing had exploded into my life, this strange bloke turned up one evening in the front room. He'd come round and sit in a straight-backed chair in the middle of us, and him and Mum and Nan and Granddad would chat while we kids were told to be on our best behaviour. After he'd been coming over for three weeks or so, we were told to call him Uncle Stan, and slowly the penny dropped that Mum had found herself a new bloke.

He came round more and more often, and my grandparents were more than happy with it. He was what they called a man's man, who was always suited and booted, and he worked at a place called Motorgear, supplying components for Ford's. Nothing skilled, just drilling holes in pieces of metal shift after shift, but steady work. Like Mum, he had a couple of kids, daughters from a previous marriage, who lived with their mother, and who he actually paid maintenance to – Mum, by contrast, had never seen a penny from Bert.

David hated Stan right from the off. Bitterly. He was in his last year at a really horrible school where it seemed like he got beaten up nearly every day, and I don't know if it was because of getting smacked in the face one time too often, but he'd got an abscess under his front teeth and his face swelled up like a football. Granddad insisted there was nothing wrong, David just needed a poultice, that was all, but the swelling and the pain got worse and finally he had to have all his front teeth out. Once again, my brother got the rough end of the stick, and once again no one stood up for him. Everyone in the family agreed he was a brilliant artist, but there was no way they'd let him go to college – as soon as he left school they pushed him into a dead-end job, then in the same breath they'd say to him *You've wasted your talent there*. No. *You've* wasted it. So unsurprisingly, David was angry and rebelling and pissed off with the world, and there was no way he was going to be told what to do by anyone, least of all Stan.

So when my Mum got herself on the council housing list and we got a flat, David didn't move in with us. It was just me, my sister Carol, and Mum and Stan in a second-floor flat on the Heath Park estate, a couple of miles up the road from Nan and Granddad. And now Uncle Stan was 'dad'.

And at first, it was great. The flat had french doors leading from the kitchen to the living room, and a little balcony – incredibly sophisticated to an eleven year-old – and outside was the community hall, the estate launderette, a playground, and a little row of shops. Everything you might need. But as with most things in the suburbs it was sterile. Mind-numbingly sterile. And these years really are the worst years of my life, for the sterility of life in Heath Park, and the aching sterility of life with Mum and Stan. Boredom and monotony. Monotony and boredom. Day after day after sodding drawn-out day.

David had disappeared off, hitchhiking around the country. Pretty soon Carol joined the RAF. So there was just me, Mum and Stan in the flat with the TV and the cocktail bar and the canary. On the surface I guess it sounds like the ideal family unit, but it wasn't. Because I was waking up to the world, becoming aware of who I was and what I wanted, and I knew this wasn't it.

During the week Stan worked night-shifts, so when I came in

from school I had to be quiet because he was sleeping. At 6 o'clock he'd get up and go to work, so a lot of the time I never really saw him. He was there but not there, if you see what I mean. But that wasn't so bad. It was the weekends that were truly awful.

To this day, I hate what I call *the dead time*. 3–6pm. Too late to be afternoon and too early to be evening. Just this horrible flat time. And if no one's around or there's nothing to do I'll head off down the pub, because I can't stay in the house. I just can't. Because every weekend, especially on a Saturday when any friends I had would be off with their family, playing football or going to Southend or whatever, I was stuck in that fucking flat in Heath Park, eleven years old and bored out of my mind.

Stan would be down the Vernon as soon as it opened. Mum would be at work down the Cables till 2 o'clock, then she'd join him there. He'd have been down there Friday night as well, but they'd both be back there Saturday for a few beers in the afternoon and come back about half three, talking in what I called their funny voices, which meant that they were drunk. For the next couple of hours they'd actually be really nice and we'd be a family together. Sometimes Stan would even talk to me. But the whole time they were there I'd be waiting for it to finish, knowing it would finish, that the clock would crawl round to 6 and they'd go out again, leaving me sitting indoors alone in the flat with a bottle of lemonade and a bag of crisps, and the dead cold weight of a long evening bearing down.

I remember walking from room to room in that flat trying to think of things to do. But there was nothing. I'd try reading a book in my room, or watching the TV, but the truth was I was stuck on my own in an empty flat, and I was lonely, and I just wanted some company. At Whitebarn Lane there'd always been someone there, Nan and Granddad, David and Carol, but now I was rattling round on my own, and I hated it. I couldn't go out because I didn't have a front door key, so I'd wander through the flat. Lost and aimless. Kitchen, living-room, bedroom. Kitchen, living-room, bedroom. Kitchen, living-room, bedroom. Hour after hour. Or I'd stand and stare out of the window – I still do it, stare out of windows – watching the streetlights come on and the streets empty. With the factory shifts the streets would fill up and empty. They'd be busy for an hour or so, and then quiet, and Saturday nights were the same. By 7 o'clock the streets would just empty because everyone was down the pub and I'd stand there in an empty flat looking at empty streets in an empty estate, waiting for them to come home.

Finally I'd go to bed, because they'd told me I had to be in bed by the time they got in. God knows why. They'd make so much noise I'd wake up anyway. In they'd come, fart about for a while, talking in those funny voices, then they'd go to sleep, and finally I'd go back to sleep. Next day it was Sunday, and Sunday meant school on Monday, and the weekend was gone.

Don't get me wrong. Stan was all right with me, I guess. He just had no interest in me whatsoever, neither good nor bad. I was just *there*. Other kids' parents did things with them, but in all the time I lived with Mum and Stan I don't remember us having an in-depth conversation, or talking at all when he wasn't pissed, truth be told. He never played football with me, and we never went on holiday. He took me to Southend twice, and that was it. It wasn't for want of money – Mum and Stan were both into looking good, and were always spending money on new clothes while I was going to school in jumpers with holes in them – it was for want of interest. Stan never cared about me, not at all. It was my Mum he was after and I was part of the package. I came with the deal, simple as that. Early on he'd occasionally take me down the pub with him on a Sunday lunchtime, and leave me outside with an arrowroot biscuit and half a shandy, but he didn't keep that up for long. As far as he was concerned, I'd go my own way soon enough, so why bother?

Mum had nailed her colours to the mast too. Before we moved into Heath Park she took my sister and me on one side and said *I don't care what you think about him, I love him, and if you don't like it you can bugger off.* It was pretty much the dead opposite of Granddad's take on life, that family should stick together come what may, and while I can't fault her for taking the opportunity to bring some love back into her life, I do think both her and Stan were pretty useless at being parents. At Whitebarn Lane it had been Nan and Granddad who took the lead role in bringing us up. Now, left to her own devices, Mum was more interested in new clothes and nights out than in her kids. I'd bring school reports home and they'd lie on the table, unopened, unread, and untouched, while Mum and Stan got themselves ready for another night out. They weren't cut out for looking after anyone but themselves, either of them. No big deal. It's just how they were.

It wasn't much fun living life in the margins around them, in the dull drudgery of that flat in Heath Park. But every cloud has a silver lining, and what those years did teach me was how to be all right on my own, how to hunker down and survive. It took me a while, but I learned how to be happy on my own and in my own skin. And when I grew older, and the chance came to grab life, I took it with both hands.

Weekends

Even though Stan worked nights because there was more money in it, and even though he and Mum always had cash for new clothes and nights out, none of that trickled down to me. So, like I said, I was going to school in jumpers with holes in them, which would have been the dog's if punk had kicked off, but which was really embarrassing when what I wanted – like every other kid in Dagenham – was to be a skinhead. To dress sharp. Instead all my clothes were cheap utility shit, stuff bought because it would do for both school and home. *Tuf* plastic slip-on shoes, charcoal-grey trousers, a stupid blazer. Even the donkey jacket I had for winter was a cheap one.

So if I was ever going to manage to dress like I wanted, and stop being marked out at school as the scruffy kid, the one everyone called a wanker, then I was going to have to sort it out myself. The question was – how? Every kid on the estate was vying to be the best-dressed skinhead in Dagenham, so every potential source of income had been thoroughly explored. All the paper rounds were taken, for starters. As for washing cars, well, maths was never my strong point, but even I knew that if you only got a tanner – six old pence – for washing someone's car, and a pair of Doctor Martens cost a couple of quid, then you'd need to wash a lot of cars before you'd be buying those boots, and not many people had cars. Or needed them washing. And lots of other kids were offering to wash what cars there were.

And then I got a plan.

Mum and Stan started letting me visit my grandparents on a Saturday, and soon that turned into me spending the whole weekend there, which suited me just fine. It was just like it had always been, except they were older of course, and a bit more lenient and easy-going. At tea-time Granddad would have his kippers while he watched the football results on the TV and checked his pools, just like he always had, and I'd sit waiting impatiently for *Doctor Who* to start, wondering if anyone anywhere really cared about the results from Scottish Division 2. And after the news we'd settle down together for the evening's telly. It was infinitely better than being stuck on my own in the empty flat in Heath Park.

What I really loved about it – and this is with hindsight – was that there was a structure to how my grandparents did things, and I found that incredibly reassuring. And I think that's how kids are. Knowing that Nan would spend every Saturday morning out shopping, and that the house would smell of Granddad's kippers come tea-time, and that these things had been like that for years, well, it was something I could rely on, and like I say, I reckon kids need that sense of certainty. Living with mum and Stan, by contrast, what routine there was went all out of kilter and out of sync at the weekends, because I didn't know when they'd be coming home, and when they did they'd be talking in those funny voices because they were pissed, and they'd be acting in a funny way I didn't like and couldn't understand, as if they weren't the same people they were normally.

Whereas with Nan and Granddad life was constant. And visiting them gave me the chance to put my little plan into operation.

I caught on to the fact that if I timed my walk to Whitebarn Lane just right, I'd be going past the Admiral Vernon just as mum and Stan came out, feeling good and chirpy 'cause they'd had a few drinks. And I'd ask them if they needed any errands running. And nine times out of ten, being half-cut they'd slip me a half-a-crown or something. Then when they sobered up, they wouldn't remember. So I sussed that out. Every week I'd catch them at the right time and use it to my advantage. And I scrimped and saved, and eventually I went all the way up to Petticoat Lane and bought my first pair of brogues. £2.20 on a pair of black brogues with leather soles, one size too big because they were all I could get, but I stuffed paper down the toes and told myself *Fuck it I'll grow into them*. For trousers I got myself a cheap version of the two-tone trousers I'd have had in an ideal world, and a cheap Stradbrook shirt, which wasn't a Ben Sherman, but it'd pass. Well, it was passable, and that would do.

And I remember going to bed that night feeling on top of the world, knowing I wouldn't have to put on those horrible plastic slip-on shoes in the morning. That I wouldn't have to face the kids at school picking on me because of how I dressed. I'd lain awake at nights for so long, dreaming of that, working out how I was going to get the money for some brogues, and what it would be like when I got them, and finally I'd done it.

Rebellion

Too many of the teachers I had at school were bullies. No good at teaching, far too keen on reaching for the slipper or the cane. Old fossils who'd never got out of the Second World War, never got over it, and were only in teaching – so far as any of us could tell – because there was nothing else for them to do when the war ended. Ok, so life hadn't given them a great deal, but what the fuck was anyone doing, putting them in charge of kids?

Even at junior school, there was this one teacher 'Westy' who drove a snub-nosed, poison-bottle green Rover, who was a bully of a man, a complete sadist. He'd slipper any kid in front of a mixed class, for next to nothing at all. He'd finish the day by reading to us from a classic kids book, but God help you if you relaxed. I remember listening to him read *The Lion, The Witch, and The Wardrobe*, listening to this quite pleasant voice and getting lost in the story, thinking *I want to be in Narnia.* Then he'd stop, point at a kid and ask *What was the last word I said?* and if you didn't know then you were out front for a slippering. A grown man wielding a slipper on a ten year old kid in front of a room full of kids just for being foolish enough to actually enjoy a story ... tell me – what that's got to do with teaching?

Nowadays he wouldn't get away with it, but back then there was nothing you could do. If I went home and complained to my Mum I'd been slippered she'd only say I must have done something to deserve it and give me a clip round the ear for getting in trouble in the first place. But the injustice of the slippering wasn't something I ever forgave, or forgot.

38

Much of the time secondary school was just the same. Teachers who'd come out of the army after the war when jobs were scarce, but who really didn't like kids and didn't want to be there. Everyone was wearing this new fashion called skinhead and they were stuck wearing this '40s utility fashion, and they'd seen people die and they had this real grudge.

And some of them were simply damaged. There was a maths teacher, a guy we called Jumbo – the story being that he'd tried to fiddle with one of the boys in school, so you can work out the origin of the name for yourself – and he was really strange. On the one hand he was renowned for his furious temper, a fearsome bully who I remember banging my desk lid up and down in front of my face screaming *Why can't you learn anything???* Well, because you're banging a desk lid up and down in front of my face and I'm scared. And I never did learn any maths, never understood the point of logarithms, never used them and never will. If I ever had an interest in maths he killed it, and to this day if I'm down the pub and I've a load of change in my hand I just hold it out and let the barman take what's right, because maths is just beyond me.

But some days we'd do no maths whatsoever. Maths would be on the timetable, but Jumbo would bring in a tape-recorder, an old reel-to-reel, and play us recordings he'd made when he was a kid, of steam trains behind his house in Upminster, telling us to listen for the squeal of the wheels slipping if the train had pulled away too quickly. And one time he played us a recording of doodlebugs, the old V-1 rockets from World War II, which he'd taped from off the TV, and I remember he said *You're not allowed to have silence on TV, the BBC won't allow silence, so you'll hear the engine stop then you should hear silence, then the explosion. But you've got some nit talking through it.* And he'd have us time it. He'd play the recording, the engine would cut out, he'd kill the volume, then after five seconds he'd turn it up again and BOOM!

So lessons like that were, well, slightly weird, but better than most. Because most of them were dull and boring, trapped in a really unjust environment where the teachers were right and you had no say whatsoever. On some level I think a lot of us realised that if you'd passed the 11+ then you were going to be the foreman at the factory, and if you hadn't then you'd be on the factory floor. For girls the options were to be a secretary, or a hairdresser, or maybe work at a supermarket. Whichever it was to be, there was no inspiration in the way we were taught, it was just a matter of keeping us off the streets and training us for our roles. Nothing more and nothing less.

Thankfully there were a couple of exceptions.

The English teacher, Mr. Stewart, was a young bloke with a really scarred face, who used to race cars at a weekend and had a really bad crash. But he was a change from teachers like Jumbo whose idea of working with kids was to bang their desk lids up and down, because he'd been to teacher training college and he really wanted to be there. He had this immense enthusiasm for his subject, for the written word, for what books could do to open up young minds, and that enthusiasm came across and I started to really enjoy his lessons. That was something which would have a real impact on my life, and my understanding of what life was about.

What's more, you could talk to him. You could talk to him in class and he wouldn't hit you. I remember going to him one time because Jumbo had really had a go at this girl in maths, banged her desk lid in front of her face, then grabbed her by the scruff of her neck, threw her up against the wall and thumped the wall by the side of her head, shouting at her *Thank your lucky stars you're not a boy!* And I went to Mr. Stewart and said *How do you make a complaint about a teacher?* And he sat me down and said *I really think you ought to think about this.* He knew it would go nowhere, that I'd just be letting myself in for a whole world of trouble, but he took the time to listen to me and talk to me properly, and believe me in our school, for a teacher to do that? Rarer than rocking-horse shit, and no mistake.

Because most of the other teachers were terrifying. This was still the time of corporal punishment, and you could be slippered for something as trivial as talking in class, or forgetting your pencil case, or for chewing gum. A teacher would slipper you there and then in class, but for more serious offences you had to go to the headmaster, for the cane. One time a mate of mine had brought a dart into school and we were larking about in the corridor. He threw it at me and it arced over my shoulder and into the heel of a teacher's shoe. We pelted, but we were caught. Cane. Another time we were in the chemistry lab, and if you remember those little tripod stands you'd put over Bunsen-burners, well the one I was using had been on all day, and was so hot it was almost glowing. And my mate was in front of me, leaning over the bench by the gas taps, and I thought *This'll be a laugh* and branded his arse. He screamed, boy did he scream, and this little triangular piece of scorched material fell out of his trousers. Cane.

The stuff we did was never really nasty, just typical kids stuff, just mucking about, but if you got the cane it was six of the best, three on each hand. Every kid at the time knew the way to curl your hand so the cane didn't hurt as much, but the headmaster, this little Welsh git, he had this way of caning you right on the tips of your fingers, so hand curling didn't help at all. And sometimes, if he felt particularly vicious, he'd hit you with a ruler on the back of your hand, and that *really* hurt. Whatever way he chose, you had to keep your thumb out of the way, because if he hit your thumb you were going to cry. No question.

I was a repeat offender. I think this was the start of me

understanding what rebellion was, knowing that I didn't like what was going on, that it was shit, and I was going to do what I could to fuck it up. I'd picked up a book called *Kes*, and it had this blurb on the cover which really struck home:

> *This is for people who think comprehensive schools and orange juice are going to produce nice children. Billy Casper is trained but he's not tamed.*

Trained but not tamed. Yeah. Trained but not tamed was me.

Books

At Marsh Green they'd never trained us for the 11+, so when we sat the test it was something we didn't understand at all, and the fact I failed was no surprise. This meant that when I went to secondary school it was the local one to me, Triptons Secondary School for Boys, which took all the kids from Heath Park, along with a nearby school called Robert Clack. (While I was there the two of them went comprehensive, and then what had been Triptons took years one and two, then in the third year you moved over to the buildings which had been Robert Clack.) Anyway, at eleven years old I ended up at Triptons along with a whole bunch of other kids from my estate. Some of them were clearly really brainy, bright kids who had real aptitude but had failed the 11+, yet it was so obvious that everyone in the school was being channeled towards work on the factory floor, regardless of what they were capable of. And it was abundantly clear that the teachers didn't care about what they were teaching you, weren't interested, and were bored with being there themselves.

I remember thinking it was such a complete and utter waste of time. If I had to be there five hours a day five days a week then why not make it interesting for me? But that was way beyond most of the teachers whose default position towards us kids was to use anger and coercion to keep us in our place, then get out of the building every bit as fast as we did at the end of the day.

In that context, Mr. Stewart was a breath of fresh air. As I've said, he was one of the few teachers who would actually listen to the kids he taught, and who was enthusiastic about his work. That in itself was remarkable within Triptons, but what really set him apart was that he went out of his way to offer us books to read which actually spoke to us about our lives.

The first book he pointed me towards was *Billy Liar.* I remember thinking *I'm not going to like this* because what book could a teacher possibly give me that would be any good? I was wrong. I loved it. I loved it so much I still have that copy on my bookshelves today. It's old and battered and falling to pieces, but I'll never throw it out. I'd get home from school and lie on my bed reading it, and loving it – Billy Fisher had a fantasy world he escaped into, just like I did – and by the time I finished it I wanted to know what else there was to read. And so it was through Mr. Stewart that I ended up reading books by all the Angry Young Men, by John Osborne, Stan Barstow, Alan Sillitoe, the northern kitchen sink writers, and time after time I'd find them writing about stuff which struck a chord with me. Stan Barstow would write how *The old man didn't talk to you, he talked at you* and I knew just what he was writing about – after all, wasn't that how my stepdad was with me?

Being exposed to that kind of writing at school revolutionised my life. For the first time I knew that other people felt the way I did, and for the first time I was given the vocabulary and the concepts to express the way I felt about the world. And one book did that above all the others: *Kes.*

The cover alone was a shock. Billy Casper sticking his two fingers up. Before I'd even opened the book I was thinking *This is the one!* And Barry Hines' writing was superb, sparse, bang on the money. I ate it up. His description of Billy Casper's school, well, that was my school. When Billy has to write a piece of fiction for his English lesson, he doesn't wish on stars like the other kids, he dreams of having eggs and chips and beans for breakfast, and carpet on the stairs. And for me that really struck a chord because of living in Stoke, where we didn't have carpet on the stairs or anywhere else, and never ate properly either. By the time I got to the point in the book where his brother kills the hawk because Billy won't put a bet on for him, reading it got me so furious at the cruelty of it I was saying to people *If ever I find that Judd ...* They'd look at me like I was mad. *He doesn't exist, Steve!* But that's how real it was for me, that's how good Barry's writing was.

Now, with *Kes* being such an iconic book, it's easy to forget how fresh and shocking it was. From the V-sign on the cover to the subject matter itself it was the antithesis of your usual kid's books, which up till then had been gentle stories like *Swallows and Amazons*, or Enid Blyton, where happy kids lived in a world where adults were friendly and everything turned out well. Fairy tales. Growing up in Dagenham, Billy Casper's world made much more sense.

There was a publishing company called Longman which did special imprints for schools, and in the back of each book they'd have questions to make you think about what you'd read, and what it meant, and they'd have lists of what they called suggested reading – an *if you liked that you should try this* kind of thing. And before long I started actively seeking out books to read. Some of it was stuff I never really expected to enjoy, but Mr. Stewart had opened my mind up to literature and I'd stick with books I'd otherwise never have given a second glance, like D. H. Lawrence's *Sons and Lovers*, and some of it was stuff that I simply drank in, like *The Loneliness of the Long Distance Runner*.

It's hard to talk about the book without giving away the plot, and I don't want to, because Alan Sillitoe's writing deserves to be read, but at the end, when the kid at the centre of the story has thrown the race, deliberately lost it to show the contempt he has for the system, I remember putting the book down and thinking to myself *Fuck me that's a statement. That really is a statement.*

And reading books like that made a world of difference to how my life turned out. Once again I was incredibly lucky. In the right place at the right time. The coincidence of being at school in the years after these ground-breaking books had been written, and when teachers like Mr. Stewart were coming out of training college and changing how we were taught, well, I can't imagine how my life would have been if that hadn't happened.

One minute I was a teenager in this dull, boring place, hating school, walking around with a permanent erection not knowing what to do with it, and suddenly this whole new world opened up to me. The world of books, of the written word. And increasingly I got into reading, into enjoying what people wrote, wondering how do you do that? How do you write like that? And for the first time in my life thinking maybe I'd find out.

God

In my first year at Triptons, there was a teacher called Mr. Padfield, who took us for RE. He was the PE teacher too, and a really likeable bloke, someone who'd listen when you talked to him, and he was a Christian. A proper Christian. He was the first person who ever confronted us kids about racism, because at that point we were all trying to dress and sound like skinheads, and he heard some of us spouting the *black people come here and take our jobs* line, the usual mindless guff, and he confronted us on it.

And it turned into a really good discussion, because that sort of crap was just something I said. I'd heard other people saying it, and I was saying it too, without thinking, without meaning it. I was eleven years old and just opening my gob and trying to sound important. And what he did made a real impression on me, and answered some questions, because I realised what I was saying was really bloody stupid. And I think a lot of other kids thought he had a point too.

So, like Mr. Stewart, he encouraged me to think for myself, and because he was such an interesting young geezer I found myself listening to him and liking his lessons. And a couple of the things he did really fired my imagination. In PE, he did a class where he had us listen to the music from *West Side Story* and pretend to be two gangs. I wasn't much cop at the dance routine, but I loved the music, and when the film came round a few months later I pestered my sister to take me. *Go on, Carol!*

Please! I was a skinhead, and anything to do with gangs got my interest. Even a musical. I sat in the cinema up the Heathway, watching as the overhead shot of Manhattan panned in to a shot of the Jets, standing in the basketball court looking cool, and I loved the way they moved, and I wanted to be like them, and I wished I lived in New York City, not Heath Park, Dagenham.

Then Mr. Padfield brought this book into class called *The Cross and The Switchblade,* which was also about New York and the gangs there, and how they give up violence and take Jesus into their lives. Now for me, this just confirmed New York was a really wild, exciting place. I'd never been there and I'd probably never go, but I wanted to know more. So I picked up the book and really got into it. And then I went home and tried to read our family Bible.

It was a big old book with all the names of the family, generation after generation, written inside the front cover. For a lot of families, like ours, it would be the only book in the house, pretty much only ever opened to record births, and deaths. I wish I could say I have it now, but it disappeared and I don't know where. Anyway, I tried to read it, but it was all *thee* and *thou* and lots of *begetting*, and I couldn't make head nor tail of it. So I mentioned this to Mr. Padfield and he said *Try this* and handed me the Good News Bible, in modern English, and suddenly it was a book I could read, full of stories.

And then myself and a couple of other kids started getting extra tuition from him at break-times, having Bible readings. When he left at the end of our first year, and the woman who took over wasn't interested in carrying it on, me and these other kids set up a Christian Union meeting where we'd read some of the Bible and try and work out what it meant and what it was really trying to say. It wasn't always easy. *He anointed their heads with olive oil* er ... what?? What the fuck is olive oil? This

Nan aged twelve.

Granddad aged thirteen on his way to Aldgate.

Bert and Pat's wedding.

Bert and Pat at Whitebarn Lane. These are the only photos of Bert that I have.

Carol, me and David.

Granddad with me at Trafalgar Square.

Granddad, Carol and Nan.
This picture for me exudes the oppressive atmosphere of those times.

Mum and 'Auntie' Lisa outside the Cables – how I always remember Mum.

Barnados' Kids – Me and Carol in a friend's garden.

Happy Families – My grandparents' Golden Wedding. Alan (on right) had arrived late,
Mum (on left) shows her displeasure.

There were some fun times too – Granddad (no 27) about to win the
knobbly knees contest on Hayling Island.

Carol and Christine Noonan – Note Carol's Ben Sherman, which I later adopted.

The shape of things to come – Stan, far right, on a boozy works outing.

The Dead Time – Mum, Stan and the cocktail bar at Heath Park.

Mum (showing a bit too much) and Stan in the Vernon.

Mum and Stan get married, Carol as witness.

was Dagenham, in 1969. I wouldn't see olive oil till the first time I went to Dial House. So far as we knew, olive oil was Popeye's girlfriend, and anointing people with her made no sense at all.

I didn't start going to church or anything like that. But for a while I did daydream about being a priest or a missionary and going to Africa to help starving black people, stuff like that. I was twelve years old, for christ's sake. How else was I going to frame these ideas? I wanted to belong, to have a place in the world, to do *something*. It might be a shock to think of Steve Ignorant ever reading the Bible, but look at it like this: I was in this stale, static, sterile school with horrible grey plastic chairs and green blackboards, and I was trying to find a way out, to know there was something more to life than that. Why the fuck wouldn't you?

I think a lot of kids that age do something similar. Then their hormones kick in. I know mine did. And my fantasies changed. I'd be sitting in maths, and I wouldn't be thinking about logarithms, or saving starving people in Africa, I'd be dreaming of the door opening and Raquel Welch walking in wearing that fur bikini from *One Million Years BC* (did that film have any plot at all? and who cares??). She'd walk up to me and take me by the hand while all my mates stared in disbelief going *Wow! Steve's going out with Raquel Welch!* and we'd walk out of school and down the street. We wouldn't go to the pub because I was only a kid and anyway I'd seen what going to the pub did to Mum and Stan, so she'd take me to the chip shop instead. Result! It wasn't a sexual fantasy, it was more a get-me-away-from-boredom fantasy. Or possibly a fantasy about chips. It's hard to say. But it was so real that some days I'd be gutted it wasn't true.

My interest in Christianity got the final nail hammered into its coffin in the third year, and not through fantasies of Raquel Welch either. We had yet another RE teacher, who claimed to

49

be a Christian, and he said we'd study other religions too, Islam, Buddhism and so on. And I thought this would be really good. So he starts talking about Buddhism and says *Gautama Buddha is meant to have lived on one grain of rice a day for nine years, which I personally find difficult to believe.* And I put my hand up and said *Sir, the Bible says Jesus raised Lazarus from the dead, don't you find that more difficult to believe?* And I wasn't being a smart-arse, I really wanted an answer, or a discussion, because that was what me and my mates were used to doing. But he just went *Shut up and sit down, lad.*

I remember thinking *Right. I'm going to go out and shag any bird I can.* Not that I could of course, being fourteen, but it was just a visceral *fuck that and fuck you.* Because up till that point Christianity had been a place where I could have my say, ask my questions, develop my understanding. And now it was just another set of rules you were supposed to go along with and keep your head down and your gob shut. Not a fucking chance. I think I'd been waiting for something like that to happen, just to blow that myth away. And I sat there, watching him at the front of the class, saying whatever it was he had to say, not hearing him at all, thinking to myself *I won't be coming to your lesson much longer. I'll be off down Dagenham Breach finding my own religion, looking at nature, watching ships go down the river.* Which is exactly what I did.

Truant

At some point I decided *Right*. These people who are screaming and shouting at me and trying to feed me all this useless information, if they're not bothered about me because I'm going to end up working in a factory anyway, then I'm not going to bother either. Sod them and sod the consequences.

So when I should have been going into school I'd play truant instead. Wander off to Green Hill with a pack of five Park Drive I'd got for nothing out of the machine by jamming a lolly stick up the side to make the slide work, and sit there watching the world go by. Or I'd head down to Dagenham Breach, which was a man-made lake from when Ford's filled in the marshland so they could build their factory, and round which was an expanse of railway sidings and air-raid shelters and stuff like that, hidden behind the factory. To get there you'd scramble under this bridge, with the railway line literally right by your ear, and be half-deafened by the din of freight trains going past, pulled by bloody great diesels, wagon after wagon of cars fresh out of the plant stretching on forever.

Or if I didn't go there I'd just wander round Dagenham, or maybe walk to Romford and back. If I thought about it in advance and saved up my dinner money, 10p or 20p a day till I had enough, I'd buy a Red Rover and fuck off into London for the day, going down to Greenwich again, or into Trafalgar Square like I had with Granddad. But mostly I'd go down to the Thames at Rainham.

It's been tarted up a bit now, but it's a place called Ferry Lane, where you can actually get to the river, and it's where all the rubbish floating down from London gets carried to and swept in to shore. A little inlet filled with wood and crap and plastic, with old concrete barges run aground. A nowhere place unless you were looking for it, with river walls made up of rocks with fossils in them, and huge piles of furnace clinker, blue-green like glass, which glinted in the light. It was a great place for a kid playing truant! I saw my first kestrel there, by doing what my brother had taught me, by just sitting and watching. I learnt so much when I was truanting. I might not be able to do logarithms, but I do know where to find a grass snake or a hedge sparrow's nest.

Green Hill and Rainham and Dagenham Breach were little natural havens in the midst of all that industry, with no one else around, and that was part of the attraction. That, and the fact I knew I was pretty safe there. I wouldn't bump into a teacher, no neighbour of my mum's would see me. If I was out on the streets or walking to Romford there was always the risk I'd be spotted. One time myself and this kid Eric Spencer were out playing truant, fart-arsing about for the day, and when it got to 3 o'clock we hopped on a bus heading back to school so we could make out we'd been there all day. Next stop, who gets on? Stan. With my sister, back on leave from the RAF, heading back home themselves from an afternoon in the pub. Eric just grabbed the top of my head and pushed me right down into the seat so they wouldn't see me, and I spent the whole journey looking at the floor, shitting myself I'd be rumbled. I wasn't, but it was a close call.

Generally though, making sure Mum didn't know I was playing truant was easy – I just headed out of the door in my school uniform in the morning and came back in the afternoon.

Dealing with the school was obviously trickier and needed a little more cunning. So one evening I asked Mum to write out the alphabet for me as we were doing a project about hand-writing at school, and I needed that and – oh – a sentence in her normal writing. Please. Armed with that it was a piece of piss to write out absence notes in what looked like Mum's writing. *Stephen has been very ill. He has not been looking for slow-worms on Green Hill.* I didn't abuse this. Well, not much. But we did have a double maths lesson on Wednesdays, and I'm sure that if you looked at my attendance record for school you'd find that Wednesdays were the day I was off with terrible migraines, or diarrhoea, or earaches or whatever. I got questioned about it one time, but wormed my way out of it, swearing till I was blue in the face that I wasn't truanting, that I really was ill, *Honestly Sir!* From then on, though, I was a little more cute about doing what I wanted.

Escape

Books had opened up a whole new world for me. I might have been skipping as many maths lessons as I could, but if there was an English lesson in the school day, I'd be there, because I knew Mr. Stewart would feed my imagination. A lot of the time, though, my real education happened outside school, down at Rainham or wherever. It's like that for most kids, I reckon. You spend hours sat behind a desk, being taught how to say *La plume de ma tante* which you're never going to use, being trained in how to endure boredom, and you're young enough to hate it, and kick back. Then you'll be at home, or riding the bus to Barking, and something will spark your interest and you'll soak it up like a sponge.

One of the things that was a clarion call to me was a film on TV: *Saturday Night and Sunday Morning*. It was in black and white, because it had been made in 1960, but right from the first shot of a young Albert Finney looking good and tasty, working behind his lathe in the factory with a scowl on his face, I was hooked. The dialogue crackled with anger, with fighting back against lives half-lived *Don't let the bastards grind you down, that's one thing I've learned ... I'd like to see anybody try to grind me down – that'll be the day. What I'm out for is a good time. All the rest is propaganda*. Bam! And he throws down his oily rag, and it's *Saturday Night and Sunday Morning* and the music starts.

After years of cowboy-and-indian films, or war films where everybody pulled together for a bigger cause and everyone knew their place, this was a breath of fresh air. It was real. The character Albert Finney plays – Arthur Seaton – is a little sod, a real anti-hero who's out for himself and fighting back against the world around him. He's sleeping with a married woman, a workmate's wife, but drops her when something better comes along; he's more in common with Fred, who's black, than with most of the others; and he's *a bit of a red*, but only because it pisses off The Establishment.

I was glued to the screen from start to finish.

So I watched the film, and then I read the book, and the book really opened it up for me. Alan Sillitoe, who wrote it, said he didn't really like the Arthur Seaton character because his politics were all to cock, because he was messed up and didn't really know what he was doing. And that's as may be. But I was an impressionable young kid reading it at 12–13 years old, and Arthur was out for birds, booze and money, and looking smart, and so for me it was *Yes!! Give me some of that!!* Nothing else would have such a seismic effect on my life till punk, because it was through *Saturday Night and Sunday Morning* that I finally twigged that you could fight back, you didn't have to conform.

I loved Arthur's contempt for his bosses, and the fact he didn't give a monkey's. That he really didn't care if he got sacked because he'd go and get another job. That his attitude to authority wasn't *Yes Mr. Robbo, no Mr. Robbo, three bags full Mr. Robbo* like the foreman, it was more *Fuck you*. All of it struck a chord, and I'd take that with me, later, when I was out in the world of work myself.

The films and books that really got my attention were all about kicking back against the system. I'd realised that mum and Stan weren't really interested in me, and that was my response. I was learning about girls, but after reading *Saturday Night and Sunday Morning* in my mind I was hoping for a married woman, just like Arthur Seaton. There was fuck all chance of it happening, obviously, but I wanted it because it was so anti-system, so anti-establishment, because it was going against everything. I was thirteen, and Dagenham's Angry Young Man.

Most of the other kids at school seemed quite happy to go along with things, whereas I didn't, but then they had a family life. They'd go out at the weekend with their parents, or go to Southend on holiday, and – as I've already said – we didn't. The stock response to anything like that was *Nah. We can't afford it* yet they always had money for new clothes, or to spend on themselves. They weren't going to say they didn't want me around, but everything they did made it clear. If Stan was watching telly I couldn't make a sound. I could be sitting reading a book and having a bag of crisps, and the rustle of the crisp packet would disturb him. If I went to my room to read it'd be *What yer doing in there? Yer bedroom's for sleeping in. Get in here!* so really I couldn't win.

As life at home got more and more stifling, I was increasingly escaping into a fantasy world. The one where Raquel Welch walked in to school and rescued me, or where I was in New York, standing in an apartment wearing a tuxedo and holding a martini glass, with a beautiful woman hanging off my arm. And we'd have made love (quite how you did that was still a bit of a mystery, but I knew we'd done it) some time earlier and now we'd be standing looking out over the bright lights of the city. The fantasy was of being *established* with her, of being somewhere impossibly exotic. And of not being stuck in a poxy flat in Heath Park with mum and Stan.

Because I looked at what they had, and what they'd achieved, and I thought *Is that it?* Was all I had to look forward to a two-bedroom semi in Gidea Park or Barking and a job I hated? Did you just get the girlfriend, get engaged, get married, have the kids, and set the whole cycle off again? It wasn't for me. I wanted out.

Alan & Dee

Uncle Alan and Dee were living down in West Byfleet, in Surrey, and I asked mum if I could go visit them, and she said yeah, so off I went and spent the weekend with them. And I thought the way they lived together and got on with their son, Malcolm, was fantastic. As you'd expect, it was simple things that struck me. The fact they played football with him, and did things together, that there was the interaction that was missing in my life. One time Alan got a tape player and recorded us all singing along to LPs and played it back. It was hilarious, and it struck me that this was probably pretty much the first time I'd had a *laugh* with adults. In fourteen years.

Alan was a great role model, because he'd moved away from Dagenham and done things his own way. When he was younger, Granddad had lined him up to marry the girl next door, but then Alan had met Dee and thrown the whole thing over. Because of that Granddad never forgave him, and he was always seen as the black sheep of the family, but having spent time with them and Malcolm, and having seen how happy they were, I thought he'd done the right thing.

So more and more I'd take the train down there and spend Saturday and Sunday with them. It was a taste of what family life could be like. Alan and Dee talked to me like an equal, and listened to what I had to say. I could talk to them like I couldn't to my own parents, and it was great. I'd dread the moment I had to leave and get the train back home, because I knew I'd walk in through the door, and it'd be *Did you have a nice time? Yeah? Well shut up then, your dad's watching High Chapparal.*

And I'd sit there in silence, knowing I had school the next day, and the idea that yet another person was going to tell me to sit down and shut up was too much. So I'd tell myself *Fuck it, I'll play truant, 'cause I don't want this weekend to stop.* And Monday morning I'd be off up Green Hill with a pack of fags instead.

Unsurprisingly, I quickly got even less happy with life with mum and Stan. At first they'd been quietly chuffed that I was out of their way at weekends and they had the flat to themselves, but when I started getting a bit bolshy and a bit lippy with them then it soon became *You're spending too much time with Alan and Dee.* It wasn't that they wanted me back, just that they wanted me back in my box. And that wasn't ever going to happen.

It all came to a head one weekend when I rang mum on a Sunday night and made up some story that the trains weren't running and I couldn't get back, because I just didn't want to leave. It was a bit naughty, because I put Alan and Dee in a bit of a position, and I shouldn't have, but I just couldn't face going home. So there was an almighty row on the phone, and when I did get back they were straight on me as soon as I got in the door *What have they got that we haven't?* So I shot back *Principles.* And their only answer was *Don't you quote big words at me* because they hadn't a clue what I was talking about or what I meant, and that just about summed our relationship up.

In their eyes, me being bolshy couldn't be normal teenage grumpiness, or because they were crap at being parents. No. If I'd started answering them back, someone had to be leading me astray. Even Granddad joined in. I remember him saying *That Dee, she doing you a good turn is she?* And it really upset me, that he'd got to take that one good thing in my life away from me and turn it into something sordid, and I thought *You shit*. He was jealous, they all were, it was that *What have they got that we haven't?*

And I'd think *Well, where do you start?* Which wasn't particularly fair, but I was sick of people telling me to sit down and shut up and I'd pretty much had it with them not understanding that what they'd done with their lives wasn't what I wanted to do with mine.

That was it really. I just knew I had to get out of there as much as possible, and I was away pretty much every weekend after that. Because what I really wanted was the normal stuff every kid wants: someone to talk to, to make me feel that I mattered, to listen to what I had to say. And what I'd found with Alan and Dee, and Mr. Padfield and Mr. Stewart, had been exactly that. But none of them had the time to devote to it, and with the teachers I didn't want to be seen as a teacher's pet, so I was too embarrassed to ask. It doesn't take a genius to work out I was looking for someone to be something like a dad, because mum and Stan were either totally indifferent or fed up with me being around. And in the end, I found the Dial House lot, and they filled that role.

Over the years, I've been pretty vicious about family life in some of my songs, and I think it's easy to see why that is. And I never wanted to have kids myself, at first because I was afraid I'd make the same mistakes mum and Stan had, and be a rubbish parent; later, when I was in a band, because I knew I wouldn't have the time to look after kids properly and shoulder my responsibilities, to play football with them and take them on holiday, to do the things with them that I'd missed out on.

Alan and Dee showed me family life could work, that the nuclear family doesn't have to be a horror show, and I'm grateful for that, but in the end it wasn't for me. In the end, the people at Dial House, and in Crass, Conflict, and Schwartzeneggar became my family, and there was no way kids were going to fit in to that picture. I had so many years of enjoyment to make up for, and I was going to get them.

Death

Before that happened though, Nan died. It was early 1972, and I came back from school, or playing truant more likely, and found Mum crying and Stan trying to comfort her. I asked what was going on, and she said *Your Nan's gone a bit funny, she's just gone really funny.* Apparently Mum had dropped in to see her, and Nan had been talking nonsense, and really confused, doing things that were really out of character, or forgetting what she'd done. Nowadays we'd recognise all these as signs of dementia, but we didn't have a name for it then, and Mum had found it really distressing.

A couple of months before that, I'd been round at Whitebarn Lane one weekend, sitting with my Nan, just me and her because Granddad was out, waiting for a mate of mine to turn up to go swimming up the Leys, and she'd said to me *Look at this. Look what I've drawn. It's a biscuit barrel.* And it was. It was a very rough, child-like drawing of a biscuit barrel. She'd never done anything like that before. Ever. I remember looking at her and thinking *You're dying.* Which may seem like a really strange reaction, but I just ... knew.

There were no more shopping trips to Broad Street market. In a matter of weeks, Nan changed from being a capable pensioner to a bewildered old lady who couldn't find her way around, who'd get part way to Chequers and forget why she'd left the house. It was a hard enough thing for us to watch, but I think it must have been terrifying for her. In the end, she refused to eat or drink anything, and pretty quickly her kidneys failed and she got taken into Rush Green hospital in Dagenham, and died.

I remember going to see her in the Chapel of Rest where she'd taken me to see Aunty Reenie all those years before. The funeral was a quiet affair, just me, Mum and Stan, and a few of Nan's friends and neighbours. Afterwards Mum and Stan took Granddad to the pub, and I went to West Byfleet with Alan and Dee. They weren't around much any more – only for births, weddings, and funerals, and there weren't many of those. For me, Nan's death underlined that things were changing, that from here on in life would be different.

Now Granddad was living on his own for the first time in sixty years. He hadn't a clue how to cook, because that had always been Nan's job, so Mum would catch the bus down every day and knock up a meal for him. What Granddad really needed, though, was company, and things got a lot better when my brother hitched back from where he'd been working in Cornwall, and moved in to Whitebarn Lane. Him living with Granddad and looking after him worked really well, because my brother got a good rapport going with the old man, which might seem strange after everything that had happened when we were kids, but by then David was saying that Nan and Granddad had been more like parents to him than Pat and Stan.

And this was what caused the problem. Mum was happy enough for someone else to take on the responsibility of looking after Granddad, but she absolutely hated the idea she was being criticised. And Mum's response to criticism was always the same. She didn't take it on board, or consider whether it was justified, she just went on the attack. If David wasn't around, then he wouldn't be there to say she'd been a bad parent, so it wouldn't be true, that was how she saw it.

So she started to look for an excuse to turf David out of

Whitebarn Lane, regardless of what this might mean for Granddad. Finally she manufactured an argument over a jar of honey. She found it in the larder, and since Granddad didn't eat honey, she decided this was proof positive that David was using his stay there to line his own pockets. There was a blazing row, which ended with both Mum and Stan telling David to fuck off. So he did. In all of this, no one asked Granddad what he wanted, and he never got a say. He'd gone – like a lot of old men when their wives die before them – from being the family patriarch who ruled the roost, to this weak, shrunken little bloke whose opinion no longer counted.

As soon as David was gone, we gave up the flat in Heath Park and moved back down to Whitebarn Lane. If this was Mum's attempt to show she could look after Granddad every bit as well as David, it wasn't very successful. Granddad had a stroke and ended up pretty much bedridden. He'd piss and shit himself, and it'd be Mum who had to wipe his arse and so on. It didn't take long for the resentment to build and for Mum to decide she couldn't deal with it. So she had him put in hospital.

The hospital sent him on to this horrible place in Hornchurch, which was a bus ride away. Anyone in Dagenham would tell you, if you went in there the only way you'd come out was in a box. Fortunately for Granddad, David was still around. He was living in Upton Park, or with the hippies in Ongar who would introduce him to Dial House, and from time to time he'd pop up and we'd go and check on Granddad. All I can say is it was every bit as dreadful as I'd been led to believe. I remember it was full of nutters and people shouting, and whenever we went I could never get out of there quickly enough.

I don't know how he did it, but David managed to persuade the doctors Granddad shouldn't be there, and got him moved from there into Rush Green hospital, which did Granddad the power of good. And from there he was able to come back home for Mum to look after him again.

Which is where it all fell down. Mum quickly decided Granddad was too much to cope with, and got him put in an old people's home. I went up there with her once to visit him, and I remember she asked him *Is there anything you want?* And he said *Yeah. I want to go home* and just burst into tears. I sat there thinking *Fucking hell. He's lived in that house most of his life and now the poor sod can't come home.*

Because he couldn't. There was no way mum would give up the time to look after him. No way she could. Anybody who's ever looked after an aged, infirm relative will know how difficult it can be. Wiping your own dad's arse is hard enough, but it's the constant demands that wear you down. I remember Mum bursting into tears because she'd only just come downstairs and Granddad would want her to go back up again because he needed something. And Mum had to deal with it all. Nowadays, as a carer, she'd get support from the council or the NHS. Back then I don't think the word *carer* even existed, and you sank or you swam on your own. When people bang on about *the good old days,* they forget how much misery there could be behind closed doors.

Whitebarn Lane was where Granddad had lived almost all his adult life, where he'd spent all those years with Nan, where he'd made his daughter welcome when her marriage had fallen apart, and now he was turfed out. Sometimes I think old people need familiar places because they're full of memories, because they can just sit in a chair in a room they know and flip through those memories like we might look through a photo album. They might not live any longer, but I think their lives are happier.

All I know is that, in the old people's home, Granddad quickly faded away, and was shifted to Oldchurch hospital and died.

And there I was at another funeral, throwing a handful of dirt and stone into the grave, hearing the *crack!* as it bounced on the coffin lid. Feeling guilty. Because I remembered when Granddad was at Whitebarn Lane and bedridden, how he'd bang on the bedroom floor with his stick if he needed anything. And one night he did, and I went upstairs. And I was a grumpy teenager, who'd picked up from his mum that Granddad was a burden. What did he want? I asked. *I just want to see you. I just want to see you.* And I told him there was something on TV I wanted to watch, and stormed back downstairs.

It's one of the things I regret. The poor bloke just wanted a little bit of company. He'd made it through the First World War as an infantryman in the 1st Essex. When so many others died, he'd gone on to have a long, full life, and a happy marriage. But near the end of his own life, when he was lying alone unable to go the toilet without someone to give him a helping hand, I told him I'd rather watch TV. What a shitty way for things to end up.

Sixth Form

Nan and Granddad were dead, but we took over tenancy of their council house in Whitebarn Lane and carried on living there. As far as I was concerned it was a much better place to live than Heath Park, which I always think of as sterile, boring, and generally crap. Whitebarn Lane was where I'd grown up, and it was just a short walk to all my favourite places – Green Hill, Dagenham Breach, the Thames. Ok, it was a two mile bus journey to school, just as it had been for my final year at Marsh Green when Mum and Stan had moved up to the flat, but I didn't mind that. If I wanted to play truant I just didn't get on the bus, I simply walked out of the front door and carried on walking. And I played truant as much as I could.

Despite this, I passed some O-levels. English language and English literature, because I'd structured my truanting around my timetable, Geography, and Art. I don't think anyone was surprised I got an *Unclassified* in Maths.

What was a surprise was that I stayed on into the sixth form. But by now, I'd been visiting Dial House, and I'd seen what they were doing for a living, which was graphic design. They worked for a publishing company called White Lion, doing book covers and illustrations for children's books. As far as I could see, this meant you sat inside all day, in this nice house in the country, you did a drawing and sent it off, it got put on a book cover and you got paid. Fantastic!

So not really knowing what I *did* want to do, I decided I'd try and be a graphic designer too, although I didn't have a tiny clue what that involved. What it did mean was staying on at school so I could get qualifications to go to art college, and building up a portfolio, so hey presto! I was in the sixth form. Straight-away things got off to a bad start – I was called into the head-master's office and told I'd have to re-take O-level Maths. *Why? I want to go to art college. I don't need Maths!* But my protests counted for nothing and they stuck me down for it. Bastards.

So I did what I'd always done, and skipped the classes. With my experience in truanting, it was the obvious thing to do. Sometimes I'd go off to Green Hill, or down the Thames, but a lot of the time I'd just slip through the cracks by hiding out in school. It wasn't as if it was difficult – none of the teachers seemed to know or care what class I should be in, and if I did get stopped wandering the corridors I'd give them the old *I'm just taking a message to Mr. so-and-so*... and be on my way. Or I'd climb up to my hidey-hole over the stage, up on the platform where the controls for the lighting rig were, and where no one would ever think of looking for me. Or disappear into the old storeroom down by the Physics department, which no one ever used.

Best by far, though, was to hang out in the Art room, where I could draw and paint. I was doing Art anyway, and the Art teacher – Mr. Bull – was happy enough to let me stay there as much as I wanted. The department had two rooms, with a little L-shaped corridor connecting them, and I'd sit in there, unseen and out of the way. If the headmaster had come round, chances are I'd have been fine pretending I was part of the Art class, because he'd have had no idea whether I should be there or not, silly old twat, but it was better not to take the risk. I was still kicking over the traces, but now I'd got smart enough not to get caught doing it!

When I was hanging around in the Physics storeroom I was just killing time, but hours spent in the Art room with Mr. Bull were something else entirely. There'd be art books to read, and that introduced me to the work of different artists, and different styles of painting, something which I was learning about from the folks at Dial House too. And Mr. Bull got me involved in painting sets for the school plays, so he was harnessing my enthusiasm, encouraging me to do something with my time, something more than simply hiding away. I'm not sure it got me any nearer being a graphic designer, but I spent a lot of time there when I should have been in Maths, or doing sport, which I hated – why the fuck would anyone *ever* want to do a cross-country run??? My official timetable might have said one thing, but my time in the sixth form was really English, a little bit of Geography, and a hell of a lot of Art.

It also – briefly – meant being a prefect.

Because I'd wised up and found ways of not getting caught, the slippering and caning of my early school years had eased off. So I guess they thought they'd tamed me after all, and the bastards made me a prefect. This meant I had to take my turn standing on the school door of a morning, taking the names of the kids who were late and writing them down in the book so they'd get the slipper or detention later. I never put in a single name, but there were other prefects – the ones who want to show they're loyal little soldiers – who always would. I'd argue the toss with them *What you doing? Fuckin 'ell! Come on!* because why drop the kids in it? What good would that do? So my attitude was seen as being suspect from the off, and when they sussed that I wasn't reporting kids for smoking either, my card was well and truly marked. Then I was *caught* smoking. A prefect with the other smokers in the smokers' union, down behind the bike sheds. And I was off the firm, which I didn't mind at all. *I really think you should take more responsibility, Williams* – oh, FUCK OFF!

It was about this time that I came back from school one day – and I'd actually been to school and not played truant – and the house was full of people, all of them with drinks, all of them dressed up. Even Stan's two brothers were there, suited and booted as always, with their gold teeth and gold rings and the bluebird tattoos on their hands. I hadn't a clue what was going on, and when my sister came over, all serious, and took me to one side, I thought it must be that someone had died. But Mum and Stan had finally got married. I couldn't believe they hadn't invited me – I could have had a day off instead of going to school – but they didn't. Thanks. I got really drunk on gin and went to sleep upstairs, and they went down the Vernon, where the party carried on.

Shortly after that Mum turned round and said *We can't afford to keep you at school any more. You'll have to leave.* My feelings were really mixed. On the one hand, I knew I was drifting – I didn't have a real burning desire to be a graphic designer and I clearly wasn't interested in knuckling down to study – so yeah, I might as well leave. On the other hand I knew this was just history repeating itself, and Mum was doing with me what she'd done with David. She hadn't a clue how I was doing at school, because she'd never asked about it or read a single one of my reports.

I never did get to art college. Instead I went into the office at school and told them my Mum said I had to leave, right now, mid-term. No one made much of a fuss. Not me, not the school, not even Mr. Bull. Education was over, and I was out in the world of work.

Bowie

In 1973 David Bowie played Romford Odeon. Tickets cost £1.50 and I went along with my mate Dave Hill. Dave had been someone I'd seen around for years, but never got to know till my last year at school, when we became really good mates. It was Bowie we'd bonded over. We were having a fag and chatting, and Dave said he was off to Romford to a barber's where he could get a Bowie haircut, which was *the* cool style to have. He could see I was tempted to come along too. *They've got nudie magazines* he grinned, and that was it. Decision made! We got the bus out to Romford and sat in the shop, waiting our turn, reading *Penthouse* and thinking life was great! Came out and strutted down the road in Romford thinking we were cool as fuck – we had the haircut, we had the baggies, we had the platform shoes – bring it on! In a year or two it would be all about having Budgie jackets, and the Bowie haircut would be out of fashion and then we'd have the Rod Stewart look, God help us, but whatever the fashion, we were always trying to look like the dog's ... Always.

Fashion had changed several times since that afternoon sitting on the doorstep with Malcolm Roberts back when I was in junior school, watching that skinhead floating up the next door path, and hearing ska for the first time. But whatever the fashion, from that moment on, clothes and music had been inextricably linked.

At twelve or thirteen, like all kids, I spent Thursday evenings watching *Top Of The Pops*, and as much time as I could listening to the radio, immersing myself in music, tuning in to Radio Luxembourg on a tiny transistor, and in later years to the then-brand-new Radio One. Buying records was something I couldn't afford – what little cash I had in those days was all going toward perfecting the skinhead look – so it was only when someone lent me a *Tighten Up* album, on Trojan Records, that I got to listen to a record for myself. Nan and Granddad had an old radiogram, so I waited for them to go out, and put the record on. Watched the arm carry the vinyl over, drop it down, and the needle drop into the groove. The sound was tinny and scratchy, but it was mine!

Ska was my first music, and I still love Toots and the Maytals '54–46' to this day. For me, it's all tied in with those two years from 1968 to 1970, and being a skinhead, like every other kid in Dagenham. The first record I actually bought, though, was 'Close To You' by The Carpenters, and I went all the way up to Woolworths on the Heathway to get it, handing over my 50p, then walking back home with it under my arm, pleased as punch. I'm still a big Burt Bacharach fan now.

But fashion changes, and skinhead bled into suedehead, and then that moved on in turn, and it was all shirts with elephant ear collars, Rupert Bear trousers with high waistbands and different colour buttons, platform shoes and stripy jumpers. This quickly led on to the Bay City Roller look, and so the whole thing evolved. And as skinhead petered out, so my musical tastes changed, and I started listening to Alvin Stardust, Elton John, David Bowie, and Slade. And so on.

Anyway, Dave and I came back from Romford with our cool Bowie haircuts, and I'd go round Dave's house and we'd sit there smoking, playing Bowie records, talking about the lyrics, really getting into it. And then Bowie came to play Romford

Odeon. I was going to say it was the first gig I'd ever been to, but that's a lie, because when I was twelve I'd sneaked into a Desmond Dekker show in Ilford with a mate. That had been full of big skinheads, proper firms from Chadwell Heath and places like that, and at the time we were scared they'd clump us. Looking back I think they admired us for sneaking in, and the excitement of being at a live gig stayed with me long after the fear had gone.

The Bowie gig blew me away. Dave and I lived off the high of the gig for weeks. I remember Bowie did 'Life On Mars', and he was wearing an outfit where he pulled off the one sleeve and then the other. He was a good-looking bloke and he was wearing make-up and all the girls were screaming at him, and I thought *Ah-hah! Right!* I never did wear the make-up, but I did get some bangles. This is one point where I disagree with Penny Rimbaud – he always said Bowie achieved nothing, it was the Beatles who did everything. No. What Bowie did was make it all right for blokes to wear nail varnish, and bangles, and a bit of jewellery. To make themselves up on council estates and not get beaten up for it. He was the first star to say *Yes. I'm bisexual.* Even the hardnuts who were into Bowie would say *Yeah, he's a bit of a poof but he's all right*. It's a classic line. *He's a bit of a bender but he's ok.* So Bowie helped change all that.

The ironic thing was that within the year I got beaten up at a West Ham game by two blokes wearing Ziggy Stardust make-up. We were playing Spurs and they got me good and proper, beat the living daylights out of me. When I found my mates they were all going *What's happened to you??!!*

I knew if I told them I'd been beaten up by two men wearing make-up, I'd never live it down.

Lads, I said, *there were these twelve geezers …*

Work

When I left school I went to the careers office, and they were a useless bunch of twats. They asked me what I wanted to do, and I said I wanted to be a graphic designer. Well there's not much opportunity there, they said. How about printing? Now I'd done a bit of silk-screen printing up at Dial House, and I thought *Yeah, all right*. So my first job was offset litho printing, just off Piccadilly, for £14 a week. I stuck it for about six months. It was an awful job anyway, but made worse by this mouthy Australian arsehole I had to work with. Never a day passed that I didn't dream of bashing him, and one morning I woke up and thought *Nah. Enough.*

Mum wanted me to go and work down the Cables. As far as she could see, it was a good, steady job with a firm that had outings for their workers and took their kids to the *Skating On Ice* extravaganza every Christmas. Granddad had stayed with them for over forty years, and she'd worked there too, and now it could be my turn. She couldn't understand why I'd want anything else. But I looked at the carriage clock sitting on the mantelpiece in Whitebarn Lane, which the Cables gave Granddad when he retired, and the framed certificate hanging on the wall, thanking him for his service, and something about measuring out the rest of my life like that made my blood run cold. I couldn't do it.

So I went back to the careers office. They were even more useless than before. If I wasn't happy to stick at offset litho they really didn't know what they could do for me. So I trotted off to the Labour Exchange, and who was there but an old mate of mine from school, Ian Jacobs, working behind the counter. It was a quick *How you doing, mate? You out of work? We'll see if we can sort you out. Here you go!* And I was on the dole, easy as that.

But it was only £10 or so a week, so I knew it couldn't last long. A few weeks later I was walking through Dagenham, down the A13, and there in one of the industrial estates was the head office for a supermarket chain called Wallis's. So without really thinking about it I popped in on the off-chance and asked if they had any vacancies. And the bloke said *Have you got any qualifications?* So I told him I've got this and I can do that, and he looked at me and said *I think we can fix you up with something.*

Two weeks later I was working down the supermarket in Chequers. And this is when life really opened up for me, because I had money in my pocket, a new bunch of mates, and I was going to West Ham. This is when the good times really started.

Not only was the job a five minute walk round the corner from the house, but I was earning £25 a week, which was a fortune in those days, and a big step up from the £14 I'd been getting at the printer's in Piccadilly. On top of that there were loads of good-looking girls, there were parties at people's houses, and we were all young and going out down the pub together at the weekend.

I was still living at home, but now I was paying Mum board and lodging Stan was off my back, and I had plenty of money left for fags, lager, and clobber. When you're seventeen, eighteen, that's a pretty sweet deal. And I was able to go down the pub with the rest of the firm (you were always a 'firm', always). There was me; Peter Edmunds who worked on the greengrocery; Tony Page, who we called 'Bookie'; Jimmy Ram, who was 'Bootsie' because he always wore big old army boots; Kevin Hawkes; Gary Young, who was a terror and a really good fighter; Bill Chivers, who got me into motorbikes; then there were the girls: Rosie Head, who taught me how to French kiss; and Cherise Meggs, the stunner that me and Bookie nearly came to blows over.

Some of us worked at Wallis's, but Kevin was a forklift driver, and through him I met his cousins, Ian Raby and Richard, who was another terror; and there were Pete Edmunds' brothers, Jimmy and Johnny who were real heavy geezers; and Phil, the Rabys' cousin. That was the core of our firm, and we'd go down the pub and have a good time, or we'd go up West Ham and look out for each other. Like I said, they were good mates, and they were great days. I had money in my pocket and I was going to enjoy myself, see girls and get my end away. *Fuck graphic design!*

Anyway, in between all the drinking and the partying, there was the work, which paid for it all. And after the printers, it was a breeze. I was working on the produce counter, selling hunks of cheese and slices of bacon, that kind of thing. *Four slices of lean and streaky, Mrs. Brown? And how's the kids?* I still know how to bone a side of pig – not that I've had much call for it in my musical career, mind. And I had a couple of little scams going, too. When the deliveries came, I'd fiddle the figures, lob a tray of yogurt or a slab of cheese in the skip by the loading bay, then pick it up later on the way home. Everyone did it. I wouldn't sell it, just take it to Dial House, or pass it on to anyone else I thought needed it. Because Wallis's weren't on the level. So neither was I.

On my first day there, this bloke George was showing me round, telling me how to set out the counter display for produce, which section was for pork pies, where the cheese went, stressing the importance of the plastic sprigs of parsley. And he seemed a nice enough bloke. Then he showed me the scales and said *This is what we do* and got a bit of bacon fat, stuck it underneath the scale and adjusted it. So, as a customer, every time you bought something you were losing, because the weight was slightly off. And I thought *You twister. That's out of order.* But those years of boxing clever at school came into their own, and I didn't say a word, just nodded, kept my mouth shut, and made my plans.

Whenever my mum came in, I'd be sure and give her a little bit extra, to make up for what Wallis's were skimming, and then I'd add some more, just to be sure. Then I noticed that a lot of the old ladies would only buy the scraps and off-cuts of fat that were sold as food for pets, because that was all they could afford. So I'd take a good look round, and if no one was watching I'd sling a couple of rashers of bacon in the bag, and pass it over. Pete Edmunds was doing the same thing over on greengrocery — he'd throw in a couple of extra potatoes or the odd onion or whatever. It was the old working class thing of looking after your own. We all used to do it. Because we looked at these old dears just scraping by, and we saw someone who could be our mum, or our nan.

And I got away with it. I'd been there a couple of months and George told me I had prospects. If I worked hard and played my cards right I could be promoted by the time I was thirty. I remember thinking *You've got to be kidding*. There was no way I was going to be stuck behind a produce counter by then. But I said nothing. Just carried on fighting back in my quiet way. A couple of rashers here, an extra few ounces of cheese there. Looking out for the ones who needed it. Let's face it, we owed them more loyalty than we could ever owe a supermarket.

The Vernon

Apparently there's something like five or six pubs a day are shutting down in this country now, and plenty of the ones still open are struggling to get by. The media work themselves into a right froth debating what this says about Britain, whether we're drinking less, or drinking more but at home, or drinking wine instead of beer, or just too apathetic to get off the sofa. Who knows? But something's changed. Because being a landlord used to be a licence to print money, and your local was a key part of where you lived, and a great night out.

Our local was the Admiral Vernon, where Mum had met dad all those years ago, and still went drinking with Stan. So it was almost part of the family. It was one of those old-fashioned pubs with a huge saloon bar, and a small public bar which is where the Irish workers – and I'm not being derogatory – where the Irish workers used to drink, and which had lino on the floor. The saloon had carpet and that's where we all went. During the day it had a big dining area for lunch and then every Saturday and Sunday evening a resident band would play on the little stage. A bloke on organ, with a guitarist, and a drummer. And they were really good. They'd play stuff like 'Begin the Beguine' which has a very difficult drum beat, but then they'd also keep up with what was new and play modern songs like 'Sorrow' by David Bowie. 'Sweet Caroline', and a bit of the Shadows. Keeping everyone happy.

Now when I first started going in there – well when we first started going in there as a firm – there was this funny hierarchy that existed in the pub. Until you were known, you could obviously buy your drink at the bar but once you'd done that you moved away. You didn't stand at the bar because that was reserved for the regulars, that sort of thing. You could sit on a particular chair till a certain time but then *You'd better get up because old Reg is coming in and that's his stool* ... So what happened was you shuffled round the pub – and the Vernon could get really rammed on a weekend, with over 200 people in there – so you'd be shuffling round the pub holding your pint against your chest, trying not to spill any, till you found your own space at the bar that no one else had claimed. All very territorial. All wonderfully, quaintly British. Finally we were regulars ourselves, and found our space. It was right round the corner but we could still see the door, so we could keep an eye on who was coming and going, and it had the advantage that we were close to the band. We'd buy them a pint and get them to play our favourite songs.

The weekend was set pretty much in stone. Friday night was always men's night. You didn't take your bird out – and we were seventeen, eighteen, so they were always *birds* – because it was men's night and that wasn't done. Traditionally, Friday had been when workers got paid, so Friday night was the one night of the week when men could go out alone, suited and booted but with some money in their pocket. You couldn't really cut loose because you had work the next day on Saturday morning, but with no women around you didn't have to watch your language. In those days, swearing in front of women was considered to be really out of order, so Friday night was something of a safety valve. And if a pub was going to have a stripper, it would be on Friday night.

Saturday night was something else. Saturday was when you got dressed up and took your girlfriend to the pub, and you'd stop at the seafood stall outside, buy your pint of prawns and bring them in, buy that first pint of lager and then get merrily pissed, all of you, sitting round a table, buying round after round. Sooner or later one of you would get up and do a turn on the mic, usually 'Bubbles' for West Ham, and everyone would sing along. And you wouldn't want to be anywhere else right then, you felt so fantastic.

One Saturday night, though, we got invited to a party in Berkhamstead. So a bunch of us piled into a couple of cars, and went over. I don't remember much about the party, but I do remember we all got really pissed. And when we were leaving, and staggering down Berkhamstead High Street, we saw the fountain. And next to the fountain, the scaffolding poles. I thought *Why not bring the two together?* It wasn't easy, but eventually we got a twenty foot steel pole standing upright in the middle of the fountain. It teetered for a moment while we all saluted it, and then came crashing to the ground. Hilarious. We were whooping and cheering and laughing – and then we saw the panda car.

Everyone pelted in different directions. Except me. Being rat-arsed and wearing platform shoes was not a good combination. I'd barely put one foot in front of the other before I was shoved in the back of the car. *Right, you fucking little shit. You're nicked. Who's your mates? Where are they? What's your name and address?* Luckily I was too pissed to talk properly, but I was really shitting it. I sat in the car while they drove round the town centre looking for the others. But unlike me, they'd all got on their toes and done one. So the coppers drove me back to the fountain, hauled me out of the car, and went *You put it in there. You get it out.*

So there I was, up to my knees in water in the fountain, stumbling around, trying to pull out this pole. It had taken half a dozen of us to get it in there in the first place, so I was getting nowhere. Eventually the coppers lost patience with it all and told me *For Christ's sake, fucking get out!* So I do. I climb out and stand there, dripping, while one of them has a right go at me, giving it the old *If we ever catch you round here again …* And over his shoulder, hiding behind a tree, I see Jimmy Ram, looking and waving and giving it the Vs. I'm trying not to laugh and this copper goes *You can wipe that smile off your face and all.* Yes, officer. *Now fuck off.*

So we could be little terrors. In our minds, we were men now. We were regulars in our own pub, and we felt pretty much untouchable – although I hadn't felt quite so untouchable in the police car – but most of what we did was just larking about, high jinks. One time we were in the Vernon and someone flicked a lighted match into Jimmy's hair. He had this nest of long hair, and suddenly there's flames going up one side of his head. June the barmaid is behind the bar going *Ooh! Ooh!* getting all of a fluster, and not knowing what to do. So Jimmy puts the flames out by picking up the water jug off the bar and pouring it over his own head, calling us *Bastards* all the while but not able to stop himself smiling because we're pissing ourselves laughing, barely able to tell him *Watch yer language, Bootsie! Ladies present!*

You had to watch your back. Just because you were being a smart-arse and putting a vodka in someone else's drink didn't mean they weren't doing the same to you. And god help you on your birthday. Everyone would buy you a pint. Maybe two. And you'd sit there with something like fifteen pints in front of you, already swilling in beer, forcing yourself to drink one of them, knowing you couldn't possibly manage them all. Your vision would start to go, your speech would be all slurred, and then you'd get that horrible feeling that yep, the pint was going down, but it'd be coming right back up again. Binge drinking? It's nothing new.

At the end of one of those nights I stumbled home and couldn't get my key in the latch for love nor money. I was running it up and down the door, vaguely hoping for some kind of miracle to get me inside, and Mum opens the door in her dressing gown, giving it *What time do you call this?* I was seeing about three of her, so I told them all *Why don't you just piss off?* and she hit me over the head with the Hoover pipe. I woke up in the morning with a lump on my head and the Hoover pipe lying, bent, in the corner of the room. I came home pissed plenty, but I never swore at her again.

Mostly we went out drinking in Dagenham, but occasionally we'd head out to Southend on a Sunday and have a blow-out on the seafront, or we'd go to Romford for the pictures. One time we were all off to Romford on a bus with the open platform at the back, one of the old Routemasters, and we're all on the platform arsing about, ringing the bell every time the conductor's back was turned, with him telling us to pack it in or he'd throw us off. Bootsie was holding onto the pole, and we pushed him off as the bus was still moving. He was holding on to the pole for all he was worth, sliding down the road with sparks coming off the hobnails in his big old boots, calling us *Bastards!* again.

It's funny that Bootsie found himself on the receiving end of this kind of stuff, because within our little firm everyone had a role, and he was the heavy one. I was the mediator who was asked to sort things out if someone's girlfriend wasn't talking to them, or the diplomat who'd make sure other firms didn't get the hump if we popped in their pub for a pint; Pete Edmunds always suggested where we should go; Gary Young was the really heavy one, even more than Bootsie; Richard Raby had a car we could borrow now and then, and so on.

So we got out and about, but mainly we stayed loyal to the

Vernon. Sometimes we'd go to the Thatched House on the A13 because they had a good band on, or there were some tasty girls down there, or just for a change we'd go to the Cross Keys which is an old, old pub in the old part of Dagenham, but then we'd always go back to the Vernon for closing time. That was our local, and you always stayed loyal to your local. Everyone did.

This meant that when you met people you could gauge who they were or what they were by where they drank. The Vernon was a social pub; anyone who drank at the Matapan was a tasty geezer. And if they drank at the Fanshawe: *Jesus Christ!* give them whatever they want and get out!

Now, there was a pub in Dagenham called the Church Elm. I think it might have closed down, but back then I never ever saw it without a cracked window. And people said to me *When you're old enough to drink* don't ever *go and drink in the Church Elm, they're all fucking hard nuts.* Of course this just piqued my curiosity. I used to pass it on the bus on the way back from the printers in Piccadilly, and it was right on the main road up by Dagenham Heathway. From the top deck of the bus you could see inside and it looked all right, and I thought *Sod it, I'll go inside for a pint, see what all the fuss is about.*

And so I did. And it was just an ordinary pub. Wednesday evening, 6 o'clock or so, a few people standing round, decent enough beer. Nothing going on, no big deal. I drank about half my pint and went to the toilet for a piss, and when I come back all the bar staff are behind the bar, holding truncheons, and these three blokes are standing in front of the bar waving broken glasses. And I thought *What the —?!* and sort of edged out trying not to be noticed ... and never went back there again. You'd have thought I'd learned my lesson there and then, but life isn't ever that simple.

West Ham

I'd been to West Ham a couple of times when I was at school – it was a mate who was a Spurs fan I'd been with that time I was beaten up – but now I was working at Wallis's with Pete Edmunds, who was a real staunch West Ham fan, we started going down whenever we could. This was when the West Ham team was packed with great players, internationals like Trevor Brooking, Geoff Hurst, Clive Best, and Billy Bonds, and had a legendary reputation for playing attractive football. Not that this always helped them get a result, mind, but they were seen as a proper footballing club.

So we went to quite a lot of matches. We'd meet up in the Vernon for a pint or two, then take the train to Upton Park. Working at Wallis's meant working Saturdays, so if we were going to a match we had to take holiday time, or work the Saturday morning but get away really quickly at lunchtime, and sprint up the Vernon to catch up with the others so we could get down the ground as early as possible.

Now, hand in hand with the Hammers fame for great football on the pitch went a notoriety for fearsome fans off it. This was the mid-70s, way before CCTV and all-seater grounds, when trouble was part and parcel of what went on. It's just that some fans were more caught up in it than others. The *Daily Mirror* published what it called a *League Of Shame* in 1974, and West Ham were right up near the top (or down at the bottom, as the *Mirror* had it). Chelsea were about the same, and if they were playing West Ham we'd definitely get down there early, because that'd be a right old tear-up.

For home matches we'd meet up in a pub in Barking called the Spotted Dog, and the leaders of the various firms would send people off round the East End. *Right. You lot go to Plaistow. You lot go to West Ham.* The police would be at Upton Park, obviously, and maybe East Ham, but seeing as they wouldn't spread out any further, and they didn't have CCTV, we just used to go elsewhere. And we'd wait for the trains to come in with the away fans on, and then we'd steam in. That was how things were, and any fans going to an away game would know what was coming, they'd know the chances were they'd be getting in a fight and they'd more than likely be outnumbered. So only the real hardcore went. It was the same for Hammers fans if they went to Chelsea, or Arsenal, or Spurs. You knew it in advance, and you went – and took your chances – or you didn't go.

Don't get me wrong, our little firm wasn't always in there rucking away. We weren't the ICF, or anything like it. We weren't ever involved with them, although we'd seen them around, and knew who they were. But the fighting was everywhere, and we had a couple of terrors in our firm, a couple of people who could look after themselves in a scrap, and who looked forward to Saturday afternoons and the adrenalin of a running battle. It was a hell of a buzz.

For all the excitement, there were a couple of things put me off going to matches in the end. One of them I'll talk about later, but the other one was something that always struck me as strange, and stupid, and which I hated at the time. And still do. Like most grounds, Upton Park had a North Bank and a South Bank (and yes, an East and a West side), and we used to go in the South Bank. Now as in all things, there was a hierarchy, and the further back up the stand you were, the harder you were supposed to be, and the top of the South Bank back then was taken over by a firm called the Mile End Mob. They were staunch West Ham supporters, and right hard bastards, and you couldn't be in their firm unless you came from Mile End. So far, so normal. But what used to happen was that if there weren't many rival supporters at the game, or if they were bored, or pissed off, the Mile End Mob used to kick the shit out of other West Ham fans, just for the fun of it. For them it was all part of being hard. I thought it was a load of bullshit.

That's why, when ICF established itself I was really glad, because it was run by people the same age as us, like Andy Swallow and Cass Pennant who we'd seen around and who were famous within the ground for being great fighters, for never stepping back. The ICF made it possible for us to go to West Ham matches as West Ham supporters and not get beaten up by other West Ham fans, and putting it like that shows you just how fucked up the Mile End Mob had been.

So by the start of the '75−76 season I'd distanced myself from it a little, and Wallis's had moved me from Chequers on to the branch in Barking, and from there to their supermarket at Upton Park. I was doing the same job each time, you just got moved on. New store, new faces, same produce counter.

And then there was this famous match where Man U came down. In October 1975. A year earlier, when the *Mirror* had published their *League Of Shame*, Man U had been top (or bottom), and before the match word had gone round the whole of the East End that the Man U fans reckoned they were hard enough to take Upton Park. So all the old guard, all the dockers and the like, came up to Upton Park specifically for this one match. It was a matter of pride, of showing the Northerners the East End wouldn't run, of sending them back home with their tail between their legs and something to think about. And a chance to sort out the Cockney Reds, traitors who didn't support West Ham. It was all bloody daft, but there you go.

I was working in Wallis's that day, and there was this guy I worked with who kept saying *Man U are coming down today*. I know. *And I can't get any time off.* I know. Because you couldn't *not* know about it. No one was talking about anything else.

And it got to 1 o'clock. Our lunch hour. And suddenly there's sirens going off and police cars flying down the road and people running, and we realise it's all kicked off at the station. Which is just down the road. So we nip out to see what's happening, still wearing our white work overalls and munching our sandwiches. And what it is, the Man U lot have arrived and they're being kicked back and punched back into the station by the West Ham fans. Running battles in the street, all this kind of thing, and we can't resist getting closer than we should. Then from a side street, another bunch of West Ham come running round the corner, and we get caught up in that and bundled along, and we end up outside the station, and now the police are involved and we're getting pushed this way and that, fists are flying and we're looking at each other thinking *Hold up – we only came to have a look!*

And there's an almighty shove and we end up down on the train platform with all the Man U fans. Me and my mate and loads of mancs.

My mate whispers *Fuckin' ell! What do we do?* And I tell him really definitely *Don't. Say. Anything.* Because I know if they hear our voices and suss we're West Ham, we're dead. I take a look around and see a couple of brooms so I grab them, give him one, and say to him *Pretend we're sweeper-uppers*. So we sweep our way out of the station, trying to blend in and look invisible, past all the Man U fans who are more interested in licking their wounds than they are in us, thank fuck. As soon as we're outside we throw the brooms down and leg it back to work. We were late and we got a bollocking for it, but we were so happy to be in one piece we just took it on the chin.

That match has gone down in football history as the one when Man U got well and truly done by anyone and everyone who had anything to do with West Ham. The poor mancs had no escape. They got absolutely battered. They got beaten onto the pitch in the ground, trying to get away from the fighting, and they got beaten all the way back out of the East End. When we shut up at 5.30 that evening it was still pretty difficult to get home, the police had cordoned off streets and that, so I just walked up the other way to Manor Park and caught a train from there to Chadwell Heath.

I got home, had a quick wash and a bite to eat, got myself tarted up, and was off down the Vernon. Saturday night. Same as always.

Beating

They say curiosity killed the cat. Well, it got me in some scrapes over the years too. There was a pub in Dagenham called the Merry Fiddlers. It's gone now and there's a supermarket on it, Sainsbury's or something, and like the Church Elm it was a pub with a reputation for trouble, but it was early evening and I thought *Sod it, let's try it*, and trotted on in. It was quite a modern pub for those times, open plan, split in two levels, with fruit machines down the far end, and a pool table. It was nice and quiet, nothing happening, just a couple of blokes in there, and a girl sat at the bar. What was all the fuss about?

So I walked up to the bar, ordered a pint of lager and lime and stood there sipping my pint. Then, as you do, I got chatting to the girl. The usual small talk *All right, how you doing? ... What do you do? ... I work at so-and-so ... blahblahblah ... Who do you know? ... Oh I used to go to school with them ...* All totally innocent. And then I ordered another lager and lime and said to the girl *Do you want a drink, love?*

And as soon as I said it this bloke appeared at my shoulder and went *You chatting my bird up?*

No. Sorry, mate. Didn't realise she was with you. I was just asking her if she wanted a drink.

What? You trying to pick her up then?

And then this other bloke appeared at my other shoulder. And I thought *Righto ...* And looked round to the woman behind the bar, but she's fucked off down the other end of the pub.

Deliberately. And I look at the girl I've been chatting to, waiting for her to explain there's nothing going on, and she's got this smirk on her face. And the penny drops, and I realise I've been set up ...

So I went *Look I really don't want any trouble.*

And the geezer goes *You're a fucking cunt aren't you?*

Yeah, I'm a fucking cunt, whatever.

You're a fucking wanker aren't you?

Yeah, yeah. I'm a wanker.

Do you fancy her?

No.

What? You think she's ugly?

I remember thinking *Oh for fuck's sake. That old one. Here it comes. I just ain't going to get out of this.* So I said *Fuck it. Do what you've got to do, mate.*

And he goes *Say 'sorry'.*

All right. Sorry.

Say 'sorry sir'.

Sigh. *OK. Sorry sir.*

Get on your knees and do it.

And at that point I went *Nah. That I'm not doing. Sorry. You're going to have to fucking do me.*

I was really shitting it. And he kicked me up the arse, and gave me a dig in the face while his mate punched me on the back of the head. *Now get the fuck out.*

So I did. I got out of there sharpish, thinking *What a dump!* And I go back and tell Pete Edmunds and the lads and of course there's all this *We'll go down there and sort them out* which was never going to happen, but which you always have to say. In the end though, it was one of those things you just had to chalk up to experience. Humiliating, terrifying, but it could have been worse. And at least now I knew never to go there again.

Now the thing was, there was one of the lads in our firm, and his mum knew my mum, and if I saw his mum around I'd say hallo and ask her how she was doing, carry her shopping home for her and this kind of thing. Now this lad had two brothers, Bill and Ben. Bill had been inside and he really was a tearaway, and Ben was fucking tasty as well, both of them always suited and booted, but in that vicious, sharp way. And so I'd got to know them, and they liked me, 'cause I helped their mum out, showed respect. So one day I'm indoors and the doorbell goes and it's Bill at the door. *All right Steve, you coming for a drink?* And I went *Well…* And he went *No. You're coming for a drink.* And I went *Er… yeah. All right then.* Thinking *What's all this about then??* Mum's yelling through from the lounge *Who's that?* So I tell her *It's ok, I'm just popping out for a little while.* And off I go.

Outside there's this car. Some geezer driving it who I've never seen before, and Ben sitting in the front. And I'm thinking *What have I done?* So I get in the car, no one's saying nothing, and I'm thinking *What's going on?* Bill asks me *How you doing, Steve? Yeah… I'm ok…Where we off to?* And he goes *Don't worry about it. We're going for a little drink, don't worry about it.* Which of course just makes you worry all the more. The driver's not saying anything and he's got a cauliflower ear and a broken nose and hands like shovels, and all I can think is *God help me.* Because I have no idea what on earth is going on, and part of me's expecting a beating but I can't for the life of me think what I've done to deserve it.

So we drive round the long way, and finally we pull into the Fiddlers car park. Now this is like two, maybe three weeks after the event, after I'd been in there for that drink. And Bill tells me *Sit here.*

And Ben and the driver get out and go in the pub. Bill stays in the car. He has to be really careful 'cause he's been inside and done time already. And they bring this geezer out, the one who'd accused me of chatting up his girlfriend, and they go *Is this the cunt?* And I say *Er ... Yeah.* And they proceed to give him a systematic beating. Which I will never ever forget. I mean they just battered him. It was brutal. They were just choosing their punches and where to whack him. And the bloke ended up on his knees with his face against the car window, his eyes swollen shut and half his teeth gone. And they said *Now say 'sorry' you fucking cunt.* And he was in pieces, sobbing, *I'm sorry sir. I'm sorry.* And they pushed him to the ground and got back in the car and we drove away.

As far as Bill and Ben were concerned, the geezer had it coming. He was one of the only junkies in Dagenham, and they told me I was lucky he didn't mug me for my money too, because this was a regular thing he had going with his girlfriend and the bar staff and his mates, that they'd get strangers – I got away with it luckily – but they'd get strangers and take them round the back of the pub and pull knives on them and rob them, that kind of stuff.

They dropped me off back at Whitebarn Lane, and I went straight to my room and burst into tears. I was in shock at what had just gone on. I'd never ever seen anything like it before and it was really truly horrible. Because they didn't kill the geezer – and I guess he had brought it on himself, so I wasn't shedding any tears over him – but they really really fucking hurt him. And that's when I packed in going to West Ham, and stopped being involved in any violence at all. I couldn't even watch it on the telly, not after what I'd seen. Up till then it had all been a bit of a laugh – the adrenalin rush of a few fists and boots on a Saturday afternoon when I was half-pissed and keeping an eye out not to get hit myself. But the incident up the Fiddlers had been something dark and ugly, and it left a mark on me.

When I was back out down the pub with the rest of the firm, I put a completely different spin on it, obviously. I had to. It was all *I did this* and *I did that*. But I didn't. I was shitting myself the whole time. And if I could have been anywhere else, I'd have gone. But it did teach me one lesson: that I'd always got help if I needed. It might be help I didn't really want, but it was there. It was that easy.

It was 1975. I was 18 or something like that. And I never went to the Fiddlers again.

Sex

Gary Young, who was one of our little firm, worked on a record stall in Broad Street market on a Saturday. The stall was run by an older bloke called Johnny Egan, who was in his fifties, and he must have had a tidy little business going, because the market was always heaving with people, and Johnny would buy and sell records, or order an album in for you if he hadn't got it, so he covered music the big stores didn't touch.

Even though he was a lot older than us, Johnny would hang out with us sometimes. Very quickly I noticed that he was always putting his hand on my shoulder, or touching me on the hip, finding an opportunity to make some form of physical contact. He was always saying *Come round, come round* and I sussed out pretty quickly that he was homosexual. It didn't take any great detective work – Johnny wasn't making a fuss about his sexuality, but then he wasn't hiding it either. We all knew he was gay – we used to call him *the bender* – but we liked him and he used to buy us drinks and he was one of the crowd, so in our book he was all right.

Anyway, one night we're down the Vernon and Gary tells us Johnny wants to invite us all to this party over in Upney. *But look,* he says, *there's going to be some queers there, so Johnny knows you'll all be on your best behaviour and won't take the piss.* I think we all recognised that the invite meant Johnny felt comfortable enough with us to ask us into his world – and that was a really big deal in somewhere like Dagenham at that time. I mean, it probably still is, but back then gay culture was pretty much invisible, and being openly gay could put you in risk of a real kicking, so for Johnny to ask us along was something of an honour. And at the same time, by having Gary tell us, he was giving us the opportunity to turn him down without an obvious snub, which was really cool of him. So we all said *Yeah, we'll go*. Partly because Johnny was our mate, and partly because we were really intrigued. We'd never been in that kind of scene.

All that might make us sound ever so right on. You know, Steve and his enlightened mates happily accepting the invite to a gay party. But it was really – as always – curiosity and friendship that took us there. Even on the bus there we were telling each other *Don't bend over!* and thinking we were hilariously funny, but really just hiding our nerves.

So we go this party, which is in a hall in Upney. We walk up and go in, and right away Johnny comes over and says hallo and it's clear he's really pleased we've made it along. Everything looks fairly normal, but we're not quite sure what to do or how to behave, so we go for what we know – we go to the bar and get ourselves a drink. And then we stand there, slightly nervous, slightly uncomfortable, looking for all the world like a bunch of people who've never been to a gay party before and don't quite know what to do. All of us feeling like fish out of water but trying to look cool and relaxed, which is the best way I know to look anything *but* cool and relaxed, but there you go. None of us wants to make a monkey of ourselves, so we're all stood with one hand in our pockets, and a pint in the other.

So the drink starts flowing and a couple of people start dancing, and this bloke comes up to me and goes *Do you wanna dance, mate?* All our little group went quiet. I could feel everyone's eyes on me, everyone breathing a quiet sigh of relief he'd asked me not them, and everyone thinking *Right! This'll be interesting...*

And I went *Er ... look ... I'm not like that, mate.* And he says *I'm not asking you to fucking go to bed with me, I'm asking you if you want a dance, all right?* Like it's the most obvious thing on earth. I felt like a right muppet. So I went *Yeah, all right then* and went and danced with him. And what a great dancer! We danced to 'Car Wash' by Rose Royce, as I remember, and it really broke the ice. We'd never been to a party like it. There was no aggro, and there was no need to keep an eye out for trouble, because there were no pissed-up blokes giving it *You looking at my pint?* And the sense of humour was great too. What wasn't to like? Apart from no women being there it was a great night out, and it changed our attitude to Johnny, too. None of us took the piss out of him anymore. In fact, we were asking him if there were any more parties we could come to.

For me, it was another one of those moments when I wondered what on earth all the fuss been about. Some people were queer, so what? When I came back from that first dance my mates were taking the piss, going *Ooooh you're one of them now.* And I was thinking *No, he was just a really good dancer. Big deal.*

I'd already had my mates question my sexuality because I listened to classical music and read poetry, so this was nothing new. One day they'd found me with a volume of Walt Whitman's poetry in my pocket, and really took the piss. Poets were queer, so if I was reading it, then that meant ... There was nothing particularly malicious in it, it was just typical teenage stuff, and anyway I'd pointed out that Walt was writing about war and death, and stuff like that, and that sort of shut them up.

We'd never experienced anything like Johnny's party before. And in its own small way I think it made all of us a little more accepting of difference than we'd been, a little less ready to point the finger. At the same time, it wasn't like we broadcast where we'd been. On the bus home we were all going *We don't tell any-one, right?* It would be our secret, because we didn't want to risk getting our heads kicked in, or have everyone think we were queer. Our views had changed, but it wasn't like we were about to man the barricades. Or even risk the wrath of Dagenham.

When it came to sex, though, I'd always been a bit slow off the mark. There was no sex education, and my mum certainly wasn't going to explain it to me. When I'd had my first wet dream all I knew was I woke up in the morning and there was something in the bed. I went downstairs for breakfast, mum went upstairs, and a minute later she was back down going *What's that in your bed??!* I told her I didn't know. *Well*, she said, *whatever it is, don't do it. It attracts mice.* Given this introduction to sexual awakening, it's no real surprise I was later than a lot of kids discovering masturbation, but then that was probably just as well. Would I have been moved by *Kes* as much if I'd been wanking myself into a frenzy every night? It's hard to say. Even in the sixth form, reading those copies of *Penthouse* when Dave and I went for a haircut had been about as close as I'd got to real sex. Now, that was about to change.

One night we were in the pub, and there were a couple of girls in there, strangers we didn't know, sitting over the other side of the saloon. One of them kept looking at me. Like I've said, I was pretty naive in those days, and the way I saw it, if someone stared at you it meant you'd offended them or they wanted to have it out with you. Either way it meant trouble. Anyway, every time I looked over she was looking at me, and in the end I thought *Fuck this* and went home.

Next morning Pete Edmunds comes into work telling the world he's copped off with her, and giving it large about what he'd got up to, telling me *I did this, I did that, you missed out you idiot.* It was typical Pete, he never missed a trick. It wasn't the only time he nipped in like that. I'd lose another girlfriend to him in the future because I was more interested in the Yamaha scooter I was going to buy than her. Back then, you'd have said he was the kind of guy who'd land on his feet whatever life threw at him, but that wasn't how things turned out. In the end, life threw more problems at Pete than he had any chance of dealing with, and he took to drinking more and more and more. Sad to say, he died fifteen, sixteen years ago, alone, on the street. But that day in work he was full of himself, the love-god of Wallis's, and who can blame him?

Anyway, the next weekend the girl was in there again. This time I made a point of talking to her, and buying her a couple of drinks, and at the end of the night we went back to her place. Michelle Stewart, her name was. Her and her mate had moved down from Chelmsford, and they were renting a place above Watson's greengrocers on Broad Street. While I'd been chatting to her, Ian Raby had fired into her mate and got himself invited back too, so now the two of them dived off into one of the bedrooms, leaving me and Michelle in the front room.

I remember thinking *I'm going to do it!* Now, the sum total of my sex education had come from films. So I had this idea that when you made love the world went a bit blurry round the edges, that there'd be silk sheets and saxophone music, or waves breaking on a beach ... No one told me that it's all fumblings, and trying to unhook a bra while not losing the magic of the moment, that it's a fight with unfamiliar underwear, that sex comes with strange noises, and smells, and sounds.

There were no silk sheets for me and Michelle – we were on the floor in the front room in front of the TV. And I remember she put on a record by the Sensational Alex Harvey Band, which had an instrumental section. It's strange, the things you remember. And then, there we were *Doing It!* and all I could think is *If I don't stop soon my wrists are going to break, they're on fire.* Plus *I can't wait to tell my mates!* and *I've got to keep it up! I've got to keep it up!* And I look up and the telly screen's right there in front of my face, and I've got this vision of myself, all distorted with a big hooter and nothing else, which was almost enough to put me off my stroke. So I looked right, and there was the ashtray on the table next to my head, with a copy of *Woman's Weekly* beside it ... Ah, romance!

So my first sexual encounter brought me down to earth with a bang, so to speak. It certainly wasn't what I'd expected from the films, but I knew I preferred the messy reality over the manicured fiction.

Michelle and I saw each other for a while. She taught me quite a few things. Things I'd only read about. And after that, once I'd found my feet, it was bloody open season. Bill Chivers fell in love with her and asked her to marry him, the fucking idiot. I said *Bill, she's not that kind of girl, she wants to have fun, you know.* And he said, in all seriousness, *No, she's nineteen now. I think it's time we both settled down.* So he asked her, and she told him to fuck off, and so he came down the pub and had a pint and got on with it. That was how it was, we were all young, none of us took anything much to heart.

Motorbikes

Bill Chivers had a Yamaha FS1E, and he let me have a go on it. That was it, I was hooked. They were just little 50cc scooters, but when you've been used to walking everywhere, or having to rely on the bus, then the freedom the FS1E (which everyone called a *Fizzie*) gave was a revelation. The top speed was 55 mph. Maybe 60 if you were going downhill with the wind behind you. But the important thing was you could just jump on and go anywhere. Anywhere at all.

I decided I had to have one. And I picked one up second-hand, for £200. It was on hire-purchase, at £5 a week, but that was fine, because I was earning good money from the job at Wallis's, and could afford it. Having a FS1E of my own meant I could get around more. It made going to Dial House a lot easier for starters, and I could head off to Southend or Basildon whenever the fancy took me, or just hop on the bike and see where I ended up, just go and see somewhere different. One of my first trips was up to Great Yarmouth with Bill. His family were off to Pontins and we rode there on our scooters, doing 40 mph the whole way, getting there and back on a tank of petrol each.

It was great, and I thought I was the dog's bollocks. Then it all went wrong. I went to start the FS1E one day, and there was nothing doing. Bill came and had a look at it, sucked his teeth and shook his head. *You need a magneto extractor* he said. Well, I'd no idea what it was, or what I'd do with it, and I wasn't the tiny bit mechanically minded. I think I'd hoped Bill would offer to sort it out himself, but that wasn't happening. So I nodded my head like it was something I'd get on to the moment I had a chance. But I never did. By now Ian Raby had got himself a Honda 175 with a top-box, and I could go two's-up with him, both of us wearing open-face helmets with chin-straps and sunglasses, and looking impossibly cool. So I'd get lifts with him. And when Bill traded his FS1E in for a 250 Suzuki, I went pillion with him too. So the FS1E sat in the garden, going nowhere.

Now at the time we were going a lot to discotheques a lot, and there was one place we used to go to all the time: the Ilford Palais, which later became Tiffany's, which was a place for meeting girls, obviously, but was also a great place for fights. There was always something kicking off down there – the Ilford lot would be taking on the Barking boys, or whatever. It was also the first place I saw racially motivated violence, blacks against whites. In fact, it was rare to have a night when there wasn't some kind of trouble. I guess it explains why Johnny Egan's party had been such a revelation.

I was there this one night when a horrendous fight started. The Palais had a balcony which ran all the way round above the dance floor, and that's where I was when this fight started over on the other side. I swear it was cart-wheeling round like a cartoon strip out of the Beano, where there's a cloud of dust and a fist or a foot coming out of it. There were people going over the balcony onto the tables downstairs and then fights starting down there too, and the bouncers trying to sort it all out, glasses smashing, girls screaming, and it got closer and closer. Pretty soon I was backing up away from it, like everyone else around me, and I ended up turning a table over and using it as a barricade, waiting till everything calmed down.

Next to me was this bloke who I'd sort of seen around, though I couldn't remember where from, and he's asking me

You all right? Obviously I was because it was nothing that serious. If you couldn't handle a bit of trouble you wouldn't ever go down the Palais. But afterwards when we'd all been turfed out, we introduced ourselves and he said *Name's Phil. I drink in the Cherry Tree. Pop down there.* It was one of those things I meant to do but never did, and then – a few weeks later – I bumped into him in Romford market. He was wearing a suit and a Crombie, just like he'd been the night in the Palais, and as he always always would whenever I saw him, even when it was unfashionable to do so.

So the two of us went for a drink. And I must have told him my FS1E was off the road, because by the end of the day he'd shown me how to break into motorbikes and get them going. I learned that Puch mopeds were easy because all you had to do was pedal them off, and Honda 50s were a screwdriver job so that wasn't too hard. As time went by I got into stealing larger bikes. Not to sell, by the way. Just to joyride, for my own entertainment.

One way or another I'd meet up with Phil quite a lot, and after a bit I found out that what he did for a living was a bit unusual: he was one of the best known getaway drivers in the area. He didn't do bank robberies, but he was really well-respected, and good at what he did. He took me out once to show me, speeding the car down Ilford Lane and into the gap between two buses coming opposite directions, a gap which looked way too small long before we got anywhere near it. Even though I was in the car I drew my knees in as if that'd make me a smaller target and give me a tiny chance of walking away when the inevitable crash happened. We made it through with inches to spare.

It might sound as though Phil was flash, all look-at-me. Nothing could be further from the truth. He was an unassuming, solid bloke. Not mouthy at all. After a while we went our separate ways, but years later, when I moved to Coopersale I walked into the pub and there was Phil, still wearing the Crombie, still wearing the suits. That was a good catch-up session! He was one of those blokes it's a privilege to know.

Anyway, for the purposes of this story, Phil taught me how to nick bikes. And it was always a real buzz. I'd take them off down Dagenham docks, where you weren't likely to get seen, or run into the old bill. Even if you go there nowadays there's always burnt-out cars and insurance jobs, because it's that kind of place, nothing but barbed wire fences and containers for miles.

On and off, I nicked bikes for about six months. I'd smash the lock, speed off, and joyride them round the docks. And in all that time I never got close to getting nicked. Not once. The way the estates in Dagenham were laid out made things easy anyway. Some roads – Orchard Road and School Road, say – had alleys running down the back of the houses, and I'd always boost a bike from in these type of roads, my thinking being that if the police came after me I'd dive down an the alley on the bike where it was too narrow for them to drive, or I'd just dump the bike and do a runner down the alley and come out on the next street. But I never had to worry about it at all.

In all that time I don't think it even occurred to me that what I was doing was wrong. I didn't think of it as stealing. I'd just found this new thing to do and it was fun, so I blocked out the fact I was taking other people's property and justified it to myself by mainly targeting Hondas. As far as I was concerned they were crap bikes, with narrow handlebars and no acceleration, so they deserved to be nicked. I wouldn't rob a FS1E because that would have been like stealing from my own. The way I saw it, this meant I had standards, which meant I wasn't really hurting anybody, which meant it was all ok. A warped logic, but it worked at the time.

A mate of mine was really into it, and carried bunches of keys round with him to make things easier. So when I went on the rob with him we were after bigger bikes. One time we got our hands on a 175 Suzuki trails bike, and that was bloody good fun, perfect for racing round the docks and over the rough ground. I really didn't want to let go of that one, but I knew I had to. It was one thing having fun, it was another to put your neck on the line.

Slowly the thrill wore off though, and eventually I stopped. I also reckoned that at some point my luck just had to run out, because I always used to end up in the same place, being the dimwit I am, down the bottom of Dagenham dock. The way I saw it, if I dumped a bike somewhere like Rainham I'd have a long walk home, and that would be plain stupid. Whereas the docks were just round the corner from home. It also occurred to me one night that none of the bikes were where I'd left them next time I went back, which meant that someone was recovering them. And that someone was probably the old bill. Suddenly it seemed like a really good idea to quit while I was winning.

Oh yeah. While I remember ... I wouldn't recommend anybody goes out stealing motorbikes. It's bad. Whoops. Nearly forgot to say that.

Giving up joyriding might have been the right thing to do, but it did mean the only bike I had was a broken FS1E, rotting in the back garden. By now I'd ridden enough bikes to know I wanted something bigger, but I'd only be able to get it on hire-purchase. Because of the money involved, I needed Stan to sign the forms for me, but he wouldn't and neither would Mum, and that was that.

Then Bookie Page and one of the other blokes in the firm each got a car. Immediately this was way cooler than a bike, because you could get your mates in, and a couple of girls, and get where you were going and still look really sharp. I couldn't afford the bike I wanted, so I knew there was no way I could afford a car. And Stan didn't have one, so there was no help there. I tried to persuade him we should get one. What a waste of time. His view was that I only wanted a car to look cool, and of course there was the usual *We can't afford it* refrain. I remember saying to him that if we had a car we could go places in it, and he said *Why d'yer want to do that? There's a pub at the end of the road.* Such small horizons, that bloke had.

Bristol

Life had really been a roller-coaster ride since I'd started working at Wallis's. I'd discovered sex, stolen motorbikes, and watched someone get beaten within an inch of his life. I'd found my feet, got in a little firm, spent a season watching West Ham, and got used to having spare cash in my pocket. But by early 1976 I was bored and restless.

Our little group had changed. Most of us had girlfriends, and that took us all in different directions and gave us other priorities, so we weren't having as much fun together as we had before. Pete Edmunds wasn't working at Wallis's anymore either, so I wasn't seeing as much of him, and Wallis's had moved me out to Upton Park, so the new mates I met through work there were too far away to go out drinking with of a night. Above all though, George's words about being promoted by the time I was thirty kept ringing round my head. Twelve more years of slicing bacon five days a week? Fuck that.

So one morning I went into work and told the manager I quit.

I popped down the dole office and Ian Jacobs helped me sign on again, then I went to the pub for a pint, and went home. Where I got into a furious argument with Mum and Stan. Aside from the predictable *Who do you think's going to keep you?* the idea that I'd just jack a job in blew their minds. Stan was still working in Motorgear, like he'd always been, and Mum was in the sweet shop across the road, which was the job she'd found when she finished looking after Nan and Granddad, and if it hadn't been for having to do that I think she'd have been at Telephone Cables for ever. They couldn't for the life of them understand how I'd walk away from a steady job with decent money, just because I didn't *enjoy* it any more.

So the atmosphere at home was poisonous, and rather than live with that I decided to go down to Bristol and find my brother. I bought a train ticket and went down there with some cash in my pocket, his address on a piece of paper, and no idea whether he'd be there or not. At Temple Meads I went into WHSmiths, looked his address up in an A-Z, and walked all the way to Bedminster. My brother wasn't in, but the people he lived with let me in so I could wait for him, and when he came back from work we went down the pub and caught up on things. I spent the weekend there and two of us got on really well, and talked about everything. I told him about life in Dagenham, how bored I was, with Mum and Stan going on at me, and he talked about how difficult he'd found things when he was there, that he felt he'd had a shit deal and that hitching round the country and sleeping on people's floors had been the best way out.

By then, David was working for the council doing gardening. Looking back, I'd say that weekend was one of the times we were closest – he was definitely about as happy and contented as I ever saw him. He'd been on the road for most of the years since Mum and Stan took up together, living in Birmingham for a while, visiting Dial House and the hippies in Ongar, and working down at a hotel in Bude where he met his wife, Rose, who was working there as a chambermaid. They'd married up in Liverpool, which was her hometown, and even lived there for a while, but now they were both working in Bristol, and it seemed my brother had finally settled down and stopped hitching round the country.

He'd taken me with him hitchhiking once, and I swore I'd never do it ever again. I'd been at Dial House and David had dropped by, he was heading up to Birmingham, and I thought it would be a great adventure. Big mistake.

Even now, thinking about Corley services just makes my spirits sink. As you come out of the services there's a storm drain, and I remember sitting on the edge of it, watching David standing with his thumb out, feeling utterly miserable. No one was stopping, it was half past eleven at night, I was starving hungry and we *still* hadn't got to Birmingham.

It never got any better. When we finally did get to my brother's flat we had to do a flit pretty much as soon as we got there because David hadn't paid the rent and the landlord was banging on the front door. So we skipped out the back, did a runner, and ended up kipping on someone's floor. Next morning it was another long day's hitching to Bristol and a night spent sleeping in a field with a view of Clifton suspension bridge, and from Bristol we crawled down to Bude to visit friends of his down there.

From Bude it took us two days to hitch back to London. Two blokes hitching together don't get anywhere fast – I know that now. I spent the whole trip tired, hungry, and wondering why I was doing it. Above all, I promised myself I'd never, ever do it again. By the time we walked back into Dial House any attraction hitching or camping could ever have held for me was stone cold dead. I've never been as glad to get anywhere, in my life. A romantic way to travel? You're having a laugh.

So anyway, I spent the weekend in Bristol with my brother, then travelled back in comfort on the train. Four hours, door to door. Bliss. The comfort zone ended as soon as I walked into Whitebarn Lane. Mum and Stan weren't about to sit back and see me enjoy my free time – if they were stuck in miserable dead-end jobs then everyone should be. So every day there were rows and arguments, and every day what relationship we'd had deteriorated a little more. Stan wouldn't talk to me except to tell me I was a waster, which was fine, because I thought he was an arsehole. Happy families it wasn't.

I spent time hanging out with a mate at his dad's carpet shop on the Heathway. That developed into casual cash in hand work to supplement my dole, so I wasn't completely skint. I was ticking over, but life was tedious, and I felt like I was going nowhere. Briefly I even thought about joining the RAF, like my sister had done. Maybe they'd teach me to fly aeroplanes! Or at least teach me a trade. But their aptitude test was full of questions like *What's the gap between the threads of a screw called?* I didn't even know it had a name. I scored so low they reckoned I'd struggle to pump up the tyres on a truck without someone keeping an eye on me, so a job as a fighter pilot was right out of the question.

I can't say I was that bothered about being turned down, but I knew I couldn't carry on staying in Dagenham. Mum and Stan wanted me out of the house so they could have the cosy little relationship they'd always wanted, with no one else around. They were looking after themselves, as always, so I thought *Fuck you!* Why hang around where I wasn't wanted? David had moved into a new place with Rose, and he said I should come down to Bristol, stay in their spare room while I found my feet. And I thought *Yeah. Why not?*

It was the autumn of 1976. I didn't know it yet, but my life was about to change. Big time.

The Clash

So in September 1976 I headed down to Bristol with a rucksack on my back and moved in with David and Rose in their new place, a flat over a betting shop down in Bedminster. At first I was signing on, but I knew that wasn't something that could continue, so I started looking for work. I heard it was easy to get a job as a porter at Bristol Royal Infirmary, so one day I walked down there and popped in. *Got any vacancies for a porter?* I asked. The bloke in the office said they hadn't, so I was heading out the door wondering what my next option would be, when he said *But we do have a vacancy for a plaster technician.* And I went *Yeah, I'll do that. Er ... what is it?*

I got the job. And my next six months were spent putting plaster of paris on people's broken limbs. It was a great job, once I got used to it. I was earning £40 a week now, way more than I'd got at Wallis's, and some days I'd sit there smiling to think that every time I shifted jobs my pay went up. Thank Christ I hadn't listened to Stan.

The job wasn't always easy. I'd warned the guy who gave me the job that I didn't know how I'd be with the sight of blood and he'd said *Nah. Don't worry. There'll be none of that.* God knows why I believed the lying bastard. Shows how naive I could be, I guess. Or how much I wanted the job. A couple of hours into my first day an old wino was brought in who'd been in a bottle fight with his mate and got his cheek sliced open. I could see his teeth through the side of his face. I remember thinking *Whoah!*

That's not right! and feeling really funny about it. But it passed, and pretty soon I got used to the sight of blood, which is always useful. I never liked it – I mean, who wants to see car accident victims? – but I could cope with it.

We dealt with a lot of down-and-outs. There were loads of winos in Bristol city centre, they used to sit outside St. James' church getting pissed, like the old bloke on my first day, and they were always coming in needing to be patched up. And they were always pissed. One day this old fella came in with a full-leg plaster which needed removing, and he was stumbling around in the room, smashed out of his head, cursing me, the world, and anything else going, giving me all sorts of abuse. By then I'd learned to just give it back like everyone else did *Get back on the bed!* because if we didn't we never got anywhere.

So finally I get him on the bed. Now, to get casts off we used a tool like a hand-drill, but with a really fine-toothed disc. It would cut through plaster but it wouldn't cut through flesh. So I cut the plaster apart, with the wino swearing and grumbling at me, and pull the two halves away from each other. And something moves. I look into the plaster and it's crawling with lice. They must be an inch deep. And I scream and throw the plaster into the corner of the room. The bloke got sent down to the de-lousing place, the room had to be fumigated, I got sent down the de-lousing place too, and had to stand there stark-bollock naked, covering myself in this paste which would kill any lice I'd picked up, and even then I still felt like I was itching, like they were still running all over me. How the old wino had managed, with thousands of lice crawling up and down his leg, I do not know.

But generally I enjoyed the job. And the money. And I was good at it, too. I was taking my first-aid course, and there was an opportunity to be an ambulance driver, which I was really seriously considering. I liked working in the hospital. Sure, there were days pulling lice-ridden casts off winos, but then there were quiet times where we'd have nothing to do but have water pistol fights with big syringes, and lark about. I was paying board and lodging to David and Rose, and I'd found a little pub in Bedminster called the Freemason's Arms, which had become my local, where I'd got to know some of the older blokes who drank there. Teddy boys who still had the quiff but no teeth, and Jerry, who was in a wheelchair and always wore a suede jacket. Characters.

So everything seemed pretty good. But the whole time I was in Bristol I was homesick for Dagenham. Which was daft, really, but they say absence makes the heart grow fonder, and there's nothing like being away from home to help you forget why you had to get out of there in the first place. And I didn't have a girlfriend, so although work was fun, once it had finished it was way too easy to remember the good times down the Vernon and nights out on the pull.

On top of that, I knew I couldn't stay with my brother and Rose for too long, because it was a tiny flat and I'd be cramping their style. If I wanted a place of my own I was going to have to start saving, but I was torn. On the one hand I knew had a really good job. On the other I couldn't stop thinking about going back to Dagenham. I'd moved towns, but it was the same old story: I wasn't happy with what I'd got. It was almost like I was waiting for something to come along. Thankfully, it did.

I was watching the TV one night, and it was Janet Street-Porter, and she was talking to Johnny Rotten, and the way he was talking, the way he looked, really made me sit up and take notice. They showed the Pistols playing a gig where there was hardly anyone there, and at the end he just sat on the stage looking bored, and I thought this was fucking brilliant! I turned to my brother and asked him *What would you say if I came home like that?* And he said *I'd tell you to have a bath and kick you out.* This from the bloke who used to be a hippy, my brother who apparently used to be a rebel. Suddenly he's turned into the right wing intergalactic father figure of all time.

And me being me, I thought *You're going back on your thing. That really is a reason to get into it.* It was typical me, doing the same thing again. Rebelling. And a couple of weeks later this girl came into the hospital with a broken wrist I had to plaster, and she was wearing old men's trousers from Oxfam, and a school tie, and an old t-shirt and plastic sandals, with her hair done strange. And I went *What's this fashion then?* And she said *It's punk rock, haven't you heard of it? It's this thing where you do what you want and wear old clothes.* I finished plastering her wrist, and before she left she said one of the most important things anyone's ever said to me. She said *There's this band – The Clash – playing down the Colston Hall tomorrow, you should go along and see that.*

And I went. I think Richard Hell and the Voidoids were support. I don't remember, I only remember The Clash. I walked in there in my nice jacket and my slightly flared jeans with the little turn-up, and my smart shoes with the leather soles, and college boy haircut (slight parting on one side, short, the kind of haircut your Mum likes), and I was confronted by, well, not many punks because it was early days, so lots of people with long hair and a few punks lying around – and if you saw them now they wouldn't look like punks – but at the time I thought *This looks really aggressive.* And I knew I liked it.

And then The Clash came on and blew me away. And I've said it before, but Paul Simenon looked twenty feet tall that night, just the way he stood there with his good looks and the clothes he wore, and I just couldn't take my eyes off him. And at the end I was blown away and I thought *I've got to have some of this. I don't know how, but I've got to fucking have some!* It was like a wake-up call. At the end there were people booing, shouting *You're crap. You're shit.* And I remember Joe Strummer stood there looking at them and said *Well if you think you can do any better, go and start a band.*

And I thought *What a great idea. I will.*

DURING CRASS

Dial House

About three weeks after the Colston Hall gig, I took a few days off work and decided to spend a long weekend in Dagenham. Ever since I'd seen The Clash I'd been getting more and more restless, because I knew this whole punk thing was something new I wanted to be part of, but when I tried to talk to my brother about it his eyes just glazed over. So I thought *Fuck it* and took the train home.

Like I say, I'd been homesick for weeks, but I wasn't back long before I remembered why I'd left. My old mates down the Vernon were up for a pint, but our lives had moved off in different directions, and most of them had settled down. I told them *I'm working in a hospital, but I'm going to pack that in, start a band. Punk rock, you know?* And it meant nothing to them. I remember Bookie Page saying *Well, I've got a wife and kid now, ain't I?*

I knew the easy camaraderie of those years we'd spent together was over, and whatever I was going to do next, none of my old mates could do it with me. I had another pint and a fag, and thought things over, and realised there was only one place to go. So I walked out of the Vernon, and went to Dial House.

It was an instinctive move, but instincts are often right. I'd been there first with my brother, years earlier, when I was still in school, stuck in the house with Mum and Stan, and bored out of my mind. David turned up at Whitebarn Lane one day, like he did, and told me he'd been staying at this fantastic place with really friendly people – he and Mick Duffield and some of the Ongar hippies had seen it from the train and decided to check it out – and he was going to go back there now, and did I want to come along?

At that point, anything had to be better than bloody Dagenham. So I went there with him. For the first time in my life I took the Tube out to Blake Hall, walked back along the line, climbed down the embankment, and into the back of the garden. There were six huge poplar trees, three times the size of the house, which ran in a line down the side of the garden to the railway, with flags and bit of rag and banners everywhere, which was what had caught my brother's eye when he'd gone past. We went through a rickety wooden gate and bumped into some bloke with long hair and bare feet wandering around in the garden, picking flowers. I was seventeen miles from home. It might as well have been another planet.

David led me through the garden, past a small concrete tool-shed, and through the back door – which naturally had a bead curtain strung across it – and into the kitchen. And suddenly there were all these friendly people saying *Hallo*, offering us cups of tea and bowls of salad, and chatting with my brother.

My first impression? Honestly? I thought they were all mad.

They all looked like hippies, and I couldn't understand a word they said because they were talking with long words, full of syllables. They had stones in their living rooms. And no telly. And they were all vegetarian, which was really weird, and they talked about stuff I didn't have the first idea about. But I let all that slide, because they had this wonderful garden with great big trees in it, and because you could do anything you wanted, and - most important thing of all – they talked to you like an equal. And *that* was a revelation.

I don't think I said a word to anyone on that first visit. I just sat there with my brother, listening and watching what went on. Everyone was David's age or older. Pen was 29. And I was 14. So I kept my gob shut and my eyes and ears open. After a bit, David showed me round. The house was like nothing I'd ever seen, but it was the garden that grabbed me. There was a vegetable patch like Granddad used to have at home, but there were goats too, a friendly dog, and loads of cats lying in the sunshine on the grass or prowling among the wild cherry and apple trees. I knew I was hooked.

So I went back as often as I could, either by Tube to Blake Hall – which I learned was John Betjeman's favourite station – or, when I had the FS1E, up over the hill from North Weald village and down through the farm to this crazy little cottage just past the cow barns in the middle of nowhere. I got to know Pen, and Gee, Richard Le Beau, and Malcolm Reading, and the visitors: Mick Duffield, Jerry Free, people like that. There were always visitors. The place was a wonderful, mad, creative hothouse, and I learned more going there than I ever learned at school.

No one would turn round and say *You've got to go to bed now* so I remember sitting round that little kitchen table till four in the morning, just talking, or listening to them talking about things and trying to stay awake, if I'm honest! For the first time in my life I watched the dawn come up, with mist on the fields, and cockerels crowing, and it felt like being part of something I'd normally only see on the telly.

Whatever I did at Dial House, it was always really interesting, because these were a kind of people who – however much I have a cheeky dig at them, saying they were all mad when I met them and a bunch of bleeding hippies – I'd never ever met before. People making films, like Mick Duffield; or George Tarbuck who was a pianist and worked in the Theatre Royal at

Stratford; Penny and Gee doing the artwork, and other people doing interesting things who'd drop by.

I learned so much there. I learned I was hungry for knowledge, that learning didn't have to be the dull, repetitive, boredom of school, backed up with the threat of punishment. I'd had a taste of how things *could* be with Mr. Stewart, but Dial House was the real deal. They'd have serious discussions, but next minute Pen would come through banging pots and pans, and we'd all pick some up and do the same, just trooping through the house after him, in a manic conga. Magic, and mad. Or they'd point a spotlight up into a tree at night, and you'd see it completely differently, lit from underneath, throwing shadows up instead of down. It was like nothing I'd ever experienced before.

I was introduced to books I'd never heard of, books by Jack Kerouac, Hubert Selby Jr. and the like. Richard Le Beau was a Walt Whitman fan too, so he showed me some other books of his I didn't know of, and some Dostoyevsky which I couldn't get on with, but because of that I did go into WHSmiths and buy a book called *Quiet Flows The Don*, which was a bloody big thick book, took ages to read, but was really good, all about the Cossacks. I'd no idea what it was about when I bought it – I just wanted to push my boundaries and read a 'highbrow' book.

Then there was the music. Upstairs there was a lounge, with a record player and a set of headphones, and masses of albums. While I started off listening to the Bowie records there, there were classical and jazz records too. Sometimes everyone would go upstairs and listen to music together, and chat, and I'd end up listening to stuff I never knew existed, and which I'd never have been exposed to anywhere else. And they encouraged my writing. I got to use a typewriter for the first time ever.

I learned you could make your writing look interesting, by,

say doing this sentence in red because it's important, or PUT-TING IT IN CAPITAL LETTERS. And Pen showed me a quick, easy way to make a cover picture for a pamphlet by pouring lighter fluid over a newspaper photo, putting it face-down on a sheet of paper, and going over it with a pencil, so the picture transferred. Or he and Gee would take time off from doing book covers and show me how to do silk-screen printing in the room they had set up for that. Later I'd learn that silk-screening with them was nothing like doing offset litho with an annoying Australian in Piccadilly, but there you go. It's all a learning-curve.

What I looked forward to most was that whenever I visited Dial House I'd be growing. Experimenting with something new. And whatever I tried, whenever I was there, Pen and the others would be going *Go for it – do it!* After so many years of indifference from Mum and Stan, Dial House gave me all the encouragement I could want. In spades.

I remember I tried to tell my schoolmates about it, but I couldn't. I simply couldn't put it into words. I'd never seen anything like Dial House, or met anyone like the people who lived there. And my mates hadn't either, so there was nowhere to start. I wanted them to love it the way I did, but at the same time if anyone did ask if they could come over I'd think *Fuck that!* because I wanted to keep it all to myself. Confused? Contradictory? You bet. I loved every minute I was there, but then sometimes I'd get back to Dagenham and think to myself *What a bunch of wankers!* Why? I'm not sure. Maybe because they had something I thought I'd never have for myself, and I was envious and resentful, who knows? But whenever I was there, I knew I wanted to live like this, I knew I wanted some of it. I just didn't think it was ever going to happen, but as it turned out, soon I was going to move in. And stay for twenty years.

Dolepunk

So there I was, all fired up about the idea of being in a punk band after seeing The Clash, pissed off no one else seemed to have any interest in it, sitting on the Tube on my way to Dial House. I expected it to be just as it was the last time I'd seen it: full, and bustling with people. But as I walked up the garden path I noticed the back door was open and dead leaves had blown into the house, and there was no one around. When I went in there were the familiar Dial House smells – incense, mildew, floor polish – and a line of slippers by the back door as always, because no one wore shoes inside, but the hubbub of noise and activity I'd expected just wasn't there.

I slipped my shoes off and went through to the work room, and there was Pen, sitting on his own, typing. I said *Where is everybody?* and he told me that he and Gee had split up and she was now living her own life in New York, doing covers for Time magazine and really enjoying it, and that he was living there on his own, with only Dave King (who'd later design the Crass logo) popping by every now and then. People had moved on, and the house was as quiet as it had ever been.

We had a cup of tea and a fag, and caught up. I told him about Bristol and being a plaster technician, and how this young girl had told me to go and see The Clash, and how it had changed my life. Pen said he'd seen them too, in Chelmsford, but that he was really into Patti Smith, who I'd never heard of. I knew The Clash and the Sex Pistols, and that was it, but that was enough for me. I remember I said *Yeah, I'm thinking of starting a punk band* and Pen shrugged and said *Well, I'll be your drummer.* And that was it. As simply and easily as that, we had the beginnings of a band. Not that either of us had a tiny clue about where we went from there, but that wasn't the point.

I ended up staying the night. Pen and I got drunk, and I had a little bit of speed and he had a little bit of hash, so we shared that between us and sat up talking and listening to music, and next day Pen said *Why don't you stick around?* Within twenty-four hours of walking into Dial House I was in a band and I had a place to live, which was better than I'd ever dared to hope for. I'd spent four days at Whitebarn Lane when I came back from Bristol, and while mum and Stan had been friendly enough, and we'd gone down the pub together, it was made pretty clear there was no way I'd be allowed to stay for too long, so Dial House was perfect.

I moved in. And the first thing we did was get the pinking shears and lose my college-boy haircut. The second thing I did was write a letter to the hospital back in Bristol, because it was clear now that I was never going back there. Originally I'd come back for a long weekend, but while the job and the money were good, the opportunity to live in Dial House and be in a band was just too good to miss, and much as I'd enjoyed Bristol in some ways, I'd never really felt at home there. So it wasn't too hard to say goodbye to it, but I didn't want to mess them around. I explained I'd decided to stay up in Essex and I was sorry I was letting them down. I got a nice letter back too, thanking me for letting them know and wishing me good luck with whatever I did next.

Which was to become a fully-fledged punk.

For visitors to Dial House from the old days, the changes they found when they dropped by were a bit of a shock. The first thing they'd see was this spotty little punk kid wearing transparent sandals, multi-coloured stripy socks, a pair of old Levi's, and an old ripped t-shirt with stencil lettering spray-painted on it. The whole ensemble topped off nicely with an old school tie and safety pins, and hair spiked up with either Vaseline – which I quickly discovered didn't work for long – or sugar and water, which did. And their old mate Pen, who'd looked like your typical hippy a year or so earlier, had spiky hair too, and was dressed all in black.

So people would walk in, and stop dead. You could see they didn't know what to think. Punk at the time – and for many years after, to be honest – was seen as being really aggressive and intimidating, and so for a lot of stoned old hippies their first reaction was fear. Martin Lee told me that the first time he met me he was sitting upstairs in Dial House and I walked in, wearing all my punk gear, and stood with my back to him, busy doing something but totally ignoring him. He was getting more and more nervous, thinking it would all kick off any moment, and when I spun round really fast and said *Whaddyathinkofthat?!* he nearly shat himself. Then he realised I was grinning, and showing him a flower-arrangement.

Playing with people's expectations, subverting them, making them question what they thought they knew, was something I learned from Pen. He's a prankster by nature anyway, and doing this appealed to him no end, and seeing as all the people we were doing it to were old friends of his, they coped with it. It wasn't as if he lost any mates because of this change to punk. It was only much later, when Crass really took off and Dial House became the centre of something very different, that there was no longer any room for them and they kind of drifted away, but for now they handled it pretty well. Some of them, of course, would join in. A lot of the people who would get involved with Crass and help us on our way were part of the loose network of artists and musicians and like-minded people that had passed through Dial House over the years.

And that had always been part of Pen's dream. He'd wanted Dial House to be an open house, where anyone could drop by and where there'd be a constant movement of people. Apparently, in medieval Japan, poets could travel the land and pay for their board and lodging by reciting their work. Artists would paint a picture, and so on. Pen dreamed of a string of places like that all over England, a series of little havens fostering creativity. But there was only one Dial House, ever.

He'd found it by heading out into Essex on his motorbike in the 1960s, looking for somewhere to live. And he came across this derelict house, empty and abandoned, a complete wreck. Local kids had been lighting fires in the rooms, the windows were gone, that kind of thing. So Pen made a deal with the farmer who owned the place, to rent it for £7 a week.

Nowadays everyone wants to live out in the country, but back then all anyone was after were new developments with all the mod-cons, and what Pen did, riding out on his bike and finding this little cottage no one wanted, was really unusual. It had taken years of work to turn the shell of a house he first saw into the really beautiful home I was living in now, but the rent was still £7 a week for the whole house, and it stayed like that the whole time I was there, right through to our battle with BT in the 1990s when we successfully fought their attempts to evict us from our home.

So living in Dial House was cheap, but I still needed to sign on. The problem was that when I was in Dagenham, or Bristol, I was just another unemployed person, and nothing to write home about. When I moved to Epping I was the only punk-rocker on the books, and that meant I drew attention.

First they sent someone round to make sure I wasn't living in what they called 'shared accommodation'. Their thinking was that this was a cheaper way to live – which it was – so if they could prove you were then they'd cut your dole. It must have cost more to send the guy round than they could possibly save, but there you go. On the appointed day I had to make out I was just living in my own room, with my own little store of food, so Pen and I made sure there was a can of beans and a loaf of bread by the bed. *Yes, I do eat separately from Mr. Rimbaud. No we don't share the milk.* I could see the geezer who was filling the forms in didn't even half believe us, but he was just earning a crust by doing his job and checking up, and I was making enough of an effort that I wasn't taking the piss. Job done.

Officially, though, I was supposed to be looking for work. And I wasn't. So then I got a letter asking me to go to the head office in Harlow. So off I went. I sat and waited there for fucking ages, getting more and more pissed off at wasting my day, and eventually asked the lady behind the desk just when, exactly, someone was going to see me. At which point she checks her notes and tells me I should have been seen way earlier, which really poured fuel on the flames. We had what you might call a 'lively exchange', and she ushers me into the interview room and locks the door behind me. There's two staff in front of me, both women. One's a trainee, the older one's asking the questions. She goes *Mr. Williams, you've been signing on for three months now. Have you been looking for a job?* So, obviously, I told her I had. And she took a long look at the way I was dressed and said *So you've got a line of work, then?* And I fired back *Yeah. I'm a plaster technician.*

This threw her right off her stride because she had to ask me what that was, and that made her look stupid in front of the trainee. So now she's as pissed off with me as I am with her.

Well, she says, *I'm afraid there's nothing in that line round here, but if you could start going for interviews, and give me a copy of every interview you go to* ... And I said *And if I don't?* I remember she almost smiled, and told me there were these places called rehabilitation centres, and I'd be sent to one of them. *It's this place up near Birmingham where we re-introduce you to the idea of getting up to an alarm clock, and help you learn a trade.*

Brilliant. What were they going to teach me? Shoe-cobbling? Basket-making? How to be a chimney-sweep? Fuck that. I turned and walked. Sod signing-on, it was too much hassle.

Owe Us

One of the things that had really annoyed me about the Harlow incident was their assumption that if I didn't have a job I must be lying around on my arse all day. I wasn't. With just me and Pen living at Dial House, there was plenty to do. The goats needed letting out and tethering, the cats had to be fed, the veg patch needed tending. And because we had a rule that you took your shoes off when you came in the house – which makes a lot of sense when you're living out in the country and don't want mud tramping through all the rooms – the lino floor would need polishing up and buffing. Then maybe I'd bake some bread, milk the goats, and – when we had them – get eggs from the chickens.

Pen would go and do his writing for a bit, and I'd write too, or go for a walk, and then we'd cook. We'd boil up a pressure-cooker of brown rice, fry it with a bit of Marmite, an egg, and some chopped vegetables and garlic from the garden. If we could have made our own wine and grown tobacco I think we'd have had it cracked, but anyway we were pretty much self-sufficient.

And people would visit, too. Bron, Pen's girlfriend, would come over, or Dave King would breeze in and out, or Pen and I would pop over to Bron's place in Stanford Rivers at night and sit around drinking wine. So life was busy, but it was a lot of fun as well. And most afternoons, Pen and I shut ourselves away in the music room and he played the drums and I shouted along.

He had a drum kit in the house already because he'd been diddling around with an awful three-piece called Ceres Confusion, with Bernard Rebors (who went on to be the Poison Girls bass player) and Peter Le Beau (whose brother Richard introduced me to Walt Whitman's poetry). They played endless noodly instrumental stuff, and featured Pen on both drums and a bicycle wheel he'd wired up to an amp and played the spokes on. It had to be heard to be believed. One thing I was really clear on – in our band the bicycle wheel was out.

Momentum built up really quickly. It wasn't as if either of us were taking it particularly seriously, we were just having a laugh and seeing what happened. Even so, in the space of a few weeks I'd written a couple of crap songs – 'Tony Blackburn', 'Heartthrob In The Mortuary' – but the first one we really practised was 'Owe Us A Living'. Richard Le Beau had written a poem called 'The Window' and in that there was a passage which read *Do they owe the chicken whose neck they chop for dinner a living? Of course they do. Do they owe me a living? Of course they do.* And that struck a chord.

I wrote the song walking back from the shop, swinging the shopping bag. Just hitting the rhythm of walking … 1, 2, 3, 4 … marching along … *of-course-they-fucking-do*. I had no idea it would become so iconic – all I wanted was a song that said *fuck you* to the Harlow DHSS! It was a useful little walk, that mile trog to the village shop and back. Ever since the days when I'd be playing truant from school, when I'd walk down the side of the A13 singing entire David Bowie albums because no one could hear me, I've associated walking with writing songs. And now, seeing as I had a two-mile round trip to the shops every time I wanted a pack of fags, there was plenty of opportunity to write.

So far the band was just me and Pen, drums and vocals. We

told ourselves this was really eye-catching because no one else was doing it, but deep down I think we both knew we needed something more. Musical history isn't exactly littered with successful drum/vocal duos. And this is where the extensive network of friends and acquaintances and people who'd drifted in and out of Dial House over the years really came into their own.

First, Steve Herman dropped by. He was an old mate of Pen's who lived in a squat at Trentishoe Mansions on the Charing Cross Road, and spent a lot of his time doing video stuff. He called himself, imaginatively, Captain Video. Anyway, he popped in to see Pen about something, and when we mentioned that we'd started a band he said *Well I can play guitar* and as quick as that he was in. Equally as quickly he disappeared off doing his video stuff and we barely saw him for the next few weeks, so nothing much changed, at least to start with.

Then Andy Palmer turned up. He was studying at the Chelsea School of Art, where he spent his time producing a silk-screen magazine, designing t-shirts, and getting wasted, and he knew the Dial House lot because he'd had a relationship with Joy de Vivre, who'd be in Crass herself, later on. Anyway, he walked in, and the first thing he said to me was *All right, squire, how you doing?* I remember thinking *Squire?!! What a tosser!*

Andy wanted to join the band too, but when we asked him what he could do he sat there and thought, and went *Er ... nothing*. He couldn't play guitar, and he couldn't sing. As far as Andy was concerned this was just a minor detail to be overcome, but it was hard to see how we could fit him in, although I hoped we could. He was about my own age, and I got on really well with him. On top of that, Andy lived in London and went to art college and knew interesting people. So I had my fingers crossed something would work out.

Finally, Pete Wright, whose little folk combo used to practise in Dial House on Friday nights, let slip that he was tired of the sort of stuff they were doing and didn't think he could be arsed with it any more. So we told him he should come and join us, and he decided he would. Pete was a great addition, because he really could play bass, and he helped pull the songs together and make them something near to tight. And when Andy Palmer rolled up again with a guitar he'd nicked from somewhere – which we all agreed showed unprecedented enthusiasm and commitment – Pete set it to open tuning in D, which is the the key I shout in, more or less.

So now Andy was in. Over just three or four days we'd gone from just me and Pen practising together to having a band. Admittedly one of the guitarists couldn't play, and the other had disappeared, but as far as we were concerned we were away! Now all we needed was a gig.

Once again, the Dial House connection came good. Martin Lee, who was the guy I'd surprised with the flower arrangement when he came to visit, lived in a squat complex on Huntley Street, just off Tottenham Court Road. There was another old friend of Dial House called Annie Brown who lived there too. She sometimes worked as an escort and had all sorts of tasty stories about politicians and high-flyers, but that's another story for another day... Anyhow, the squat was having a festival, which sounds grand but was really just a tinny PA set up in the courtyard at the back of the squats, and Martin sorted out for us to play.

We had five or six weeks to get ready. Steve Herman would turn up, rehearse, and disappear again, Andy got to grips with making some kind of noise with his guitar, Pete slotted in. By the time of the gig we had five songs. We didn't look particularly punk – not least because Steve Herman was a balding, bearded, sandal-wearing hippy – and we'd never played in front of anyone before. The only time I'd ever been on stage was doing a singalong down the Vernon when I was pissed, and now I'd be doing my own material, and I was shitting it. I always do before a gig, even now after all these years.

We played to about a dozen people – two of whom were dressed as teddy bears for some reason I never got to the bottom of – and a whole bunch of kids, which made me even more uncomfortable about the swearing in my lyrics. *Of-course-they-fucking-do!* sounded great when I was walking back from the village swinging the shopping, rather less cool in front of a bunch of ten year olds. And the whole place had a generally hippy kind of vibe, so I remember we started 'Owe Us' and people were trying to dance to it in that usual hippy wafty stoned kind of a way and getting absolutely nowhere.

We got halfway through the set and some old bloke from the rent-paying houses on the other side of Huntley Street marched over and switched the sound off. And we all went *Oh. All right. Sorry.* and trooped off stage. None of us had a clue how to deal with it. We'd had five songs, and we played just three, at 2 o'clock in the afternoon, to half a dozen hippies and a couple of bears. It was clearly the start of something monumental.

London

We spent the rest of the day at Huntley Street getting pissed on cans of Skol, and telling each other we were going to be famous. Then we went to Martin's flat and got stoned. The gig had been a buzz, worth all the anxiety beforehand, and now I was on a massive high.

At the time, though, the really big thrill for me was walking down somewhere like Tottenham Court Road with, say, a ripped t-shirt, and having people stop and turn to look at you in the street. Punk created that much of an impression. Later on, if people stopped and looked you ran as fast as you could because there was going to be trouble, but in the summer of 1977 what we were doing was just really shocking, and people didn't know how to deal with it. The music was just a part of what punk was all about, not the main focus. As a punk you were a walking artwork, and how often does that happen? At the Huntley Street gig a couple of kids had asked us if we played any Buzzcocks and we'd told them *No. But we are punk*. Because that mattered, because we were part of this new and edgy and liberating scene, and like nothing that had gone before.

What we were part of felt like absolute revolution. You'd see another punky looking person walking down the street and you'd quietly acknowledge each other as being part of something truly powerful and exhilarating. And you have to remember the way punks looked, and the music punk was creating, provoked massively hostile and hysterical reactions in the media and among the general population. If the teachers I'd had at school hadn't been able to cope with skinhead fashion, they hadn't a hope of dealing with this. I'd get on the Tube and people wouldn't sit next to me. They'd rather stand up. Or I could walk into a pub and be told *Get out!* just because I had spiky, coloured hair. It was that extreme, and it was an incredible thrill.

I was 20 years old, and I loved it. Whenever I could, I'd head in to London and just immerse myself in this wonderful, brave, new world. There were bands to see, and pubs to go to, and girls to meet, and when I wasn't doing that I'd hang out with Andy and Pete, or wander round to Martin in Huntley Street. If he wasn't in I'd think nothing of shinning up the drainpipe, climbing in through the window, and making myself at home. He always said he knew if I'd been round because he'd come back and find Mahler on the record deck and the headphones still plugged in!

I felt I had the best of both worlds. I lived, cheaply, out in this beautiful little house in the countryside, but I was within striking distance of everything that was going on. At Dial House I had responsibilities – if Pen was away I had to be there morning and evening to make sure the cats got fed and the goats were tethered out or locked away – and in London I could be as irresponsible as I liked. Which was quite a lot, as it happens, because I really enjoyed getting wasted and causing a stir.

Pete Wright was great for that. He was – in the nicest possible way – a nutter. It seemed to me that he'd woken up one morning and just decided to say *No* to everything. If there was a door that said *push* he'd pull it. If it said *no entry* he'd go through it. Wherever there was a rule he'd do his best to break it, because he was just into rebellion in any shape or form. He always has been and he always will be. One day we were walking down

Tottenham Court Road and this woman stopped him. *Excuse me, would you like to*— and Pete leant down and screamed *PISS OFF!!* right in her face because she was a Scientologist and he didn't see why he should have to listen to her bullshit, or be polite about not wanting to. Point made. And heads turned as well, all along the road. Which was all part and parcel of being punk.

So I'd either catch the Tube in from Blake Hall of an evening when the chores were done, or – if we'd been rehearsing – I'd get a lift into London with Pete, or with Andy in his Ford Escort because he drove really fast and would get there sooner. And then we'd go out, and see where the night would take us. Quite often I'd be wired – of all the drugs, speed was always my favourite. By far. The cheapest thing you could get was 'blues'. They'd give you a buzz for about ten minutes and then you'd drop another couple. Some people were into downers, but I didn't go for that at all. I wanted the rush. I could be in a shit pub, take a couple of blues, and suddenly everything would be brighter and more interesting, and life was just a big adventure where I'd think to myself *Yes! I'll do that! I'll go there! I'll talk to you!* And, of course, I'd be brimful of confidence. Ready to deal with anything.

After the boredom of growing up in Dagenham and feeling trapped in Heath Park, this new life was exactly what I wanted. And I was busy grabbing it with both hands. It felt like I was right in the centre of things, in a world where everything was changing, and anything was possible. I was meeting interesting people, and seeing different ways of life which were a million miles away from the dull safety Stan aspired to. The old life was over, and with it went my old name. When I moved into Dial House I left Stephen Williams behind. From that moment I became Steve Ignorant. It made perfect sense, because I didn't know much about anything, and – and this was important – it sounded good. Johnny Rotten, Joe Strummer, Steve Ignorant. Yeah, that'll do.

Like everything else, my political ignorance in 1977 was pretty much total. I was vaguely aware that Jim Callaghan was Prime Minister – not that I'd have wanted to put any money on it – and that was about it. This was changing, though. You couldn't live in a house with Pen and not learn about politics. And because a lot of the people Pen knew were political too, I quickly found out we were living in interesting times, and I soaked this new knowledge up, like I always do.

That's how I ended up at Grunwick's. I was over at Martin Lee's one night in June, having a drink and a smoke, and he told me he was off there in the morning with Mick Duffield, who was going to do some filming. Did I want to come along? Well, it sounded like it could be interesting, and I had nothing much else to do, so why not? *Er, by the way, what's it all about?*

The Grunwick's strike had been going on for a year already. It was centred round a film processing plant which had sacked a quarter of the workforce – which was largely asian and female – because they'd wanted to join a union. And because they wanted proper pay, an end to compulsory overtime, and an end to racial harassment in the workplace. Little things like that. They'd been picketing the plant for twelve months, trying to stop the blacklegs going into work, and now they'd asked for a mass picket to show support for their fight. The miners were coming down, and the police were going to be there in strength.

I didn't have a clue about any of this – I was Steve Ignorant, remember? – but Martin explained it all to me as we shared a couple of cans and a spliff. Next day we headed out to Willesden. We turned into the street where the plant was, and there were coppers lined up all along it. As we walked towards the gates they just took the piss, spat at me, and stuck their legs out to trip me up. One after the other. My political education didn't just come through people like Pen and Martin, a lot of it came from the Metropolitan Police. I remember thinking *I always knew coppers were bastards, but you've just confirmed it*. When the scab buses arrived, and all the pushing and shoving started, I was on the sidelines with Mick, who was filming it all, but a lot of people – including Martin Lee – got nicked. The police were never too fussy about who they arrested in these situations, and some of them just relished a chance to put the boot in. I watched, and I learned.

I was still Steve Ignorant, though. There's no point in pretending otherwise. It's there on film for all to see. On the *Autopsy* film Mick Duffield shot, there's a scene where I'm round at Martin's, talking to Annie Brown. She's chatting with me about the Baader-Meinhof group, and it's really really clear that I'm trying to talk about something I have no fucking clue about. None whatsoever. I'm just too embarrassed to say.

So one way or the other, for better or worse, there was plenty to learn. A lot of the people I was meeting now – like Annie and Martin and Pete – were squatters, living in central London, taking huge empty buildings and turning them into homes. Pete was in Gower Street. Martin lived in one of more than fifty squatted flats in Huntley Street. Mick Duffield and Steve Herman were in another huge squat in Trentishoe Mansions on Charing Cross Road. And so on.

These squats made living in London affordable for musicians and artists and families who otherwise couldn't have done it, and allowed them to live the same sort of creative, imaginative lives we were trying – in our small way – to have at Dial House. Some of what they did was pure genius – there was one squat in west London which announced to the world it was declaring independence from the UK. They wrote to the United Nations demanding recognition as a sovereign state, sent ambassadors to negotiate with the GLC, and made everyone who lived there a minister. They had six or seven Ministers for Alcohol, and The Minister of State was just four years old!

The press and the TV loved it, and the story got international coverage. And the serious point, that councils were leaving buildings standing empty when people were on waiting lists for homes, got heard too. The authorities hated it. And they determined to act.

In August 1978, 600 police, with bulldozers, made a dawn raid on the Huntley Street flats and evicted the inhabitants. Martin Lee and the 150 other people who lived there were thrown onto the streets. The local paper called it *scandalous*, but the crackdown on the big London squats was underway.

Like I said, they were interesting times. If I wanted something to rebel against, I didn't have to look far.

Roxy

Life in the summer of 1977 was good. We'd had our first gig, which made us a proper band. In my eyes at least. I was settling into Dial House, looking after goats and chickens, and writing songs. We were rehearsing and getting a proper set together. And I could hop the Tube into London and immerse myself in the excitement there, too. Perfect.

My only problem? Steve Herman. From the moment he'd joined the band alarm bells had rung because – as far as I was concerned – image was really important, and he wore sandals. And had a beard. And looked like a hippy. And was going bald – not that I hold that against anyone nowadays. I told myself punk was meant to be inclusive, so yeah, let him in. What the fuck, but I wasn't happy.

The final straw was when we went into a little studio just off Tottenham Court Road, run by a mate of Steve's, and recorded a four track cassette. Listening to it gave me the first chance to really hear what we sounded like – when we rehearsed I was too busy keeping to the beat, and when we gigged I was way too nervous – and I didn't like it. Steve's *plink-ker-plink-ker-plink-plink* guitar playing was just wrong. It sounded like Bert Weedon meeting the Sex Pistols. Having him in the band didn't just make us look like hippies, we sounded like hippies too. It couldn't go on.

Before we had a chance to sort it, though, we got our first gig at the Roxy. I think Pete got it us by taking one of the cassettes round, but I'm not sure. Anyway, we played, and it went well, and afterwards I was having a beer or three and I remember going up to this girl and saying *Can I sleep with you tonight?* and she said *Yeah*. So at the end of the night I went back to her place in Deptford, and because of that I ended up getting to know the Deptford punks and started hanging out with them. It felt slightly weird sometimes, as an old West Ham fan, to be walking around Millwall at all, never mind being there dressed as a punk, but I never got any bother. Whether that was down to it being a real hard working class area where people just accepted what punk was about, or whether they just thought you had to be a bit mad to have the balls to dress like that, I don't know. But I never got touched.

So when I came back from Deptford a day or so later, Steve Herman was out. He didn't take it well – who likes being thrown out of a band? – and there was a bit of a row and a kerfuffle, but anyway he was out. And Phil Free – who was another Dial House connection – was in. He was everything we needed: he had a guitar, he had a van we could carry equipment in, he was a nice guy, and he looked like he fitted in better. Bingo. Things were definitely on the up. And then we had our first gig with him, our second gig at the Roxy, which was a total fucking disaster.

I was really excited to be getting another gig there, especially as the last one had gone so well. That afternoon I'd met up with my new Deptford mates, gone to the pub with them, and had a bit of a smoke. Then I went on to Martin Lee's and had a joint or two with him and Andy, and drank some more beer. Pen was sitting there working his way through some bottles of wine, and we were all of us having way too much fun to think about taking the gig seriously. Which was our big mistake.

Later, after the fuss had died down a little, Pen wrote about it all. And, as happens with history, his version of what happened, by being written down, became the 'truth'. The truth was messy and complex, and none of us came out of it smelling of roses. Nobody's flat got trashed, for starters. A stack of 7 inch singles got knocked over. There was no rock and roll madness, just a bunch of people in a band who'd had too much to drink and smoke. Pen was so out of it on three bottles of wine, he didn't even know what he was doing when he was putting his kit up. I was a mess. Andy was no better.

So the gig was shit because we were all too twisted. All of us. It was an absolute shambles from the start. The sound was never that fantastic at the Roxy anyway, but if there's one thing for sure, it's that we didn't help. There was one song where I started off singing one track, and Pen was doing drums to another, so it was a god-awful mess. I realised and changed songs just as Pen swapped to drum to what I was singing, so we missed each other again and were out of time in a new, different way. And it all just fell apart. No one was *telling* us we were shit, but we were shit. No one *told* us to get off stage, but the management turned the sound off, which – in anyone's book – is a huge clue. Phil was so pissed off he put his elbow through a speaker. And Pen tried to whip the audience up, waving their fists in the air and shouting to let us play on.

The result was we got banned from the Roxy. Which is where the song came from, obviously. We weren't the first band to have a crap gig, and we certainly haven't been the last, but heading out of the Roxy with our tails between our legs didn't feel great.

I tried to tell myself it was just a laugh, but I felt a bit of a twat. We weren't getting gigs left, right and centre – they were few and far between, in all honesty – and now we'd blown one of the few chances we had. We were all pretty miserable. On top of that, as we were leaving, Pen somehow got himself separated from everyone else and got lost. He woke up hours later, still pissed, underneath a bench in Tottenham Court Road tube station, with the sweepers sweeping round him. All he could do was make his way to Mick Duffield's place in Cambridge Circus in tears and then get a cab all the way to Dial House. Fuck knows how much it cost. I know Pen didn't like to talk about it.

Things were rocky for a few days. Pen was that pissed off he left the band. For about two hours. Then, being Pen, he wrote his article, which really annoyed Andy because he felt it made him out to be a proper knob. So he decided *he* was going to leave, and we had to sort that out and make peace all round. In the end we sat down and talked about what had happened and all agreed we wouldn't get fucked up before going onstage to do a gig, because we had these really good songs, but we had to be able to play them, else the whole thing was pointless.

So after the Roxy gig we just straightened up our act a little bit. It was a learning curve, that's all. A storm in a musical teacup. And time to move on. It wasn't as if we suddenly went straight-edge – we still liked a drink and a smoke and, like I said, I always had a soft spot for speed – but we weren't going to mess up a gig through being trashed again.

Anyway, too many of the people we knew liked a drink and smoke too, and were happy to share. Martin Lee came round one day with three tiny dope plants, and we planted them in big pile of goat shit down the bottom of the garden where it was overgrown and wild. They grew and grew and grew. In the end these things were bloody enormous. If we fancied a smoke we'd just wander down, pluck a leaf or two, dry them under the grill, and roll a joint.

It was our old self-sufficiency ethos coming good once again. Then one day I was coming back to Dial House on the Tube, and as the train passed I looked down into the garden. *Holy shit*. There was a very well-beaten path through the undergrowth leading straight to these three bright green bushes. We might as well have had a big sign and an arrow pointing them out. Did we want to get busted? No. So we chopped them down, dried them out, and ended up with a big old Quality Street tin packed full of grass. And every now and then we'd dip into it and have a little smoke.

Thing was, this stuff was really vicious. Smoke a bit too much, and your heart would start racing, your eyelids would flicker, then you'd start getting paranoid about what you had or hadn't said – if you've ever been there you'll know the score. It was really swirly, and I think it turned me off smoking dope for life. None of us could cope with it, and eventually we gave it all back to Martin. He did well out of that – we grew it, we took the risk, and then he was visiting one day and we thrust the tin into his arms. I remember he looked at us and asked *How much do you want for it?*

And we said *Just take it away. Please.*

So he did. He was living in a flat near King's Cross now the Huntley Street squat was gone, and his mate Bill – who I got on really well with and dropped my first acid with – had found a flat nearby, so whenever I was in London and dropped in on Martin you could be sure the three of us would end up on some kind of drug-enhanced adventure. And, because it was my favourite, there was usually speed involved.

One night I was there someone had got their hands on some coke, which was a massive deal in those days, so we mixed it in with a load of speed, and took the lot. Immediately we're massively cranked, speeding our tits off, gabbling away at each other and completely incapable of staying in one place. Before we know it we're out of the flat and on our way to Jack Straw's

Castle, this pub in Hampstead which has oak beams which are *the thing* on the planet we really need to see. Nothing else will do, nothing at all, we've got to get ourselves over there *Right now! Come on, let's go!*

So we're marching towards King's Cross station in the early evening, jabbering nineteen to the dozen and then some, having the time of our lives, and we turn the corner and there's all these coppers giving some bloke a right pasting. *Fuck*. Then they throw him in the back of the van. *Oh fuck*. We've bumped into the SPG, the Special Patrol Group, who have a right rep for violence and brutality and generally beating people up. *Oh fucking hell, we've had it*. At the very least we're about to get stopped under the sus laws and searched, but we've seen what's happened to the bloke they threw in the van, and things don't look that good.

My heart's beating so fast I think it's going to burst, but we try and sneak past without being noticed, which is next to impossible with me looking like a punk rocker, and sure enough this copper with two pips on his shoulder stops us. *Nothing to worry about lads.* 'Course not. Nothing at all. *You've heard about the terrible fights round here at night?* We just nod. None of us dare to make eye contact with him, we're too busy staring at the ground in the hope he won't notice how totally wired we all are. *It's the Scottish pimps* he says, *beating up on their toms.* Cue more nodding. *Where you off to then?* Now one of us has to say something, so I tell him *Just off down the pub. Have a pint, game of pool, you know...* still not looking at him and being as vague as I can while my heart rate goes off the scale and I try to fight down the urge to run, because this is just the calm before the storm and any moment now I know we're going to get a monumental kicking.

Just then this bloke comes walking down the other side of the road. I can see him looking over, wondering what's going on.

My childhood haunts: Chequers Lane and Ferry lane.

The Bowie years.

Steve Ignorant arrives – first passport photo.

Out for a good time – Doing well at Wallis.

In Cricklewood with
Aphrodite 1977.

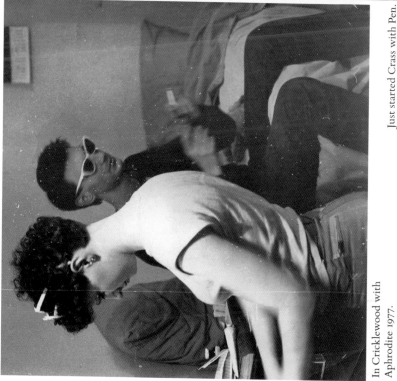

Just started Crass with Pen.

The only photo of Martin Lee. From right to left: me, Bill (with back to camera),
Martin, unknown friend, Annie Brown. First Conway Hall gig.

Live at Wembley Cricket Club.

Action Space –
Andy does a
great impression
of a young
Elvis.

Action Space.

Sound checking
in Pen's
'Seditionaries'.

Eve belting it out between me and Andy.

Annie Anxiety does her thang.

Trying to work out what Pen's playing –
Digbeth Civic Hall.

John Loder.

A break in recording *Stations*. Andy, Joy, me and Pen lunching under John Loder's pants.

The look of love. Islington Bingo Hall.

He's nothing to do with nothing, he's just innocently walking past, wondering why the police have stopped the punk rocker and his two mates. The copper sees him and yells to his team *Get him!* They steam across the road, grab the guy, and slam him up against this corrugated iron fence. We don't move. We daren't. If we keep still enough maybe they'll forget us and go away.

The copper's screaming at the bloke *Open your pockets, you dirty fucker! Come on! What's in this pocket?!* They reach into one pocket, and bring out all these sticks of Wrigley's chewing gum. The next pocket is full of Wrigley's gum. Every pocket, one after the other, is full of Wrigley's gum. Even the guy's turn-ups have Wrigley's gum in them. The copper goes *Right. Nick him!* So they throw the guy in the back of the van, and the copper turns round to us and goes *Have a nice night, lads*. And off they go.

We got to Jack Straw's Castle eventually. But we were so cranked on speed and terror I spent ages at the ticket machine for the Tube trying to feed a pound note into the coin slot. And when we did get to the pub we just stood there with pints in our hands, dazed, disorientated, disbelieving, asking each other *Was that real? Did you see it? Did you? Really? I haven't gone mad, have I?*

The beer never touched the sides. I didn't notice the oak beams. And I have absolutely no idea at all what was going on with the Wrigley's gum.

Moving In

After all those years in the doldrums in Dagenham, wondering what I was doing with my life, to be involved – and actively involved – in a band, however small it was, with just the odd gig here and there, meant I felt anything was possible. We could feel it in the air every time we went into London – this idea that the world was changing and anything could happen, and that we were part of it. We were young and we were punk and life was an adventure. And all of it, all of it, was just great.

We rehearsed at Dial House, which wasn't too bad for Phil, who had a place in Ongar, but a bit of a trek for Andy and Pete who had to drive out from London by car. For me and Pen, of course, it was ideal, because we could just work on songs whenever we had the time and present them to the others. With something like 'Owe Us' ... I'd know the tune I wanted, and I'd hum it to Pete, and he'd play it on the bass, then Andy and Phil would add guitars. Pete was a good enough musician he could work on his own material – like, say, 'Securicor' – and then bring it along, but generally the songs were worked out at at Dial House.

We were getting a good little set together, and we got a chance to try it out at a festival to save the old Covent Garden, which was about to be pulled down. The whole area was just decaying buildings and cobbled streets, rather than the faceless tourist trap it is now, and we got a slot on the main stage. I think Mick Duffield managed to arrange it. Anyway, Pen had an ear infection and couldn't make the gig, so I got in a guy called Charlie, who I knew from Deptford and who drummed in a band called This Heat, to cover.

Someone was videoing the event. I remember looking out from the stage and seeing one of those big old video cameras, a big unwieldy thing about the size of a rucksack which weighed a ton. So someone somewhere has a mouldering, rotting video of one of the very first Crass gigs. And not only is it Crass performing without Penny Rimbaud, but it's Crass in the days before we all wore black. Hard to believe, I know, but we used to just go on stage in whatever we wanted or whatever we had on. For me that was pretty much always jeans and a ripped t-shirt, and plastic sandals. Only Pen wore black, right from the start. He had a pair of Seditionaries that cost £40 – and this is back when £40 was forty quid! Way out of my price range – I just waited till Pen's were too ripped for him and grabbed them.

That was pretty much the last gig where we didn't wear black, though. The myth doing the rounds at the time – which I remember as being true, by the way – was that one of us put a white and light wash in with some black clothes on a hot wash, and everything came out a dirty grey. After that we decided black was the way forward.

Bit by bit, our image was coming together. And image was important. Next, Pete put some scrim over all our equipment and sprayed it black. Then he painted the Crass symbol on the front. The symbol pre-dated the band – Dave King had designed it for the *Christ Reality Asylum* booklet which Pen had been writing when I first moved in to Dial House – and represented power devouring itself. It was a brilliant piece of design, and became an iconic punk image. You could love what Crass stood for, or you could hate it, whatever, but you couldn't fail to recognise that symbol.

But that was a way off. For now we were wearing black, and the equipment was all black, and I thought we were looking really good. I loved it. I can't say often enough how much fun all this was. Fun was something that got a little bit lost later, but for now I was having the time of my life.

At some point Andy gave up his flat in Holland Park and joined us in Dial House, and later Pete moved in too, which made the whole process of writing and rehearsing loads easier. Now, when we came up with ideas we could just nip into the music room and hammer them out. I was writing loads of songs – and for every set of lyrics we used another two or three got screwed up and thrown in the bin – and it was all a total buzz. Even talking about it now gives me a rush. It just felt so good to be doing something.

What I felt – and I can only talk for myself, though I think the others felt it too – was that anything and everything was up for grabs. It wasn't just about people stopping and staring at you in the street. I'd go into London and someone would give me a new fanzine I'd never seen before. Better Badges came into existence. Rough Trade sprang up. The music press was full of punk rock, and there were always gigs to go to. It was a really exciting time, and it felt like the world was changing. Afterwards, of course, the dust settles and everyone gets that perfect 20/20 vision that comes with hindsight, but when you're there, living it, caught up in it, there's no clear pattern, no sense of where it's all going or how it'll all turn out. I just felt that something great was happening. I didn't necessarily know what it was, but I wanted some!

So if I was in London, I used to do my best to get to as many gigs as possible. The Nashville Rooms in West Ken, the Vortex in Soho, the back room of any pub with a punk night. I remember I saw the Damned and the Adverts at the old Astoria.

I wasn't that impressed by the Damned, but I fancied Gaye Advert something rotten. Years later, when I did the gig at Shepherd's Bush, I got my photo taken with her, thinking *Do you know that for years your picture was a real turn-on for me?* But I just saw bands, wherever and whenever I could. It wasn't that I was trying to watch and learn, or hone my skills as a frontman, or anything like that. I was young, I was after girls, good times, and excitement, and all the rest, my friends, is propaganda!

Living out in Essex, mind, we were sort of one step removed. And it was pretty tough being a punk out there, because you were such a target. I used to get so pissed off listening to people tell me how punk was all about being streetwise, and living in the city where life was really hard, and how easy we had it, living out in the country. I'd look at them and think *Bollocks. You've no fucking idea.* We had no public transport, and no corner shop – I had to walk a mile just to get some fags, for christ's sake. For six months of the year you tramped through mud, with shitty trouser bottoms, and as for a pint in your local, forget it – you try that in Epping without getting your head kicked in.

For the most part, though, life was good. I was living in a house with my mates. And now that Andy and Pete were there, not only was rehearsing a whole bunch easier, but the chores were shared out and it wasn't just down to me and Pen to look after the place. Then Andy started seeing an old girlfriend, Joy de Vivre, and she moved in too. Dave King would drift through from time to time, so there were five or six of us living there. Phil was down the road in Ongar. Eve was in Stanford Rivers. Sometimes Gee would fly back from New York and everyone would meet up at Dial House and sit up in to the night drinking and sitting round the kitchen table, talking, partying and having a laugh.

The pieces of the jigsaw were falling into place. We weren't gigging a lot yet, but as a band and a group of friends we were getting somewhere. I really didn't think things could get any better. And then they did.

NYC

At first, I thought it had to be a wind-up. Then, when I twigged that it wasn't, and that no one was pulling my leg, and that we were going to fly to New York to play some gigs – well, I was so excited I just about burst. Being in Dial House was good, being in a band was better, but this was just incredible. Just a couple of years earlier I'd been bored out of my mind with my life feeling like it was going nowhere, and now *I'm going to New York! I'm going to New York! I'm going to – bloody hell – I'd better get a passport.*

So there was a bit of a run around – off to Ilford to get my birth certificate, then to the passport office to sort out a passport, and finally on to the American embassy to queue for a visa – but I didn't mind any of it, because *I'm going to New York!* The way I looked didn't raise any eyebrows, even though you'd have thought it could, my brand-new British passport had a US visa stamp in it, and I must have looked at it a hundred times on the train back to Essex, just to be sure it was really true. *I'm going to New York!*

It was Freddy Laker who'd made it possible. He was the Easyjet of his day, this guy who'd come up with the idea of no-frills cheap flights to the States. When they started in 1977, charging £59 one-way from London to New York, it revolutionised travel across the Atlantic. Suddenly it was simpler and more affordable for Gee – who was living over there – to pop back and visit us at Dial House. So she did. Then she realised it

151

would be just as easy for us to visit her. So she stumped up the money, sorted out five gigs, and told us to come over.

It was summer. And quite often, if the weather was good, we'd sleep out in the garden at Dial House in our sleeping bags. Sometimes I'd wake up and look at the night sky and see planes flying over on their way in and out of Heathrow, and think to myself *I'm going to be on one of those! I'm going to New York!* At the same time, seeing as I'd never ever been on a plane, had never actually been out of England in my whole life, I couldn't quite believe it, whatever that stamp in my passport promised. It was too impossible to be true.

Finally the great day came. The night before, we stayed at Mick Duffield's place up on the top floor of the squat in Trentishoe Mansions. Everyone else slept, but I was so excited I couldn't. I sat staring out of the window, looking out on this wonderful vista right across London, looking down on the roofs of Soho and their hundreds of chimney pots, watching people milling in and out of the amusement arcade across the road. 2am. Awake. 3am. Still wide awake. 4am. Still wired with adrenalin. And then dawn came up and my excitement levels went up even further. Just that one sentence running round my head *I'm going to New York! I'm going to New York! I'm going to New York!* like a kid on Christmas morning.

We all went for breakfast in a cafe in Old Compton Street, but I couldn't eat anything. I just drank coffee and smoked cigarettes and watched the world go by while everyone else tucked in. Then the bloke out of *Doctor Who*, Tom Baker, walked past, and before I could stop myself I pointed him out and shouted *It's Doctor Who!* He just rolled his eyes and grimaced as if to say *Can't I even go for a morning walk without some idiot pointing at me?* And instantly I wanted to run out and say *Sorry for being a numpty but I'm going to New York in a few hours and I'm really excited!*

I guess you could say I was kind of manic. I was like a cat on a hot tin roof, waiting for everyone to finish eating, and say goodbye to Mick, and get going. Nothing and no one was moving fast enough. It took an hour – to me it felt like days – for us to get to Victoria, find a train to Gatwick, and trundle off south, and I swear the train was going so slowly it seemed to be moving backwards. Then at some point in the journey they announced that at the next station the train would split. The front half would carry on to Gatwick and the rear half was going to be, I don't know, scrapped or something. We were in the front half, but we looked round, and Phil had disappeared.

He'd done his usual trick, which was to head to the bog with a good book and nest there for the best part of the day. But the bog was in the rear half of the train, which meant Phil ran the risk of spending the rest of his life in a siding. So we dashed through and banged on the door to warn him and he came stumbling out with his trousers round his ankles wondering what the hell was going on. Probably the quickest shit he ever had …

We got to Gatwick. I felt like nobody in the history of travel could ever have anticipated anything as eagerly as I was looking forward to this trip. For me, trooping onto the plane and taking our seats was the height of exotic. I was practically beside myself with excitement, thinking *I'm going to New York!* Everything in my world was wonderful. I had a window seat! There was free beer and peanuts! And cakes! Blimey, could life actually *get* any better?

When we came in over JFK the sun was low on the horizon and they put us in a holding pattern. I remember looking down at the suburbs of New York, swimming pools in back gardens, open areas of marshland, about to land in this city I'd dreamed about ever since Mr. Padfield had introduced me to the music of *West Side Story*, but which I'd never really believed I'd ever get the chance to visit, and suddenly I had a Joni Mitchell song

'Refuge Of The Roads' running through my head, and even now if I hear it I'm back on that Laker Airways flight, circling over New York in the golden evening light.

Getting through immigration took a bit of doing, because I didn't have a penny on me, and they wanted to know exactly what that was all about, and how I intended to get by. So I promised not to bankrupt the country or rob old ladies, and finally they let me in. I can't remember how we got in from JFK to Manhattan, whether it was by train or bus or what, I was just so cranked. But whatever, we got off at the other end, and there I was, the boy from Dagenham, in New York. I just couldn't believe it.

There was so much to take in. The big obvious stuff – the skyscrapers, the cars, the traffic, police with guns, yellow snub-nosed cabs, street-corner delis, the endless noise – was incredible enough, but add that to the countless tiny differences that let you know you're somewhere that isn't home, and the effect was overwhelming. We'd no sooner got to Gee's than she asked me to nip to the deli over the road for some butter. By the time I came back I felt like I'd explored a whole new world.

The butter didn't come in a block, but in a stick. But that wasn't the half of it. When I asked for a pack of Marlboro the guy gave me a book of matches too. When I said I hadn't asked for them, he told me they were free! *Wow! Free stuff!! Thanks!!* And then he told me you never say *Please* or *Thank you* in New York. Right. That was going to take some getting used to. *What are those cigarettes? Lucky Strike? Untipped? I'll have to try them – they'll be really cool.* The guy was staring at me like I was a martian, dressed in all my punk gear, and I barely noticed. Everything was new, and wonderful, and exciting. I was in New York, and I loved it!

We were there for ten days, and I never calmed down. If we

weren't playing a gig, or rehearsing, I was off out the door, exploring New York. On our first night Gee had taken us to the Grassroots Bar on St. Mark's Place, and I'd met up with a mate of hers called Johnny Dynell. We got on like a house on fire, and he became both my guide to the city and my partner in crime. He was a really good-looking geezer, with a girlfriend who was a female bodybuilder, and he knew how to party. Hanging out with Johnny I ended up in the best and most interesting places, meeting the kind of twilight people who live on the fringes, the quirky folks you only get to meet in New York.

It's amazing how much I packed in, but then I barely slept. I'd go out with Johnny late at night and sit in Washington Square Park, listening to all the black guys there harmonising with their singing as they passed round joints, being asked *Hey man, what's with the hair?* and having a laugh. One night Johnny took me on from there to a club called Two Twenty, on MacDougall Street. All up the stairs on the way to the bar were pictures of really stunning women – Raquel Welch had nothing on them, even the Raquel Welch of my schoolboy fantasies – and I was thinking *Oh yes!* I walked in the bar, the barman's got no shirt on, and all these beautiful women were strutting round. Blokes of course. It was a transvestite, transsexual, gay bar.

One of them came up to me and asked *Do you want some tea?*
No. I'll have a beer thanks.
No, honey. Tea.
What?
Tea. Pot. Marijuana.
No thanks. Got any speed?
You're funny!
Yeah. I know.

What you doing later, sweetie?

Er ... going home with Johnny. My mate.

I remember my thoughts went back to Johnny Egan in Dagenham, because – once again – here I was in this really friendly place, having a laugh with a bunch of homosexuals. Only this time I was a few years older and wiser and there was none of the *Don't bend over!* awkwardness and nervousness we'd had on the way to the party in Dagenham. We sat around drinking and chatting, and they'd ask *So what's with the hair?* and I thought it was really fantastic you could go to a place like that and no one gave a shit.

One of the many, many things I loved about New York was that we could go somewhere like Two Twenty at, say, two in the morning when the regular bars closed, stay there till six, when it shut, and then go on from there to an early bar and carry on drinking. Or if we couldn't handle that, we'd go to a diner – one of the old-fashioned diners which still existed back then – and have pancakes, or omelettes, or french fries, or hash browns, exotic food I'd never even seen in England. Then, after a few hours crashed out, we'd be off again.

It was during all this bar-hopping and exploring that I met Annie Anxiety. I came out of the Grassroots Bar one night, and I was just walking round the block, pissed, enjoying being in New York, taking everything in. I saw this girl with green hair, sitting on a doorstep. Next time I came past I started talking to her. We ended up spending the night together, drinking, chatting, and smoking spliffs. And she became another part of the big New York adventure. We headed out to catch the Staten Island ferry about four in the morning only to discover it wasn't running; we caught cabs across the city; we had fun. Next day Annie came to the Quando gig. By the end of the year she'd flown over to England, turned up at Dial House, moved in –

briefly – and started her own musical career. All of this from a chance pissed-up meeting on a New York street! How could I not love the place?

Most of the time, though, I was with Johnny, and seeing the city with him was an education, like living in a cross between *French Connection* and *Saturday Night Fever*. We'd be walking along and he'd say *Fancy some amyl nitrate?* and go up to some guy on a street corner and score. And it'd be really good! *Don't worry* he said *If the police catch you with dope, they'll just take it and smoke it themselves. Or sell it.* And then he'd take me off on another great adventure.

He took me to one club, and my heart sank. It was full of ordinary people, businessmen in suits, nothing exciting, just three DJ decks on stage. I told him it looked like a right dump and he said *Give it a chance, give it a chance.* Then some guy walked up to one of the decks and did the first bit of scratching I'd ever heard. *Nigga–nigga–nig–nig–nig–nigga* and then this drum beat started up from two drum kits that were hidden behind the curtains across the stage *Boom-ka! ka-boom-boom-ka!* and all these sober business people suddenly went absolutely crazy, ripping their shirts off and dancing like loons. I'd never seen anything like it – remember this was 1978 – and I just stood there with my mouth open, thinking *Fuckin' hell!* You had to hand it to Johnny. He knew where to go.

So with all this going on the gigs dwindled into the background, I'm afraid. We were originally supposed to do five, but one got cancelled, so we ended up with four. By this time we were wearing black, we had a proper set – which we'd later record as *Feeding* – and we knew what we were doing. And we were still a five-piece. There were no women in the band yet. Eve and Joy only joined when we got back to the UK.

Our first gig was memorable for two reasons. One was a

whiny American kid who reckoned his band should have been headlining, and who was being a proper little arsehole, giving it the I'm-more-punk-than-you bollocks, telling me America invented punk. I wanted to knock him out, but decided to wind him up instead. *What football team do you support, sunbeam?* Soccer? *It's not soccer, you little prat. Come on, name your team!* We had a running battle which went on all night.

There was also a reggae band on the bill, but when they turned up at the front door of the club the white doorman wouldn't let them in. Blacks could only come in through the back door. I couldn't believe it. I went outside and did my nut. If they had to go round the back then we would too. The doorman didn't get it at all. *Guys, it's not you. You can come in this way.* No. Fuck off.

The reggae band were great. The snotty-nosed kid's band? Shit. I wouldn't have wanted to like them anyway, just because he was such a tosser, but they were really really bad. And then at the end of the night he was shouting at Gee that he wanted more money, which was way out of order. Gee had sorted the gigs out and put her own cash up, hoping to recoup it out of the door money on the shows, which was a huge ask, and clearly wasn't going to happen. We were an unknown band from England with a handful of gigs behind us, and while there was some interest, Gee was going to end up out of pocket. She'd done this out of the goodness of her heart, and now this selfish little shit was having a go. I did my nut for the second time that night. Andy stopped me from knocking seven shades out of him, which was a shame. It would have been no more than he deserved.

I don't remember much about the second gig. There were maybe twenty or so people there. The third gig was in a place called Quando's, which was a Puerto Rican community centre down the road from Gee's apartment. One of the women who lived in her block was in a band called The Contortions, so Gee put them on the bill. The lead singer was James Chance. Now James' idea of being 'punk' was to wear a suit with a little square cut out of it, and to intimidate the audience by rushing into them, arms flailing, and maybe wrestling someone to the ground, safe in the knowledge they wouldn't dare to do anything. All very contrived, and typical of the arty States new wave scene, in my opinion.

Anyway, James made the mistake of doing his party piece a bit too close to Andy and Phil, who obliged him by putting the boot in, which wasn't part of James' game plan at all. His show got stopped. I thought it was hilarious. We went on after, and I was still laughing. The kerfuffle with Mr. Chance meant our second gig there was cancelled, but that was fine by me. I went out and got pissed with Johnny Dynell again. What else would I do? I was in New York!

Although I was out all night, going round people's apartments, drinking, meeting people and going places, I turned up for whatever gigs or rehearsals we had planned, because the band was the whole reason we were there, and we'd all learned from the fiasco at the Roxy. But if we hadn't got a gig, I was going to party! I can't say whether the rest of the band were having the great time I was, but I know there was some discussion about what I was up to, and a bit of a disapproving *tut* when I walked in. Pen told me I was living my life like a dog, and I remember asking him what he meant by that. He said *You're always out, doing all these drugs and things*. As if it was something wrong.

I remember thinking *Pen, I'm 20 years old. It's the first time I've been out of the country. I'm meeting all these people and seeing all these new things and having all these new experiences, for fuck's sake. It's all right for you. You're thirty-something, you old fart, you've been through your thing. Let me have a little taste of it, will you?* But I did quieten down a little bit. For a day or so. Then I was off out again. I just couldn't resist it. I couldn't believe I'd gone from leaning on the bedroom windowsill in Whitebarn Lane, bored out of my mind, to being out and about in New York. I was like a kid in a sweet shop, and I don't regret any of it. At all.

Southern

Dial House was absolutely central to the creation of Crass. It didn't just provide us with a place to live, it gave us an incredible network of connections to tap into. And one of the most important of these was John Loder.

In 1978, John was running a studio called Southern, up in Wood Green, and recording jingles for radio. He was another old associate of Dial House, and back in the pre-Crass days he'd recorded Pen and Gee's awful, avant-garde rubbish which sounded nothing like music and entirely like a furniture van turning over on the M6. But we didn't hold that against him. When we came back from New York and decided we needed a new demo tape, one which showcased some of our new songs, and didn't feature Steve Herman's guitar playing, John was the obvious man to turn to.

He instantly got what we were doing.

In part, I think he clicked straightaway that something could come out of it, but on top of that, having us in the studio was a change from the humdrum routine of doing endless radio jingle bollocks which paid the bills but had no excitement in it whatsoever. So he was very encouraging, right from the start, full of suggestions, and always really enthusiastic. It wasn't about the money, either, because we were skint. The demo was done by barter. We swapped some of Gee's artwork for a couple of hours studio time. And John was up for that. He was a lovely, lovely bloke, and became a really good mate. People talk about him being the ninth member of Crass, and I think that's fair enough, because more than anyone else, he helped make us what we were.

So we recorded the new demo tapes and started sending them out to people to try and get gigs, like a thousand other new punk bands were doing. And once again, luck, chance, fate, and the Dial House network all came into play.

Tony Lowe, a mate of ours, was working doing window displays for record stores. One day he was working out in Walthamstow, doing a display for Small Wonder records, which was run by a guy called Pete Stennett. And he gave Pete one of our demos, and told him *Listen to that*. He was barely home at the end of the day and Pete was on the phone asking *How do I get in contact with these people? I want them to do a record!*

Tony phoned us, we phoned Pete Stennett, the rest is history.

The offer from Small Wonder couldn't have come at a better time, because things were a bit quiet. Pen, Phil, Andy and myself had got some work painting someone's house in a nearby village to bring in a bit of extra cash. After the excitement of New York I was back to feeding the goats and the cats and tramping down to the village for the shopping.

Despite this, Dial House was thriving. Half the band had moved in and we were in a honeymoon period. Not only was the workload shared, but suddenly there was lots of different input, different ideas, different songs being written. We'd sit around the table talking till three or four in the morning, discussing things, throwing ideas in and seeing what came out, knowing we were going to be making a record soon and that something was happening. That was hugely important. We were going to be a real band!

Some of the pre-Crass visitors still dropped by, and we had the occasional little party. The strict *No alcohol* line hadn't yet come into play at Dial House. Gee was coming back and forth from New York to visit, and had started up a magazine called *International Anthem*. Annie Anxiety dropped by. Mick Duffield had got involved and started making Crass visuals, so he was coming over quite a lot, or we'd go into London and he'd film me walking round somewhere like Top Shop, looking punk and shocking people. Or he'd take loads of photos and disappear into our dark room for hours. So the place was a little hive of activity, very creative.

I was really enjoying it. Before, if Pen had been away at Eve's I had to be back to put the goats out. Now there were other people doing it too, so I had a bit more freedom if I was out in London partying. How did Dial House work? Easy. Consideration for others. If you listened to the one record player we had, you didn't play it too loud, out of decency towards everyone else. You didn't go in each others' bedrooms, but the other rooms were a free-for-all. When it was time for the evening meal, I'd just start cooking, or Pete would and I'd help out because he'd done it yesterday, or Pen might take over. It was the same with the washing-up. It just got done. Everybody pulled together, and cut each other some slack, and it all worked. I never remember anyone turning to someone else and saying *Pull your weight* – we just did.

It was a shared workload, a shared lifestyle, but with no rota. If you never cooked that wasn't a problem. So Andy Palmer never cooked because that wasn't his strength. His speciality was ringing round for gigs, because we'd finally got a phone installed. BT, bless them, put it in the larder. Before, if Pen and I wanted to speak to Gee in New York we had to walk up the road to the phone box in Toot Hill with a huge pile of change and feed it in like it was going out of fashion. Now we just froze our arses off standing by the fridge.

The way we lived worked. But we were never – however

much we got labelled with it later – ever, a commune. That particular millstone got hung round our necks after *Feeding* had come out, when a journalist rang Pete Stennett and asked *Who are these Crass people? What are they like? Where do they live?* And Pete, in all innocence, said *They're a bunch of ex-hippies who live in a commune out in the middle of Essex*. From that point on I spent the rest of my Crass years explaining that we did not live in a bloody commune, we were just a bunch of mates living together in the same house. But certain press people jumped on it, and used the commune tag to dismiss us and play to people's preconceptions. Still, what do you expect from the music press? If there was one thing I was to learn over the years, it was never to be surprised.

All of that, though, was off in the future. In October 1978 we went back into Southern and recorded our set from start to finish, just the way we played it. Apart from a few vocal overdubs after, the whole thing was recorded live. Overnight, because that was cheaper, and we had no money.

A couple of months later I was holding a copy of our first ever record.

We called it *Feeding Of The 5000*. Partly because that was how many we'd had pressed, so it might be how many we'd sell, partly because it was taking a biblical reference and turning it on its head, which was what punk was all about. I remember holding the acetate – the metal version of what would become the vinyl record – putting it on the record player at Dial House, and thinking *Five thousand? We won't sell five*. Because to me it didn't sound punk. It sounded crap, it sounded tinny, it sounded weak. It wasn't the Sex Pistols. It was going to bomb.

What did I know? *Feeding* came out and flew off the shelves. We sold all 5000 and went to re-press. I was stunned. We had a success. I don't think any of us quite believed it.

Success

Undoubtedly, part of the success of *Feeding* was because we made it cheap. It was £1.99 at a time most albums cost £3.99. That shocked a lot of people, but it intrigued them too, so they went out and bought it. After all, what had they got to lose? We consciously chose to go down the *Pay no more than* route, not just to encourage people to buy our records, but also because that was the punk ethic, to keep it cheap. We were short of cash, and a lot of the people we knew were skint. We wanted them to be able to go out and buy our records and still have the cash left for a pack of fags. Right from the start, Crass lived its ideals. And right from the start, that put us on a path for confrontation, whether we liked it or not.

Small Wonder had sent *Feeding* to a pressing plant in the Republic of Ireland. Trouble was, Ireland's a Catholic country and there was a track on the album called 'Asylum'. The workers at the plant took umbrage and refused to have anything to do with the record while that track was on it. So in the end we withdrew it and replaced it with a track called 'The Sound of Free Speech' which was two minutes of silence. Point made. We hadn't backed down, but while that was getting sorted the release date got pushed back. Meanwhile Gee had moved back from New York and was busy doing the artwork for the cover. I remember standing, looking over her shoulder as she did it, watching it take shape. It looked great, but finding a printer who was prepared to print it was a whole other ball game. In the end we found someone, in Brentwood I think, who was really excited and up for it, and finally everything was done.

And when it came out, like I say, it sold like hot cakes. I don't think any of us grasped the implications of this – I know I didn't. But about six weeks later we played a gig at the Aklam Hall, out under the Westway in London, and suddenly all these people came to see us. Some of them were wearing raggedy black clothes, like we did, and some had the Crass symbol on their jackets. I remember thinking *Fucking hell!* I couldn't tell you how many people were there – it's easy to exaggerate numbers, and I know the place wasn't packed out – but it was way, way busier than any gig we'd done before. A month or so later we played Conway Hall for the first time and it went like a dream. The whole place was rammed, totally filled out, including the balcony, and everyone was jumping up and down. It was brilliant! I've been back since and it's a tiny little venue, but that night it felt like playing Wembley!

Getting *Feeding* released had been hard work, but the explosion in the number of people at our gigs showed it was worth it. Now, we wanted to release 'Asylum', the missing track the pressing plant in Ireland had refused to touch. So we set up Crass Records, found a different pressing plant, and released 'Reality Asylum/Shaved Women' as a 7 inch single. For 45p.

This had two immediate consequences. One was that we lost money on every single sold, because we'd forgotten to include VAT in our costings. We'd been so busy following the Crass ideology about not ripping people off that we stitched ourselves up completely. The second was that we had to end our relationship with Small Wonder.

Some fifteen year-old kid had bought the single, and his mum had heard it. She was so offended by the lyrics she called the police. And they went to see Pete Stennett. Small Wonder might not have put the single out, but Pete's connection with us was enough for the police to put pressure on him. He was getting visits from the Obscene Publications squad, and he wasn't comfortable with it. He felt we were too hot to handle, and we realised we couldn't put him in a position where he was risking losing his livelihood. And the other bands on his label, like Cockney Rejects and Patrik Fitzgerald didn't deserve to suffer because of what we were doing, either. At the same time, there was no way we were going to stop doing it, no way we were going to change. We were having way too much fun. So we agreed we'd go our separate ways. From now on everything we did, for as long as we did it, would be through Crass Records.

We got a visit from the police too, of course. Two of the Obscene Publications squad came round to question us about our lyrics. We decided in advance we'd say we all wrote 'Reality Asylum'. That way, if they prosecuted us for it later, we were all in it together. We also got a lawyer from Epping – Mr. Leonard, who worked with us for years – to be there when they came round. And, being Crass, we taped it all, with a hidden microphone. The police would ask a question, and the lawyer would say *Don't answer that* or take us into another room and tell us *Right, the way to answer this is …* It all felt really nerve-wracking, but he told us they couldn't really do anything, they were just fishing. And some of it was almost comical – I remember them pointing at our record collection and saying *Bet you won't find any Rod Stewart in there*. No, officer. But we do have some Mahler. Now is that proof of innocence? Or guilt?

So we came off Small Wonder, got some money back from the sales of *Feeding*, though it wasn't a lot after costs – and even less once the VAT on 'Reality Asylum' had been paid – and decided the obvious thing to do was put out another record. So we went back to Southern Studios and recorded *Stations Of The Crass*. We did it overnight again, because John gave us a cheaper rate. It took a bit longer, but now we had a record of all the new songs in the set. And then we decided to really make it value for money and release it as a double album. One studio recording, one live. We did a gig at the Pied Bull in Islington in the summer of 1979, and stuck a microphone at each side of the stage. Bingo. Job done.

Unfortunately The Bull never had great sound at the best of times, and the album we ended up with was virtually unlistenable. But when *Stations* came out, it still sold well. When *Feeding* was released it had been heavily and viciously slated by the music press. With a few very occasional exceptions, they clearly didn't like us, they just twisted what we said and took the piss. So with *Stations* we thought *Fuck 'em*. And we went straight to the fanzines, which was where most of our growing fan base was anyway. Straight to them, and straight to the people who were buying the records. And we showed that could work.

By early 1980, *Stations* was number one in the indie chart, we were playing bigger venues with more people, and we were gigging in Birmingham, Leeds, Manchester and Hull, all round the country and not just round London. Crass was going places, and my life was changing.

Fans

From very early on, Crass had decided we had a responsibility to our fans, and we took that very seriously. Other bands might taste success and be seduced by the rockstar lifestyle, we wouldn't. Even before we'd produced our first record, we'd decided it was going to sell at a price anyone could afford. When *Feeding* came out, and went to re-press, and people had come to our gigs with the Crass design stencilled on their jackets, you'd have thought we might be tempted to change, and run for the good life. But we didn't. The discussion around the table till three in the morning was about how we mustn't let it go to our heads, mustn't sell out, mustn't start feeling like God Almighty.

We stuck to our guns. Which was the right thing to do. But somehow this meant we couldn't allow ourselves to enjoy what we were doing, which didn't make sense to me. We couldn't say to someone *Great! You've got our symbol on the back of your jacket!* No. We couldn't even mention it. Instead we'd buy them a drink. Don't get me wrong, I'm fine with buying people drinks, but it felt like false modesty. We were putting on a show, and we *wanted* people to come along, we *wanted* people to like it, and it was great that they knew the words to our songs.

For fear of selling out, though – or being accused of selling out – I think we took the first steps down a long road where even our best would never be enough. Our motives were great, but we were so focussed on *not-being-a-rockstar* that in the end it jumped up and bit us on the arse, because in the end we couldn't move. In the end we were trying to be so perfect for so many people for so long it became impossible to breathe.

But that's with the benefit of hindsight. At the time we were learning as we went along, and trying to do the right thing. And let's face it, that's more than you can say for some, and it's not a bad way to live your life. So when people told us they couldn't understand the lyrics because the songs were so fast, we went back to Dial House, cranked up the Roneo printer and printed up thousands of leaflets by hand. They had the lyrics on, and they explained what we were about too, and we gave them out. When people asked if we had badges, we designed some with the Crass logo, and gave those away too. And when people started turning up at Dial House, we welcomed them.

Bands we'd played with, or people who wanted to put on gigs, would drop by. Young punks would turn up, wanting to see the Crass house. And there were lots of interviews with fanzines. Because we'd chosen to ignore the mainstream music press, the fanzines were our only way of telling people what we were about, so this DIY publicity was really important to us, and we were always doing interviews. Some of them were bullshit – kids turning up with a biro and a piece of paper saying they had a fanzine because they wanted to come and see Crass – but that was fine. I'd have done the same.

The farmer and the villagers were slightly bemused by this influx of young people with mohicans, black clothes, and brightly coloured hair, but there was never any trouble. Even the local police were generally ok. Sometimes they'd go as far as giving people a lift up to the house if they were lost. One time we got a delivery of five Italian punks who couldn't speak a word of English and assumed they'd been arrested when they were picked up outside the train station in Epping. Their surprise – and relief – when they got dropped off at Dial House had to be seen to be believed.

A lot of these people stayed over, and then they needed somewhere to sleep, so they'd end up in the upstairs room with the record player, or in the studio. Dial House isn't the biggest place, and it was a bit chaotic, but it was great for people to see how living there worked. And they all wanted to be involved. They hadn't come for a holiday, or for free bed and breakfast, they were there because of what Crass was, and they all mucked in and helped out. Sometimes though, living there was like being on a rush-hour Tube. God knows where everybody went. Or how they all got fed.

And then it got even busier. In a twist so bizarre you couldn't make it up, Eve's house got compulsory purchased by the grandson of Idi Amin. Honestly. So she and her son moved in. She bought a little garden shed, put it up in the garden, and that became her space. Then Phil lost his place, because it got sold off, so he came to Dial House too. With his three kids. His daughter was 13 or 14, and needed a bit of privacy, so I said she could have my room – which was a tiny box-room we'd made by putting up partition walls – and for the next two years I slept wherever I could. I was in a relationship with Gee, so sometimes I'd sleep in her room, but if she wanted her own space I'd end up on the sofa, among snoring strangers. Ridiculous, in a way, that I didn't have a room of my own in the house where I lived, but the place wasn't big enough. As well as all these people, there were twenty-five cats, a dog, two goats, and a bunch of chickens. The cats had the sense to fuck off all day, into the hedgerows, and only come back to be fed. But whichever way you cut it, the house was full.

Not only was the house full, but being in Crass had become a full-time job. And now we started getting fan mail. At first it was, say, ten letters, so we'd sit down and write back. And because there were only ten, we'd be really chummy. Next time it was 30. Then 50, 100, 200. Then sackfuls. And because we were writing back, people would write to us again, and the whole thing just snowballed into a fucking nightmare.

A lot of the time we were answering the same questions *Have you got a badge? What bands do you like? Why do you wear black?* And, because it was Crass, *How can anarchy work? Can you really have anarchy and peace?* so we printed out a leaflet that covered these questions and wrote a little message at the bottom of each one so it was still individual. If we hadn't we'd have been overwhelmed. As it was we still had to designate two nights a week purely for writing back to people. We'd sit round the table, pick a letter from the pile, read it, answer it, and move on to the next. Christ knows how much it cost us in postage. I dread to think. You'd just grab a stack of letters *That's for me, that one, this is for Pete, that's for Eve* and get on with answering them.

Some letters were just addressed to Crass. I remember opening one which turned out to be for Eve, but she was in another room and I couldn't be arsed to go find her. So I wrote back *Sorry Eve can't answer this letter but she's got really bad diarrhoea.* A little while later she gets a letter back saying *Sorry to hear about your diarrhoea* and you could see the confusion on her face when she was reading it, going *What the hell is this all about?!!* Another time I wrote back that Joy de Vivre had fallen down the stairs and couldn't hold a pen. Anything just to liven things up a bit because sometimes I was just so bored with it, with sitting there hour after hour, answering letters.

Quickly, very quickly, we stopped calling it *fan mail*. Because among the piles of letters would be ones from people turning to us because they'd nowhere else to go. *I'm so fed up with living at home, I just want to get out. What should I do, Steve?* Letters like that really hit a chord with me because of my own loneliness growing up in Dagenham. If I'd ever thought of writing to David Bowie it would have been the same sort of letter *Dave, what can I do? Please help me.*

So we were getting letters from people with serious problems. Young blokes who were addicts. Girls contemplating suicide. And then we got a phone call asking us to go and see a kid in a coma.

He'd been pushed into the road by a couple of skinheads, and a bus had hit him. And now he was in hospital in Portsmouth, and his mum wanted us to come and talk to him. So Gee and myself went down. It was a very weird experience, to sit by his bed and talk to him while he lay there with a tube in his throat, not moving. I didn't really see how it could help, but then again, what harm could it do? And if it made his poor mum feel better, then that was something. He did come out of it about four weeks later, thankfully, but I don't think we had anything to do with that.

It happened again a couple of years later. Some kid climbed out of his bedroom window late at night to go somewhere, and got hit by a car when he was crossing the road. So I went to see him too. Once again, thank fuck, he recovered. He left me a note at the Shepherd's Bush Empire show, saying *Wa-hey! I'm still here!!* Another happy ending. At the time, though, when you get a phone call asking you to visit a kid who loves your music and is in a coma, and you don't know whether he'll live or die, it's really intense. But of course you go and do it. To us – and certainly to me – if we were putting ourselves out there, then that was part and parcel of it. That's something I still believe. However horrible it might be, however much you might not want to do it, however much it pisses you off and you don't want to see it, you've got to do it. Because it comes with the job.

As for the letters, I thought – and I always have thought – how great it must be to write to someone and you get a letter back. Not an impersonal note from their secretary, but a handwritten letter from the person you wrote to replying to *your* situation. Especially if you're writing to someone about how shit life is, because then you don't feel so alone. If we got a letter from someone in Nottingham telling us they were going to commit suicide, there wasn't a lot we could do. We couldn't physically stop them. But we could write a letter back and hope they didn't do it.

And I think the fact that even now people will come up and say *Crass changed my life* is partly down to all those long dull hours we spent sitting round the table in Dial House, answering each and every single letter. Taking our responsibilities seriously. Even something like 'Owe Us', that simple song I wrote walking back from the village with the pet mince melting in the bag, had something to do with it. It struck a chord with a lot of people, and it's the biggest song Crass ever did. The one everyone always remembers. A whole nation of kids clicked into that.

At a time when we were being told there was no such thing as society, and that making money was the only good, and that it didn't matter if you threw whole communities on the dole, Crass stood up and said there was another way of doing things. That people were more important than power, that there was no authority but yourself. I think that what we lit up in people was the feeling I had the first time I picked up *Kes* and saw that picture of Billy Casper giving it the Vs. The realisation you didn't have to do things on their terms or live in the boundaries they set you. So when people come up to me and say *Thanks*, I think it's more *You inspired me to do something*, and they're saying thanks for that. Nothing less and nothing more.

I still think they owe us a living, by the way. *Us* being everybody in the world, *they* being those bastards.

You know who you are.

Violence

Not everybody liked Crass. Some people really fucking hated us. For a lot of young punks – who listened to our lyrics, or read our leaflets, or came to our gigs, or visited Dial House – Crass was an inspiration. To others we were a threat. And if there was one line the music press loved to push, one stick they repeatedly beat us over the head with, it was the idea we were spoilt, privileged people mouthing off, and so could be ignored, or laughed at. It saved them from having to think. Or listen.

With my background, this idea that we were just playing at what we did – that we were really nothing more than a bunch of middle class wankers living in a mansion in the countryside – used to infuriate me. But since we were trying to break down class barriers, I couldn't turn round and go *No. I'm working class.* How the fuck could I when I was arguing for a world where there was no class at all? How could I fight it without getting caught up in their petty little tiff? Without playing on their terms? It used to do my head in.

The fact is that if you stand up and say there's a better way of doing things, and that the system we live in is wrong, there's always going to be people with pens and print who are going to murder you for it. Pen was in his thirties. He talked with a middle-class accent. He lived in a beautiful house. *Put the pieces together, dear reader. Crass are a con.*

It was bullshit. All we ever did when the royalties started coming in was let Southern handle it, and pay ourselves £500 a year each, £10 a week, the same as the dole. A lot of that went into the kitty. Most of the rest got spent on printing the leaflets and badges we gave out for free. Or on postage, answering letters.

I'd come back from a gig and find myself wandering round a cafe in a motorway service station in the middle of the night, eating the chips people had left on their plates because I had no cash to buy food. We got enormous support from our audience and people who liked what we did, and the way I saw it, that was our reward. Of course there were people who didn't like us – that's life. But being accused of being rich, rip-off bastards? That used to really get on my hooter. I never had any fucking money.

But seeing as the press were slating Siouxsie and the Banshees for being from Bromley, they'd have hell freeze over before they gave us a fair crack of the whip. And some of the criticism thrown our way was hilarious. I'd quite liked Adam Ant in his early days, with his decadent Berlin cabaret routine, and his idea of a sensual revolution. Then he did the Royal Variety show and bowed to the Queen. The fucking knob. He still had the nerve to say Crass weren't anarchists, because we were giving people cups of tea at the Anarchy Centre when we should be giving them machine guns. *Yeah. And shoot you, you fucker.* You had to laugh, you really did.

After a while, anything the press said was like water off a duck's back anyway. We had other things to worry about. Like violence at our gigs.

It wasn't as if we hadn't seen trouble before. Back in the early days, about the time of the trip to New York, Andy Palmer had got us a gig at the Chelsea School of Art. It was unforgettable. There were about 300 people there, and as soon as we walked in I knew it was going to go off. You could just feel it in the air.

We went on stage after some typical student rock band. I started 'Owe Us', turned round to Pen to get the *1-2-3-4*, turned round again – and apart from Eve Libertine the hall was empty. In three seconds we'd cleared the place.

We did the whole set, but we did it to an empty hall. As soon as we'd finished, everyone piled back in again and suddenly there were fights breaking out all over. I don't just mean a bit of pushing and shoving either, this was serious rucking. People running at each other with broken bottles. It was utterly bizarre, and to this day I don't know what it was all about. At first I thought Andy might have bullshitted, said we were something we weren't, but then I'd have expected the bother to be coming our way, and it didn't. None of it touched us. We just stood and watched lots of blokes with beards having a go at each other, utterly confused. Was this what students were like?

But now the violence was different. The NF were at one of their electoral high points, their headquarters was in Great Eastern Street in London. Fascist skinheads disrupted our London shows. This wasn't about two idiots in a crowd having a pop at each other. It was more serious. One night we played the Moonlight Club, in West Hampstead. The gig was fine, everything went well, we went off home. Then next day we started getting reports that after the show skinheads had been waiting for the Crass fans down at the Tube station. They battered them and chased them all down the line, and were threatening to do the same again next time we played.

And then there was the battle of Conway Hall. It was the third show we did there, and this time we were playing with the Poison Girls and the Rondos. I was backstage and I heard this huge noise. I came out to look, and the world and its dog were fighting. Apparently what had happened was that a bunch of skins had turned up and were giving it *Sieg Heil* and threatening to throw bricks at us when we started playing. The usual bollocks. Now one of the blokes on the door was in the SWP and a bunch of his mates – the Cockney Reds, really staunch geezers – were having a meeting round the corner, so he nipped round to find them, they came back all tooled up, and *Boom*. It all went off.

Hand on heart, I don't think Crass dealt with it too well. We believed in non-violence. We saw the ideology of the left as being as bad as that of the right. And we never saw the difference between the violence of the attacker and the fist thrown by someone who fights back. After the ambush at the Moonlight Club we had this ridiculous discussion where we tried to work out what to do. Someone suggested we should hire coaches to ferry punks into our gigs and maybe hire a security firm to look out for them on their way back home … And I remember thinking *This is fucking stupid*. I was from Dagenham. Yes, I'd seen how unpleasant violence could be, but not fighting back just didn't seem right. And Crass never saw that. Even people who were fans of the band, like Colin Jerwood, found it hard to understand.

As a young punk, Colin was a big Crass fan, and came to loads of our gigs. Once, we were playing Hastings, and some skinheads kicked off, broke some mirrors and were holding the broken bits of glass like weapons, threatening people. So Colin goes and grabs a screwdriver, and the rest of his mates got tooled up as well. Gee comes flying out into the middle of it and has a pop at Colin for what he's done, but doesn't have a pop at the skinheads. And he always saw that as an injustice. And to be honest, I did too.

Another time, at Bristol, a big fight started. Andy Palmer's at the bottom, me and Colin are trying to pull people off him, Colin thumps someone, and the first thing Andy said when he got up wasn't *Thanks for helping me out lads*. He went up to Colin and said *What d'you hit that bloke for?* Which really hurt Colin, because he was trying to help, and he was dealing with trouble the only way he knew how. I remember a huge part of me was thinking *He's right. Andy's talking bollocks*.

But after the Conway Hall gig, we put out a leaflet condemning the fighting. And I think that said to a lot of people that we didn't really care. That they got the shit kicked out of them at the Moonlight while we drove back to Essex, and we didn't have a fucking clue what it was like for them. But god forbid they should fight back.

The music press having a pop at us was neither here nor there, but that leaflet was a huge mistake. When you tell your fans they're wrong to hit the people who are steaming into their gigs and beating them up, then you really haven't got it right. It was almost as if we were saying we should feel sorry for these fucking twats who were coming along to disrupt our gigs and throw bricks at people and chase punks down the railway line, that we should be giving them tea and biscuits and understanding. Fuck that. We should have organised ourselves and given them a bloody good hiding. We shouldn't have let those bastards ruin one fucking gig. Pacifism may be a great ideal, but in reality it just doesn't always cut it. And if one thing should have brought that home, it was what happened at Stonehenge festival in the summer of 1980.

We'd played Stonehenge the year before, and everything had been fine. There weren't many people and most of them were hippies. But the year it all kicked off it was a bigger deal, and there was a big punk presence. We were there, and so were Flux and the Poison Girls, and Colin from Conflict was there with a few of the south London lot. And of course there were the bikers. These big fucking lumps.

Afterwards, when I was trying to make sense of it all, I told myself that maybe they'd got jealous because there were loads of punks there. Or that they'd had some bad drugs. But in the end I could only find one explanation that rang true. Fuck trying to make excuses for them. They were just a total bunch of wankers.

The atmosphere had been a bit edgy anyway. Then when Flux were playing, someone threw a bottle at them. It hit one of the band, and Derek Birkett goes *Right. Whoever threw that, fucking get up here now!* Then he turns round to whoever's next to him and says *These bikers are a bunch of cunts, aren't they?* A biker standing behind Derek bottles him, and all hell breaks loose.

I'd never liked festivals anyway. There was never anywhere to wash or take a shit, everything stank of woodsmoke, and you were always in earshot of some idiot playing the bongoes. But what sticks in my mind from Stonehenge that year is hearing the screaming through the night as these bikers – and what heroes they were, these 30 year-old blokes, these big lumps – hunted in packs, chasing and beating up punks who were half their age.

Anyone who looked like a punk was a target. And there was nowhere to go. All you could do was hide and hope for the best. If you hid in your tent, the bastards rode a bike over it. Running just took you into the next field, and a motorbike was faster. I managed to hide in the van with some other people, and spent the most terrifying night of my life, lying there listening to what was going on, hoping we'd all be safe. Pen, bless him, because of his age and his looks, was able to pass unnoticed. So was Gee. And the two of them, along with Phil and Joy, spent the night trying to save people, to bring them back to the van, or hide them with old friends. It was one of the bravest things I've known anybody do, ever. I've had my disagreements with him over the years, but for what he did that night alone, Penny Rimbaud deserves a medal.

We got through the night and got the hell out of there. All of us were in shock. The festival had been started up, years before, by Wally Hope, who was a good friend of Pen's, and we'd had this naive belief that even if we didn't all listen to the same music, even if we weren't all into motorbikes, whatever we looked like or believed, it was a place where there was room for all of us, because we were all anti-establishment. Punks, bikers, hippies, the lot of us.

The bikers' violence proved us wrong. Apparently they offered a half-arsed apology through one of the festival organisers later, saying it had all been *A mistake and a misunderstanding*. As far as I'm concerned that was worth fuck all. They'd desecrated Wally's memory. They'd defiled his dream. They were no better than the fucking police.

They lost in the end, because punks went back to the festival the next year, despite what had happened, and soon punks and new age travellers were the norm there. But I never went back. After what happened at Stonehenge I swore to the rest of Crass that I would never do another outdoor festival again in my life.

And I never have.

Out On Tour

When Crass started out, it was fun. Pen and myself didn't really think it was going to go further than the garden gate, but *Feeding* changed all that. Suddenly we were successful, and people wanted to know what we stood for, and hear what we had to say. Slowly, as we tried to tell people what we thought, and do what we believed in, Crass took over our lives. By 1981, it was really full-on. Twelve hours a day, seven days a week. Exhausting.

We were in Thatcher's Britain. The miners' strike was coming up, the Falklands War was about to kick off. And as a band, we'd gone down the line of confrontation and having a meaning and being against the system. By now, the leaflets we turned out were political, trying to organise people, to create a movement, and the conversations we were having were political, and the gigs we were getting offered – especially in Italy, because the Italian anarchists are really hardcore – were very political.

Dial House was a headquarters, not a home. A nerve centre, not a place you could relax. The phone was always ringing, there was always someone there, there was always something to do. It didn't ever stop. Whether we were at home, or on tour, we were working ridiculously hard, and not sleeping enough, and living on sweet f.a. Now even if, as a bunch of people, you're doing everything right, absolutely 100% right, under that kind of pressure you're going to burn out.

And we didn't do everything right, by any means, because no

one can. And because sometimes there was no *right*. Take one example, the decision there would be no alcohol in Dial House. Our motives were bang-on. With all these people visiting, we felt it made sense. The way we saw it was that if someone was going to put the time and effort into visiting us, and make a long journey from wherever, then they deserved not to find us sitting round pissed, or too hungover to talk to them. There was no getting stoned, either, for the same reason. And because the last thing we wanted was to be busted by the police over something as trivial as a little spliff.

So, no alcohol. A good thing, because we were taking our responsibilities to our fans seriously? Or a bad thing, because we were saying to ourselves that we could never, in the privacy of our own home, lay our public role aside, take an evening off, and blow a gasket? Remember, this wasn't something that went on for a week or two, it lasted five years.

I'm not blaming anyone else. We did it to ourselves. But we went too far, and we put ourselves in a situation where we were constantly under pressure, constantly laying ourselves open to criticism, constantly in danger of being seen to make a mistake. I couldn't write songs any more, because I felt I had to scrutinise every word to be sure I could justify and defend it, and it couldn't be taken the wrong way. The pressure was on, and it was really intense.

Tours could be fun – we played some great places, and I had definite favourites – but they were hard work too. We didn't make a penny from them, because all the gigs we did were benefits, to raise money for various local causes. And since we were trying to keep the costs down so as much cash as possible went to that night's cause, we ended up sleeping on people's floors. And what you get then, for better or worse, is pot luck.

There was one night we played Liverpool. After the gig, some bloke tells us *Yeah, I've got somewhere you can stay.* So we all go back to his. We get there and he can't open the door. He's either lost the key or he's too drunk to find it. So in the end he just boots the front door in. I don't know why we didn't turn round then and leave right then. But no. In we troop behind him, up the stairs and into this room. There's no carpet, just bare floorboards with nails sticking out, and one iron bedstead in the corner, which Phil and Joy commandeer. It squeaks every time they move, so it's *eek eek eek* all night, but they're comfy in their sleeping bags. Or as comfy as it gets. The rest of us are scattered round on the floorboards, freezing our nuts off.

The bloke who's invited us round then sits in the open doorway of this room, trying to talk to us while we're trying to go to sleep. Out of his head, sucking on this rustling crisp bag full of glue. Then there's a bit of commotion downstairs at the front door.

And he shouts *Hey!*
And someone shouts back *Wha'?*
You'll 'ave to be quiet!
Wha'?
So he shouts louder *You'll 'ave to be quiet!*
Why?
'Cause Crass are in 'ere!
Who?
Crass! And the crisp packet rustles. *Is that you, Julie?*
Yeah.
Gizza fuck.
No. Fuck off.
Go on. Gizza fuck. Rustle rustle.

I'm lying there on a cold, hard floor, listening to this, with the stink of glue wafting over, thinking *You've got to be kidding.* Next morning I woke up really early, tired and aching after a shit night's sleep, going *I don't want none of this* and went downstairs to the bog. There's no seat, there's no bog paper. *Fuck's sake.* The door shuts. There's no handle on the door. I had to kick my way out. I couldn't wait to get out of the place. This went way beyond what was acceptable. This wasn't punk, this was genocide. Suddenly the flat in Heath Park was really attractive, with Stan and the cocktail bar and Mum and the canary.

So a tour could be really, really hard work. And then the next night I'd be at the next gig – which would be a benefit again – cold and tired after a long drive, hungry and desperately in need of a shower, and someone would have a moan at me about having to pay £1.50 to get in. I remember thinking *What the fuck am I doing this for?* And I couldn't turn round and say *Well don't come then* because that wasn't the way Crass did things. I had to explain it to them, talk it through, have a sodding debate when all I wanted was a square meal and a good night's kip. There's some people for whom nothing you ever do will be enough, it's just how they are, and more and more I found myself telling these people to piss off. Because I'd had enough.

Don't get me wrong. We met a lot of great people. People who helped us and fed us and bought us pints, people who put a lot of work into sorting out gigs to raise money, people who were trying to change the world for the better, and I haven't forgotten any of that. But I'm just trying to show how, over the years, what we were doing was exhausting and unsustainable. We had a laugh on tour, but it was bloody hard work too, and then when we got back to Dial House it wasn't as if we could say *Right. Shut the door. Let's have a week off.* Someone would be round, there'd be an interview to do and letters to answer, and then the phone would ring. And it just didn't stop.

And for me, that unrelenting pressure turned me into someone who felt everything was shit, that life was shit and it was never going to get any better. I remember thinking *This is all a load of old cobblers*.

Crass had laughs and stuff, but we never let off steam. We never had a piss-up or a party, and I don't think you can live like that, long-term. I know I couldn't. I'd head into London and go out partying with my mates. But even when I did go to the pub I could never be seen to be drunk because I'd be letting Crass down. If I fell in the gutter it wouldn't just be me falling in the gutter, it would be all of Crass. It couldn't be done. It wasn't something that was explicitly said to me – it was my personal decision – but that silent, unspoken pressure was always there.

In the end, it just burnt me out. I remember one girl I was going out with, I remember really opening up to her about it, and saying *I don't think I can take much more of this, because I'm just a miserable bastard, you know?* I stopped going to gigs. I got fed up with seeing people wearing raggedy black clothes. I got fed up with hearing songs about nuclear war. I got fed up with hearing, at the end of a track, the *BOOM!* of a nuclear explosion. I got fed up of that classic punk bass line you'd always hear. And I got fed up with being given leaflets at gigs, and being deafened by a shit PA and drinking crap lager from a plastic mug.

And then the end came.

It wasn't pre-arranged. Not at all. It was during the miners' strike, in 1984, and we were doing a benefit for the Welsh miners in Aberdare. I remember before the gig, standing outside with these two big miners – massive blokes, built like brick shithouses – having a bit of a laugh. And a police car went past. And one of these miners went *Oh we cracked into them lovely last week, boyo. Gave them a bloody good hiding! Go on, you bastards!*

Anyway, we did the gig, and the gig went fine. The miners

came, we got presented with a miner's lamp, everyone had a good night. It was one of those gigs when you knew just why we did what we did, what Crass stood for, and what we were all about. We got in the van to go home, started driving back down the M4, and Andy Palmer said *I want to leave the band.* Literally like that. There was a chorus of *Why?* and *That's a surprise!* But I remember thinking *If you hadn't said it, then I would have.*

A couple of days later we sat down and talked about it, and I said *Well, I'd been thinking about leaving the band anyway.* And a couple of the others said the same. We'd all got to that point. And all Andy wanted to do was have a relationship with his girlfriend. He'd already moved out of Dial House and was living in a squat in King's Cross, in the same place as Mick Duffield, and seeing this girl. We had no more gigs booked in, and so on the way back from Aberdare, Andy had seized his moment.

When I woke up on the morning of 12th July 1984, Crass was already history.

AFTER CRASS

Exeter

When Crass disbanded, my overwhelming emotion was enormous relief. Six weeks later I had itchy feet and wanted to go out on tour again. And there was no band. It had been a central part of my life for six or seven years, and now it was gone. Suddenly, Steve Ignorant was just that bloke who'd been in Crass once. It was a hard thing to get used to.

For a while I resented the fact that I'd spent so much of my twenties in this staunch anarchist band who did everything right and took the world on, when all that part of me really wanted was to be in a punk band, get pissed, and have a good time. As the years go by, though, it becomes easier to look back on the years Crass spent together. To take pride in the things we did well, and hold my hands up to the mistakes we made. Because we did make mistakes, even if they were with the best of intentions. And how could it be otherwise? We were just a bunch of people living together and making music, not a collection of plaster saints. Nobody's perfect, whatever they tell you.

There's no doubt about it, what we tried to achieve sounds incredibly idealistic. And it was. I'm really proud of what Crass did. But the downside was that – without intending to – we put a host of expectations upon ourselves, and ended up having to live up to this image we'd created. This made it extremely difficult to just go out and say *Fuck it, I'll be me*. Because we could never let the image go.

As early as the visit to New York, that was true. I remember

Phil nipping out of Gee's apartment in a t-shirt and shorts, and coming back in really worried he'd been seen by one of the women in the Contortions and he wasn't in our regulation black. And everyone went *You idiot! You've spoilt it now!* Looking back, I can't help but laugh, but at the same time I think *What a bunch of tossers!* We took ourselves so seriously.

No one can live under that kind of burden for ever. The only reason we were able to keep going as long as we did was because we were a really really tight group of friends, a really tight family. All of us were always looking out for each other, and we were all involved in Crass together. But that was also one of the downsides. When you're that close, and living like a family, little niggles can really grate, and small differences of opinion have huge significance. Like the book clear-out incident.

Dial House was always full of books. We had regular clear-outs, so we didn't end up buried beneath them, and it was interesting to see what went, and what stayed. There were some really obscure books that had been there forever, which should have been chucked out way before, books which were just collecting dust in the corner and no one was ever going to read. Like the ones about politics in America, which Pen's dad had given him – nobody ever read them, but they were still there. Ray Bradbury's science fiction writing, which I liked, went, while the J. G. Ballard stayed because it was more highbrow. There was a whole row of *Inspector Maigrets* by Simenon – we used to take them on tour because they were easy reading. But *The Sweeney*, which I got, that went.

So this one time we're having a clear-out, and the Maigret stayed. But there was great hilarity when I decided that *To Sir, With Love* should stay on the bookshelves.

Now, for those who don't know, *To Sir, With Love* was written in 1950-something when this guy E. R. Braithwaite, who was from British Guiana, and one of the first black immigrants to come over, was looking for an engineering job. He couldn't get one because of his colour, because of the colour bar. In the end, the only job he could get was as a teacher in a secondary school, a job no one else would take, in East London. And the book is about how he had to really struggle to overcome – obviously – the prejudice and the racism around him, but also how he got through to these kids who were absolutely uncontrollable. And he did it. It's a true story. And in parallel with anarchism, it's all about being taught how to respect yourself and other people as human beings.

Now surely, if you're in Crass, being an anarchist trying to respect yourself and other people, then *To Sir, With Love* is a pretty valid book to have on the bookshelves. At least as much as *Inspector Maigret Solves It Again*.

Anyhow, everybody had a good laugh when I made a fuss about *To Sir, With Love*. But I put it back on the shelves. Then I went back to Dial House a few years later, to a jumble sale, and there it was in the jumble sale, being sold, along with a couple of my other books. And I had to buy the bloody things back! I did my nut!

I've mentioned this before in interviews, and I don't want to turn it into some huge Crass myth, but it just struck me that there was almost a literary snobbery. An unconscious bias because of the background of the people there. To me, that just illustrates that Crass weren't perfect and infallible. And I wonder if we'd have done better to own up to that. Would it have killed us to say we were having Dial House to ourselves for a week or two so we could shut the world out and recharge our batteries? Or shut it out and party? Or to say we needed a hotel for the night because lying on wooden floorboards in an empty room with a glue-sniffing buffoon was just too much, and we wanted a proper night's kip? We might have copped some flak, but we might have made room for ourselves to enjoy life too.

We'll never know, because we didn't do it. We tried to be the perfect band who never sold out, and never showed a flicker of weakness. And what happened eventually – of course – was that being in Crass took over to the extent there was no room for a personal life and no room to fall out either. It was an enormous pressure, and yeah, in the end it got us. To be honest, I'm surprised we lasted as long as we did, but I think the records show what happened, because the last ones are dreadful. We'd said what we had to say. We'd said the system's shit. We were just saying it again, going over the same old ground, but with different backing. And the images were dark and depressing – cattle trucks and gas chambers, crucifixion and nuclear bombs.

I don't want to use the benefit of hindsight to beat Crass up. A lot of what we did was good. All the time we were confronting things and breaking taboos. So *Penis Envy* was the women in the band singing, and a feminist agenda, and why not? Why not stir up the bucket of shit? Why not throw a spanner in the works? God knows it needed doing. But for any bands thinking of doing the same today, I'd say yes, confront what's wrong, but never let the fun go out of what you're doing. Somewhere, Crass stopped being a laugh, and I never understood why you can't do something meaningful and have fun at the same time.

I think the hope we had was that we would be an example. That people would pick up on what we were doing and then do it for themselves. And they did. When bands like Flux and the Chumbas started, I remember thinking *Thank Christ for that!* Because it took the pressure off a little. I guess I hoped that sooner or later we could just retire quietly and gracefully, and let others carry on. But we'd driven ourselves too hard, too relentlessly, for too long. All the way through to the end our ethic was to give the people who were buying our records value for money, and so we went over the top with that, giving away badges and leaflets and booklets and using whatever money came in for the next project while we scraped and got by.

I realise it's hard for some people to believe, but – really, honestly, truly – for any sceptics reading this, there was never any money around. If there had been, do you really think I wouldn't have gone and bought a motorbike? Or taken driving lessons? Or I wouldn't have gone and bought Seditionary clothing? Or gone to the Wag Club? Or taken really top quality pharmaceuticals instead of the shit I was taking? Really? Of course I fucking would. All that and more.

So I say three great big hairy cheers for Crass. And a couple of pints on the side. Yes, we made mistakes, but so what? At least we stood up and did something. We were a bunch of mates who took on this incredible responsibility and the workload that came with it. We believed in classlessness, that everyone was equal and should be living free. We believed that if you wanted a better world, you got off your arse and did something about it. We were brilliant and flawed, and whether you loved us or we got up your nose, I tell you this.

We lived our ideals. We didn't change the world, but we had a bloody good go. And on the way, some cracking things happened.

One time we played in Exeter, St. George's Hall. I walked into the bar and there were these three skinheads standing there looking pretty menacing, like they always used to. And I got annoyed all of a sudden, because I was fed up with it. I was a skinhead when they were still in nappies, first time round. Maybe I never had the Docs and only got to wear monkey boots, but *I was there, you fuckers! You will rue the day!*

So I'm all umpty, and glaring daggers at them, and they're looking at me. That day was a turning point for me. I wasn't going to be scared of skinheads no more, I was just going to steam in and get the little bastards out, because I'd had enough by then of them coming to our gigs and causing trouble. I thought *If they kick off, if they do anything at all, that's it. I'm going to be on them.*

And there was a spare mic stand, so I unscrewed the three legs and hid them. That way if anything happened I'd know where to go and grab one. I thought *I'll do them in the knee first and they'll go down.* So anyway, before the gig starts people are coming in, then – *BOOM!* the door bursts open …

… and about twenty Down's Syndrome kids run in. And they're running round in circles, shouting and hollering, and they burst into the bar, and one of them runs right up to the biggest skinhead, throws her arms round him and goes *I love you!* And he stands there with this little girl hanging off him, and goes *Yeah. I love you too.*

And then he looks over at me, and smiles. *You all right there, Steve?* It turned out all three of them were fans, and I'd just got the wrong end of the stick. And what was really lovely was all three of these skinheads just mucked about with the Down's Syndrome kids. Everyone did. All the punks, everyone. It was just absolute chaos, left, right, and centre. Noise, and screams, and laughter. The bloke who'd brought them out was working at a day centre for them, and I asked him *How the bloody hell did you get them to a Crass gig then?* And he said *I just told the management I was taking them to a concert. I didn't tell them what sort.*

So anyway, we got on stage, and we're doing the set. I'm doing 'Owe Us' and I look up and then one of the kids is there on the stage next to me, clicking his fingers and going *Yeah! Yeah! Yeah!* and hugging me, and laughing. Having the time of his life!

And after, when the gig was over and we were taking down the gear, I remember dear Fox, the drummer from Dirt – who's dead now, sadly – I remember him having an instant rapport with these kids and going *Come on then! Who wants a go on the drums?* And he sat there and gave them the sticks and let them play the kit. Some of them would just give one of the cymbals a timid *tink!* and giggle and run off. Others would give everything a good old hammering ... Everyone stayed around afterwards having a real good laugh, and of all the Crass gigs we've done that's the one that stands out, that's the one.

There was something about what we did sometimes. Really special.

Love

As I've said, life in Crass could be pretty demanding. So it's hardly a surprise that my love life was too. I was young, and single, going out as much as I could and making amends for my late start with girls, and trying to fit all that in round our schedule of touring and recording.

It sounds fantastic. Like I was living the dream. And on one level I was. I liked sex, there were plenty of women who liked sex, everything in the garden was rosy. Or it should have been. But the whole time there was this complex, unhappy triangle I was caught up in, because there was me and the girl, and there was me and Crass. If the girls got too close I ran off with Crass, if Crass got too much I ran back to a girl. And I struggled with that more than anyone. I'd walk back into Dial House, or into the studio, and expect myself to walk out of one set of emotions and into another set cleanly, just like that. Trust me, it can't be done. Or at least I can't do it. So, for all the fun I seemed to be having, trying to keep these two worlds apart in my own head was bloody hard work.

Don't get me wrong, I had some great times. A couple of the most erotic nights I've ever experienced, and some incredibly fond memories. Times when I felt so close, so connected, it blew my mind. And you can't make those nights happen. They come along once or twice a lifetime. And you just have to enjoy them when they do.

But if you expect a kiss-and-tell, all the gory details about what happened where, and who with, then you're reading the wrong book. There were relationships I fucked up, and ones that did the same to me, same as happens to everyone. No big drama, move along. The truth was I was committed to my band, and Crass were a full-time job. If I couldn't find time for myself, how on earth was I ever going to make the time for someone else? I tried a couple of times, and I couldn't make it work.

While Crass and I were still an item, the simple, easy, un-complicated relationship I was looking for was never going to happen. Not the way I wanted it to. Instead I found myself caught on this perpetual yo-yo, bouncing between nights down the pub with a girl, holding hands and kissing, being affection-ate, and days arguing about the military-industrial complex and the threat of imminent nuclear war. Is it any wonder I didn't know whether I was coming or going?

If I had to pick one good memory out – and there's no names, no pack drill, so don't even think of asking – then it's of being with a girl in the top floor of a block of flats in East London. Everyone had gone to bed, and out of the window you could see West Ham station with the underground trains running in and out, and there was the gas works, and smoke coming out of factories, and orange sodium lights blazing as far as the eye could see. A really great industrial landscape. We were both stood there, naked, looking out over the whole world, her eyes were shining, and it was just one of those moments when all your barriers are down and all pretence is gone. I'd just touch her, run my fingers over her, and it was like our skin was what joined us together, not what kept us apart, and that with a sim-ple touch I was sinking right into her ...

Even to this day when I think about it, I get a rush, like a faint echo of that night, and realise it's the memories of the good things we've done and the great times we've had that keep us going in darker times. You. Me. Her. Everyone. That's just the way it is. You've got to have some love in your life. I had love – sometimes – and when there wasn't love, there was Conflict.

Conflict

In 1980 we were doing a gig somewhere up north and this young, fresh-faced, good-looking punk came up to me and said *All right Steve, my name's Colin. This is Paul. Is it all right if we print off some of your leaflets and hand them out at other gigs that we go to?* And that's how Colin Jerwood first started getting involved with Crass. Pretty soon I knew that there were two really important things in Colin's life – his vegetarianism and the band he was just starting, called Conflict. They had their first gig coming up in a few weeks, and he asked me to come along.

So I went all the way down to Mottingham, in South London. Colin met me at the station, took me back to his parents' house, where I met his mum, Iris, and his dad George. Iris took one look at me that first time I walked in, shook her head, and said *We're going to put some skin on those bones.* Straightway she started feeding me sandwiches and cups of tea. She used to call me *meat pudding 'arry.* I went down there a lot over the years, and I really had a lot of time for his parents. George used to have me in fits with the politically incorrect things he'd say, and Iris was always telling me to eat more, and asking *What is it with the 'air, 'arry?*

That first visit, once Iris was happy I wasn't going to starve to death, we went off to the gig which was in a little church hall somewhere in Eltham. And I should have realised at the time, but Colin did what I was to learn was one of his classics – *Steve, you don't need to do nothing, but would you mind standing behind the mixing desk for a minute while the sound guy nips out for a drink?* Of course the sound man had gone home because they weren't paying him to stay. Thanks. And he wanted it taped, of course. Typical Colin.

And they got up on stage. Colin, Big John, Paco on drums, a guitarist. Now, on the way there Col had been really clear *Right, the way we're going to start is I shout 'Conflict!' and you come straight in, no hanging about, right?* And everyone went *Yeah, yeah, yeah, got it.* So they're on stage, everyone's waiting, Colin yells *Conflict!*

Silence. Nothing happens. The band just stand there. Col's furious. He shouts *You cunt!* And suddenly they wake up and start playing. It wasn't a bad gig, to be fair. Afterwards, we headed back to his folk's house, with Colin all excited and wired because he'd done his first gig. I couldn't help remembering how I'd been, after Huntley Street, when playing to a couple of bears and some hippies meant we were going to rule the world. Anyway, Col's full of himself, and his mum says *Let's hear it then.* He puts the tape on, and of course it starts *Conflict ... you cunt!* And his mum goes *Oooh! We haven't got that bleedin' swearing all the way through, have we?*

And that was it. Conflict were up and running. They did a few more gigs, and then we offered them a record deal. I think it was the single they did first: *The House That Man Built.* Then we did an album with them, and they'd come to our gigs and we'd go to theirs, and about a year later they were in the studio and Colin said *Will you come and do some vocals with us?* It was for an animal liberation single they were doing. He told me *I've got the chorus for it, but I ain't got nothing else.* We were in Southern Studios, and this was Colin getting an inch and taking a mile, again. So I had a couple of hours to write this bloody song, all about fox-hunting, which became known as 'Berkshire Cunt'. One of the best sets of lyrics I've ever written.

I started hanging out with Conflict a lot, going down their local pubs and getting into scrapes, as you always did with that lot. Paco was a fresh-faced young punk we used to call Elvis, there was Big John and the rest of the crowd, there were parties round people's houses, stuff like that. I could let my hair down a little bit round that lot, and there were substances around, and I liked to dabble, so it was all good, and it was about as big a change as could be from Dial House, where there was no booze at all, and from being in Crass in general. By then I was already known as Steve-Ignorant-Have-You-Got-10p-Mate? because I'd be at my own gigs going round asking people *Got 10p? Got 10p?* collecting enough money to buy a pint or two, because – as I've already said – all our gigs were benefits and we never had any money. Sometimes I even bartered t-shirts for a drink. Ridiculous, when you think about it, but that's how staunch and hardline being in Crass could be. So Conflict were a breath of fresh air, and certainly not for anyone who liked a quiet life ...

Just outside Sidcup station there was a pub called the Iron Horse, where Conflict used to go. Sidcup's a suburb of Bromley, in South London, and I don't know what it is about the place, but every geezer there wants to know, they all want to have a go. One day we'd been recording up at Southern, and we went down to Sidcup when we'd done. This particular occasion it was a Bank Holiday Monday. Millwall had lost their match, and West Ham had won theirs, and Sidcup's south of the river. Millwall territory.

So we're in the Iron Horse, and it fills up and it fills up and it fills up. There's us lot, Conflict and that, in there, and all these well-dressed soul boy hardnuts with their birds, out for a good night out. There's some live music, and for whatever reason the bloke on the guitar starts playing 'Bubbles'. A huge roar goes up, 'cause this lot are all Millwall, and a West Ham song was the last thing they wanted played in their pub. And Colin, quite softly as it happens, points at me and goes *He's only bleedin' West Ham!* He thought he was having a laugh, but my heart was going nineteen to the dozen. It felt like he was going to get me killed. *That bloody mouth of yours, Col!*

So the atmosphere was edgy as if it would kick off any minute, but then the whole pub emptied because two gipsies were having a bare-knuckle fight outside – which says pretty much everything you need to know about what kind of a pub it was – everyone was tooled up. But for all that I'd been on edge while I was there, it was a scene I knew from growing up in Dagenham. It felt like taking time off from being a hardline anarchist and enjoying my youth. And if I was lucky, I'd come out in one piece.

Another time we went down the Iron Horse after a day in the studio, it was early in the evening and the pub was really quiet. There were just a couple of skinheads sitting there playing cards. Colin walks in, turns his back to the bar, stares right at them and says *I fuckin' hate skinheads.* I'm going *Leave it out Col, will ya? They're just playing cards.* But he's having none of it. *Nah, I fuckin hate 'em.* I'm really not in the mood for bother, so I smooth everything over, and we go and sit down by the stage with our pints. The DJ turns up, he starts putting on records, and the place fills up, as usual. Then a whole bunch of skinheads come in. They're looking at us, we're looking at them, the tension starts to build.

Then one of them asks the DJ for a tune – Gary Glitter, 'Leader of the Gang' – and they all climb on the stage dancing to that and then they go back to glaring at us. Fucking great. Now Colin decides he's going for a piss, pushes his way through the crowd, and disappears. He takes ages to come back. I notice half the skins have sloped off too, and I start wondering if they've followed him to the bog and are kicking the shit out of him, so I tell Paco to keep an eye on my bag and start making my way through, to see what's going on. Just then, Colin comes back. I asked *Everything all right?* He went *Yeah. You see that wanker there? I've just told him, you look at me like that again, I'm going to put that glass down the back of your fucking throat. Anyway, gotta shoot now, Steve. See ya tomorra?*

And he's out the door. I can see him through the window, trying to start his rusty old van. And I look round, and there's all these skinheads wanting to kill me now. So I think *Bloody hell. Better get out.* So I'm squeezing my way through this packed pub, all these blokes holding their pints at chest height, limbo-ing my way through, trying not to knock into them. And I spilt one, of course. *What you doing, you cunt?* Really sorry, mate, did-n't mean it. I'm trying to placate him, but keep moving, and all these skinheads are weaving their way through the crowd after me. So I got out, managed to catch up with Col, jump in his van, and we drove off, laughing. *That bloody mouth of yours, Col!*

But that was the kind of situation which you tended to get into with Conflict. And, like I say, it was the total antithesis of how life in Dial House was. Time with Conflict was never dull. For better or worse, there was always something to keep the adrenalin going, and keep you sharp. And I was the member of Crass who straddled both worlds. There was Crass, which was full-on, hard work, with lots of purpose to what we did, but then I could fuck off down South London with Conflict and guarantee someone was going to have some blues or a bit of speed or whatever. I could have a few nights out, cop off, pos-sibly have a few hairy moments, but it was life. It was exciting, it was fun. Which is what you want when you're that age.

But then – unfortunately for Colin – it dissolved into not

being fun, because he got glassed for mouthing off at a couple of bikers. He ended up in hospital, had to have an operation on his eye, and lost part of his sight forever. And along with that, Conflict got themselves a reputation for being violent. Like us, they had trouble at their gigs. Unlike us, they wouldn't back down, or condemn it. They just took it on. Maybe that made them more of a target, I don't know. I do know there was many a fight at what used to be the Woolwich Tramshed where Conflict and Combat 18 would have it out. It was almost a regular event. I was never involved in that – I didn't want to be, and anyway, that's Conflict's history, not mine.

I understood where Col was coming from though, because where he lived reminded me of how life had been in Dagenham. You've just got to be hard. No question. You've just got to be like that. There were skinheads on Col's estate, and every day he'd get shouted at in the street, someone would always be causing a problem, there were endless fights. And he either stood up to it, or he gave in. That was the choice. So he stood up.

And he brought that attitude with him to Crass gigs. Your mates were in trouble, you helped them out. If that meant thumping someone, you thumped them. End of. Except Crass didn't do things that way. The two of us would talk about it, about how he'd get yelled at for standing up to skinheads or whoever else was causing trouble. Col knew I had a lot of sympathy for his position, but at the end of the day that wasn't going to help *What can I do? What can I say, Col? I'm in Crass*. And that was that.

And at one point Conflict got so hot, that it wasn't feasible for them to perform with Crass, because it would just have ruined it. It wouldn't have been a Crass gig, it would just have been a fight. And I thought that was a real shame. Because I really wanted to support Conflict. I thought what they were doing was good, and I liked them. But I remember having a talk with Colin and saying *Look mate, you're going to have to go your own way here, because we just can't work together.* And he said *Yeah I know.* There was an understanding there. And also, quite rightly, they didn't want to be controlled by Crass, and be told *You can do this but you can't do that.* In the same way, really, that Rubella Ballet didn't. Rubella Ballet's take was they weren't dressing in black like everyone else, they were going to be a riot of fluorescent colours instead. And thank god they did.

Conflict were going to do things their own way. I admired that, and I respected it. And a couple of years after Crass had split, I ended up being part of it, too.

Change

Sudden, unexpected change can really do your head in. Someone in the family dies, or your relationship breaks down, or you lose your job, and in that moment the world changes completely. The bed is empty, the house is silent, all the old routines are gone. You adapt eventually, of course, but it takes a lot of getting used to.

And that's how it was for me. One minute I was lead singer of one of Britain's biggest punk bands, living and breathing what we did, totally immersed in the way of life. And then it was gone. All over. History. No more sleeping on floors, no more benefit gigs, no more tapping people for 10p so I could have a drink at my own gig. At first, I was almost elated. Before long I found myself thinking *Fuck it. What on earth do I do now?*

More to the point, who was I? I'd been part of Crass for years, but Crass had been a major part of me too. Losing that felt like losing my identity. While this had its plus side – I didn't have to study the paper or watch the news any more, looking for depressing stories or horrible images we could use – it also meant I felt lost, completely fucking lost. I missed going on tour, missed the intensity and the adulation that went with it, missed being part of something.

I think all of us were in the same boat, more or less. We were all trying to work out what it was we'd just been through, how it had changed us, and where we were now. Crass had been so all-consuming that we hadn't had time or space to think about ourselves, and now we finally had the time we didn't know what to do. We were stressed. We were exhausted. We were burnt-out. The phone would ring and people would offer us gigs, which just reminded us what was gone. Finding our feet again was going to take time.

I spent quite a bit of the next year wandering round in a daze. Like someone let out from an institution who doesn't quite understand the world or how he fits into it. And then one day, that changed. I was on the top deck of a bus, in London, still dressed in my raggedy black clothes, and I looked out of the window and there on the street were these punks, posing for photographs. I remember thinking *Nah. I don't want to look like this no more*. I got off the bus, walked to Carnaby Street, and splashed out on a pair of peg trousers and some brothel-creepers. I bought a bowling shirt from a second-hand shop, got my hair cut and combed it with a side-parting, and had my ear pierced. And felt a whole lot better, as if I'd chucked the past in the bin with my old clothes.

For a long time I'd been listening to nothing but punk. Now I started listening to whatever was on the radio, to pop music, lovers' rock, ska, reggae, and a bit of dub. And above all, rap. I'd heard 'The Message' by Grandmaster Flash and that had turned me on to rap in a big way, because the way he wrote lyrics hit me as being the way I wrote lyrics, and that really excited me.

Little by little, I was finding my voice again, and starting to write. I even recorded a rap record called 'Get Your Elbows Off The Table', and got Johnny Dynell to come over from New York to help, because he knew more about rap and hip-hop than anyone else I'd met. There's a copy of it somewhere, but it never got released. I just wasn't happy with it. I'd been used to songwriting with a bunch of mates, but those days were over. Back at Dial House, things were falling apart.

We hadn't realised it at the time, but Crass had been the glue that held us all together. Crass was why we'd all moved in to the same place. With the band gone, it slowly became clear we didn't actually want to live with each other any more. The process of unravelling and separation wasn't easy – there were lots of discussions, just as there always had been, but now they got increasingly heated and escalated into arguments. I tried to be involved as little as possible. When tempers flared, I slipped away and went to my room.

By the time the dust settled, we'd handed the record label over to John Loder because no one wanted to carry on looking after it. Phil and Joy had moved out, and Eve was living in Brixton. Andy had already left, of course, and Pete Wright was off in Harlow. Pen, Gee, and myself stayed on in Dial House. Twelve months earlier the place had been a whirlwind of people and purpose. Now there'd be days when I rattled around it on my own.

To me, this felt like a body blow. A loss every bit as big as the end of the band. Any hopes I'd had of starting something new evaporated. I'd been writing lyrics, and diddling around on a guitar and keyboard, and I guess I'd assumed that at some point I'd start working with Pen, or Andy, or whoever. But they'd all had it with music, and everyone else I knew was into punk and punk alone, and none of them had the slightest interest in rap. I couldn't see a way forward. And as for the world of work, well, I was 27 years old, with no qualifications to speak of, too old for an apprenticeship, and with no real skills. The very thought was depressing.

So I withdrew. I stopped going out, stopped going to gigs, stayed at Dial House, and read. I read a lot. I picked up *Bury My Heart At Wounded Knee*, and was astounded at the way Native Americans had been – and still are – treated. That led me to read more about them, and that, in turn, led to me buying a tipi. I loved the idea you could take it with you, put it up somewhere, stay a night or two, and then – when you left – no one would ever know you'd been there. Fantastic. About as far away from Heath Park as I could imagine.

I went down to Hatfield Forest in Essex, chose my trees for the tipi poles, stripped them down, sanded them, and put the tipi up in the garden at Dial House, with wooden pallets on the floor so I wasn't sleeping on damp ground. I'd already got into wood-carving, so cutting and trimming the poles wasn't difficult, even though I had a grand total of two chisels, a straight one and a crescent gouge, and spending the night in something I'd built myself, so close to nature, was incredibly satisfying. It just felt right.

If there's been one constant in my life, it's been that my curiosity always leads me to explore new things, that I'm constantly hungry for new experiences. So while it might seem strange that I ended up living in a tipi after being in a staunch anarchist band, I was just following my nose, and seeing where it led me. It was that old thirst for knowledge again. I didn't believe our society had things right, didn't accept the things they told me, so maybe older cultures had something to say? Maybe another way of looking at the world made sense?

I was devouring books. Reading everything I could about Native Americans, of course, and Celts too, because of the figures and sculptures I carved in wood. And then I started reading Carlos Castaneda. I loved the stories, all the tales about shamen, and magic, and drugs. It all sounded very interesting. Maybe it was time for Mr. Ignorant to explore his spirituality?

Curiosity, I was about to learn, could be a blessing and a curse.

But first I went back to Iceland.

Iceland

I was living in my tipi, carving wood and marking time, and the phone rang. It was Einar from the Sugarcubes. *Steve, why don't you come over to Iceland for a couple of weeks and see the midnight sun?* Well, it was hardly as if I was doing anything I couldn't put on hold. I was on my way.

I'd met Einar in 1983, when Crass had headlined a massive peace festival in Reykjavik. He'd been one of the organisers, and from the moment we met him he was a top, top bloke. Iceland had this weird relationship with alcohol, where you could get your hands on spirits but beer was like gold dust, so when Einar had met us at the airport he was more interested in pushing wads of notes through to us while we were still in Arrivals – so we could buy crates of duty-free beer – than he was in saying hallo. He was running a festival, and *How do you do?* could wait. But beer? Beer was vital.

From start to finish, he looked after us, showed us the sights, and made sure we were ok. Nothing was too much trouble. The only time he took a break was when his band, Kukl, who were huge in Iceland, took the stage. Their lead singer looked like she was about nine years old, but her voice and her stage presence knocked me sideways. I'd never heard anyone quite like Björk. I stood watching them, thinking *Fuck me, this bird can sing!*

The crowd loved Kukl. I wasn't so sure they'd like us, because we'd chosen the Reykjavik gig to perform *Yes Sir I Will*. In its entirety. For the first time. I have no idea why we did this. We had all these great songs, like 'Owe Us', or 'Big A Little A', or 'How Does It Feel To Be The Mother…?' stuff people wanted to hear, and had invited us over for, and instead we gave them this avant-garde semi-jazz bullshit. Martin from Flux was filling in for Pen, who was tucked up in bed in Essex with an ear infection, and personally I thought Pen had by far the better deal.

To make matters worse I had to have the words to *Yes Sir* written out, which meant I was stood on stage with all these pieces of paper, not knowing what to do, or how to stand, or how to move, feeling really stilted and unnatural. Unable to be a front man, and acutely aware that where Björk had prowled the stage I was looking like a shop dummy. If I'd have been in the audience I'd have demanded my money back, because I felt we really short-changed them. I hated every minute. We never did *Yes Sir* from start to finish again.

Anyway, after that gig, Einar and I kept in contact. When he came over to England to study for a year, not long after Crass split, I popped down to visit him and his wife at their flat in Stoke Newington. We spent evenings talking and drinking, and I escaped the post-Crass fallout for a night or two. Then he'd gone back to Iceland, and now he was inviting me to come and stay.

I was keen to go, because Iceland had completely bowled me over, like nowhere else I'd ever been. My memory of 1983 was of getting off the plane and thinking *I could live here*. The whole time we were there I felt this instant and overwhelming affinity with the place, as if I'd come home, as if I'd finally found where I belonged. There'd even been tears in my eyes when we boarded the plane to leave.

So I told Einar *Yes!* and flew over. He and his wife met me at the airport and we drove up to his brother's farm in the northeast of the country. I stayed there two weeks, and in all that time it never got dark. Not once. The sun would set, just before midnight, and bounce back up into the sky a little later, day after day. It took some getting used to, this perpetual daylight, and I lost all sense of time. Morning, afternoon, and the middle of the night looked pretty much the same. It was like living in a dream. I spent all day helping with the farm work in the blazing sunshine, then I'd sit up through the bright nights talking, or reading the Icelandic sagas which – being a soppy romantic – were right up my street. Life couldn't get any better.

I looked like Superman. I was fit, tanned, and content. And the cherry on the cake was that Icelanders love to party. There was a hotel in the nearby town, and the hotel bar was the only place you could buy a drink, so most nights we'd drive over, through this incredible landscape, with the sun shining down on us, and see who else was there, which generally turned out to be pretty much everyone. We'd drink, and party, and pile out in the small hours of the morning, bleary-eyed in the 2am sunshine.

It was surreal. And just when I thought I'd got my head round it, there'd be something new. Like the night we all left the hotel, drove off into the middle of nowhere, and stopped at the side of the road. Next thing, everyone's taking their clothes off and disappearing into this hole in a nearby cliff. So I strip off and follow them through a gap in the rock face, down a rope, following the sound of laughter, and suddenly I'm in a thermal spring in a cave, up to my waist in water, and everyone's pissed and naked, and passing round the bottles of booze. *Blimey. This isn't the Vernon.* I'm in a natural sauna, there's some very good-looking women, and I'm not moving anywhere till I can stand up without embarrassing myself. *Come on Steve, we're going!* Er ... I'll be with you in a minute. Soon as this erection's disappeared.

So, yes, I loved Iceland. It was magical. Adni, Einar's brother, who ran the farm, asked me *Why don't you stay?* And I seriously considered it. He warned me that it wasn't always summer, that in winter there were only three or four hours of half-light, that after a blizzard there might be twelve feet of snow and we'd be trapped in the farmhouse, and that sometimes the isolation could send people stir-crazy, but even so I was really really tempted.

Unfortunately I had to get back to Dial House. There was an important meeting I'd promised I wouldn't miss. All too soon it's my last night in Iceland and we're back in Reykjavik, having one last party. We're down a nightclub and the drinks are flowing. My flight back to England's at 9.30 in the morning, so before the night gets out of hand I decide I'd better check with Einar that he's picking me up and taking me to the airport.

You're coming to pick me up tomorrow?

Yeah, yeah, Steve.

Don't give me that 'yeah yeah'. You're picking me up, so don't be late, and don't get pissed.

Yeah yeah Steve. No problem. And he stumbles off with a bottle in each hand. Half an hour later I'm having the same conversation with him, but now he's absolutely slaughtered. *Look Steve,* he says, *why don't you just stay another week?* It's tempting, because we're having a great night out, but I can't. I've got to go back. Then this girl comes over and we end up chatting. She asks me if I want to go back to her place, and obviously I do, but I know if I do that I'll just miss my flight, so I can't. And no sooner has she wandered off than Einar's back. *Steve, come on! Stay another week!* He really isn't prepared to take no for an answer, and between him and the girl I'm struggling to say *No* anyway, but I tell myself I can't give in, because I've got this responsibility to go home.

When the club shuts we go our separate ways, and Einar promises to pick me up at 8am. I stay up all night anyway, partly because it's my last night in Iceland and I don't want to miss a minute, but mainly to be sure I don't sleep through and miss my flight. 8 o'clock comes and goes. No Einar. 8.30 and he still hasn't shown. I wait till 8.45 and I ring him. He's overslept – of course – but he orders a cab, and five minutes later we're on our way to the airport, which is good. The airport is forty kilometres away, which is bad. And neither Einar nor myself look anything like our perky best.

What time's your flight, Steve?

About half an hour, mate.

Oh. That's not so good.

Yes I think. *Tell me about it.* Then he leans forward, says something to the driver, and the driver just floors it. He turns to me triumphantly. *It's ok. I phoned the airport and they know you are coming. I told them you are English and you overslept and they say you can just run through check-in.*

And security, Einar?

They say ok, you run through security too, but you have to move. Because the plane will be out on the tarmac and ready to leave.

Jesus. Right.

We get to the airport, the taxi pulls in, and the race is on. *'Bye, Einar!* Every second's going to count. But as I leap out of the car I snag my trousers, and the seam rips all the way up one leg. They're flapping around and tripping me up, and I look like Robinson Crusoe, racing through the airport waving my passport, with all the security guys waving me on *Go through! Go through! You're the crazy English guy. Go through!*

I pelt out onto the runway. And there's two planes. *Bugger.* Back into the terminal with my flapping trouser leg, asking *Which plane for England?!* It's the one on the left. *Quick, crazy*

English man! Quick! I run back out on the runway, race across the tarmac, pelt up the stairs, and into the rear of the plane. Everyone is sitting there, waiting to leave, and they've heard me thumping up the steps, and they all turn round. I'm standing there panting, sweat pouring off me, stinking of last night's beer, my trousers falling apart, and I can see them thinking *You're the reason we're waiting???*

I turn to the stewardess.

Sorry – gasp – *sorry* – gasp – *sorry I'm late.*

She's got a face like a sack of chisels and just points to the seat. *Sit. Down.*

I slump next to these people who recoil away from me, spend the whole journey trying to fix my trousers with safety pins while my hangover takes hold, and finally – not a minute too soon – I'm back at Dial House. I walk in through the door, and there's Pen and Gee, looking puzzled.

What are you doing here, Igs? We weren't expecting you till next week.

Argentina

I should have turned round and gone back to Iceland. But I hadn't the cash. I was still living on the £500 a year we paid ourselves from Crass sales, and I'd taken it as a lump sum to go to Iceland in the first place. Now I was skint. And going nowhere. It was back to messing about in the tipi, carving wood, and reading whatever I could get my hands on, and after the excitement of the last two weeks that just didn't measure up. I was bored.

Now, whenever I'm bored I'll look for something to shake life up, some kind of little adventure. Something new to move on to. That's just how I am. As far as I could see, Crass had finished, and I was never going to be in a band again. Everyone had their own stuff to deal with – Pen's dad was ill, Eve's mum had died, Gee's mum wasn't well – so we'd all withdrawn from each other. Whatever I was going to do next, I'd be doing it on my own.

And what I did was quite a departure.

In early 1983 I'd got a letter from a woman called Maria, who lived in Buenos Aires. This was just after the Falklands War, and I was really interested in chatting with someone from Argentina and hearing what they had to say, so I wrote back, and over the next two or three years we kept up quite a correspondence. By the time she told me she was involved with healers, and that one of the professors she worked with was well-known in Argentina for his work with cancer sufferers, I was living in my tipi and reading Carlos Castaneda, and way more open to the idea than I'd ever have been before.

Our letters got more intimate. Then she sent me her front door key, and a photo. And she was quite good-looking. Finally we chatted on the phone, and she told me her teacher had a vision of me surrounded by silver light. Did I hear alarm bells? No. I thought *I've got to get to Argentina!*

This was a complete turnaround from getting pissed and stagnating. It was as if I decided that – now Crass was gone – I could allow myself to explore more spiritual things, and see what the fuss was about. Maybe I'd get my mind opened, and enter some altered state. Maybe this was my Carlos Castaneda moment. And maybe I should have known better.

I scraped some money together, and bought a return ticket to Buenos Aires. I got a visa from the Argentinian Embassy, and told Maria I was on my way. It was early 1987, and I was going to visit her for two weeks. I didn't tell anyone, but I didn't think I'd come back. I was going to have an experience so intense it would completely change my world. I was totally sure of that.

The night before I was leaving, Gee drove me down to London. We parked the car near Trafalgar Square, went for a drink, came back fifteen minutes later, and the car window was smashed and all my stuff was gone. Rucksack, passport, visa, everything. All I had left were the clothes I was wearing and the flight ticket in the pocket of my jeans. There was no way I was going to Argentina, no way I could get a new passport and a new visa and still catch my flight. And not much hope of finding the scumbag who'd robbed me, either. I was never going to find enlightenment. We got back in the car and went home.

One week later, with a new visa in a brand-new passport, I flew out of Heathrow. Re-booking my flight had only cost me £50, but that was because I was taking the long route to

Argentina, via New York and Brazil. Twenty-one hours in the air, two changes, three queues for immigration. By the time I got to Buenos Aires I was destroyed. I staggered out into Arrivals – and Maria wasn't there.

I was so tired and jet-lagged I could have sat down and cried. I don't speak a word of Spanish, and I've flown halfway round the world to be here, and the person I've come to see – the only person I know in the whole country – hasn't shown up. I can't believe it. I'd imagined us rushing into each other's arms when we met, and instead I'm standing in the airport wondering *What the fuck do I do now?*

Eventually Maria saunters up. *I got bored with waiting* she says, *so I went for a walk.* It's not the best of starts, but at least she's here. We get a cab back to hers and on the way there's a massive thunderstorm. It sounds like God's throwing bowling balls up and down the sky. Huge flashes of lightning one after the other, and rain coming down in lumps. Incredible weather. And somehow it just makes me feel tired and edgy and overwhelmingly homesick.

What I really need is sleep. And lots of it. But that isn't going to happen because Maria wants to show me the city. Which is fair enough. I'm exhausted, but let's see the place. She tells me there's a gig we can go to, which I'm fine with. *There's one thing though* she says. *I don't want everyone to know Steve Ignorant is staying with me, because everyone will want to come and visit.* Even as she says it she's ringing her friend to tell her I'm there, and that we'll be down the club later, but hey, it's her call. She lives here.

Up to this point we've been dancing round each other, all stiff and formal, and not really hitting it off. But I've told myself it's nothing a couple of hours chilling out, and a few drinks, and maybe three days sleep, won't solve. Then Maria comes out of her bedroom holding two dresses and asks me *Which one should I wear?* and I know the evening's doomed.

I don't mind I tell her. I don't have an opinion.

No, Steve. Which one should I wear?

I really don't mind. Honestly.

No she says. You must tell me because I want you to enjoy this evening.

Ok, well ... wear the one on the left.

So you don't like the other one?

I didn't say —

What's wrong with it? Why don't you like it?

It's lovely, I just —

But you say you don't like it!

Look, I really don't give a shit what you fucking wear! Can we please just go to the club?!

The club, when we finally get there, has just one entrance, down some wooden stairs. My brain is fried to a cinder with exhaustion, and all I can think is that the place is a death-trap. A fire waiting to happen. There's twenty or so punks waiting to talk to me – which pisses Maria right off, because she knows her mate's blabbed and she can see where this is going – and from then on the whole night is spent with Maria translating questions for me and translating my answers back while I keep my eyes peeled for anyone dropping a lit match or a smouldering cigarette. I've been up for nearly two days straight and I'm jittery with lack of sleep. By the time some argentinian skinheads come in and start scowling at me across the bar I'm convinced I'm going to die here, it's just a question of how. Will I get an almighty kicking? Or burnt when the place goes up like a torch? Will I just die of exhaustion? Or will it simply be the strain of having flown all the way over to meet this woman I'm just not getting on with? It's a tough call.

Against the odds, we get out alive and make it back to Maria's. At last I can get some rest. But no, Maria wants to know whether we're going to sleep together or not, so there's an hour or more of discussion before I can finally lay myself down. We're in the same bed, and she tries it on. Nothing doing. I'm struggling to keep my eyes open and I don't fancy her at all. Cue another big discussion. It's the middle of the night, I'm desperate for sleep, and all I can think is *When do I get my lesson in learning the art of knowledge? I could get this earache, this domestic bullshit in Barking if I wanted.*

Next day I feel a little better. At least I've slept. Maria's friend, the professor from the institute, is over, and they're chatting away in Spanish. When he leaves, she tells me she must do some healing on me. Well, all right. This is what I came for, after all. She sits me in a chair, puts a bowl of water underneath it, and starts doing her stuff. She lays her hands on me, and suddenly I feel this incredible surge of emotion, this amazing realisation.

This is all a load of bollocks. I've flown halfway round the world for this crap. I've really done it this time. *Ignorant, you twat!*

Maria stops what she's doing. *Steve,* she says *I can sense you getting angry.* I went *Angry? You bet I'm angry! Fucking hell!* And it all kicked off. We had a blazing row. A proper shouting match. She told me I was aggressive because Crass had been evil. I told her I was sleeping on my own while I was there. She said my friends had damaged my aura. Really, Maria? Up your shakras.

So I spent fourteen days in Buenos Aires hating the person I was staying with. I spent the days reading and re-reading *Brighton Rock* by Graham Greene because it was the only book I'd taken with me, and at night I slept on my own with a baseball bat down the side of the bed, just in case. I'd gone over with high hopes of enlightenment and altered states, and I ended up ticking the days off, drinking whisky, and watching Maria's pet tortoise crawling round the flat. I hate tortoises.

It was such a disappointment. I went all the way to Argentina and I didn't really meet anyone. And I didn't really learn anything, except that I can be a muppet, which I already knew. I couldn't wait to get back on the plane and start that long journey home, and when we landed at Heathrow I knelt down and kissed the ground. I was done with that healing bullshit, and my aura felt better already.

Brixton

It was time to get back to something I knew. And what I really knew was music. I'd been sitting round Dial House for two years, listening to the radio, feeding the goats, and generally taking time out to find my feet again after the intensity of Crass. At last I was writing lyrics again, and I'd started thinking maybe I was ready to do something with them. But how?

I picked up the phone, rang my old mate Colin, and made him a proposition. I wanted to do a single. Would Conflict be prepared to do the backing for it? *Steve,* says Colin, *I'll go one better. We was thinking that Conflict would like to perform at Brixton Academy as a tribute to Crass. Would you be into that?*

This was right at the start of '87. I thought I might well be living in a hut in Argentina having visions left, right, and centre before the gig came round. But on the off-chance things didn't work out it couldn't hurt to have a back-up plan. So I went *Yeah. All right.* And that was how it started. The first gig I did with Conflict was that dreadful gig at the Academy in April 1987, where everything got trashed.

The whole thing was a farce from start to finish. Col had booked the venue with a little sleight of hand and a touch of wheeling and dealing, busy with his usual ducking and diving to get us in, but that was where the problems began, not where they stopped. The venue didn't understand how we did things or what we wanted, and we didn't see why we couldn't run our show our way, so there was one argument and disagreement after another. Over door policy and ticket price, guest list and stalls, soundchecks and fees. And so on. If we'd said *Today it's Tuesday*, they'd have told us *No*.

All that was annoying, but we could have dealt with it. The real problem lay elsewhere. In the week leading up to the gig we got asked to go down Brixton police station, and meet with the police. They'd heard rumours that there was going to be trouble, that 5000 punks were going to pile out of our gig and riot, and they wanted to put big metal barriers all the way to the venue from Brixton tube. We told them that was ridiculous. It was never going to happen.

The day of the gig comes, and somebody's printed up a flyer telling people they should go out and riot once the gig's over. I've a good idea who produced these, same as I have with who started the rumours. I won't point the finger – that's not my style – but I will say it was a stupid and irresponsible thing to do. Because the police were already expecting trouble and were ready to deal with it. Because people had got coaches from all over the country for that gig, and some of them were from Devon, or Norfolk, and the only copper they'd seen in their lives was the local bobby, and Brixton was full of SPG in full riot gear waiting to get stuck in. And because I don't believe for one minute – not a single minute – that whoever put that leaflet together was out there running the risk of getting their head caved in like they were asking others to do.

The gig itself was a shambles. At some point during the day it became fairly clear no one was going to get paid, so the sound guys didn't give a shit, and the sound was awful. Fights were kicking off. People were climbing on stage. Security started beating someone up in the crowd and when we shouted at them to stop they came to the side of the stage and threatened to beat us up too. It was dangerously out of control. And as soon as it was over and the lights came up, security just linked arms and cleared the building, kicking everyone out onto the streets of Brixton at the same time with tempers running high. A few windows got broken, and then the police waded in. Or the other way round, depending on who you talk to.

It was an embarrassment. My first gig in nearly three years and I had to borrow some money to get home. Nobody ever got paid. There weren't any accounts to speak of and the income from the gig just disappeared into an ever bigger series of black holes. I don't think anyone ever got to the bottom of what went on. It was a fucking disaster.

A little while later I met up with Col and Paco and the rest of them down in Woolwich and they asked me *Do you want to do some more?* And I thought *I might as well.* Which might sound surprising, but what else was I going to do? I couldn't live on the memory of Crass forever, and here was the chance to do what I wanted, to get back on the stage with a bunch of mates and sing. And surely, after Brixton, things would have to get better, wouldn't they? After all, my social life had improved. Being in Conflict had already kick-started that.

I'd started going into London again, and catching up with old friends. Annie Anxiety was living in a squat down in Vauxhall which had its own little bar. They only sold cans of beer, but it was a bit of a social hub and a meeting place, so I hung out there quite a lot. And I'd also started dropping in on some of the squats up in Islington. Phil Free's daughter lived in one, and there were friends of Andy Palmer's in another, so sometimes – on my way back from rehearsals with Conflict, or between dates when we were on tour – I'd stop there. I'd spent too long sitting at Dial House with my head in a book, and that had just led me to the Argentina fiasco, so this was just what the doctor ordered. I was going out with a Japanese girl, called Yazoo, who lived in a squat in Cross Street in Islington, I was having a laugh, and life was good.

And then I got married.

I'd been seeing Yazoo for about six months. It wasn't anything particularly serious – we weren't the loves of each other's lives, or even anything close – but now her visa was about to run out, which meant she'd have to go back to Japan. If she got married, she could stay, but time was running out. Every other day she'd mention it, and in the end I went *For fuck's sake! Shall we get married then?* And why not? Yazoo would get to stay in the country, and we'd all have a day out on the piss. It would be a bit of a laugh.

So on 22nd January 1988, I married Yazoo at Finsbury Park Town Hall. The congregation was a motley crew of punks and squatters, I was wearing a borrowed suit which was a bit short in the legs but just about fitted me, and Colin Jerwood was my best man. Typically, he was late. I'm standing outside, smoking a fag and thinking *Where are you, Col?!* when a metallic green Cortina comes pelting round the corner. There's furry dice hanging in the windscreen, one wing's full of filler, and as it screeches to a halt it sounds a comedy horn. Col parks it on a double yellow, and bowls over *All right, Igs! Let's get this done!*

Twenty minutes later, it's all done and dusted. We're out of the registry office, into Col's car, and we're off down our local for the reception. The Islington squatters all used to drink in this pub called the Old Queen's Head, and that was where we spent the rest of the day. The people from Cross Street had made sandwiches and cake, Paddy the landlord gave us a free drink once we'd produced the certificate to prove we really had got married and weren't just having him on – the fact everyone was covered in confetti proved nothing in his book – and we stayed in there playing pool and partying till the place closed, and Paddy threw us out. Then we went back to Cross Street and carried on through the night.

Yazoo and I stayed together another few months, then we drifted apart and went our separate ways. Each of us had moved on. And I was busy with Conflict.

I was with Conflict for a year and a half. A lot of the time – especially in the early days – what we did was fun, but in the end I chose to leave. I thought about it long and hard and realised that, musically, I wanted to do something different. But Conflict was Colin's band, his baby. I couldn't push myself forward and start calling the shots. It would just be wrong. I'd enjoyed writing songs for them, but now I needed to move on.

That was part of the reason. The other thing was that, having seen them at first hand, I could see where a lot of their bad publicity came from. And I didn't want to be part of it. I really didn't like the way Col surrounded himself with what I call the lunatic fringe. Friends of his who'd do anything he said. One of them would be his personal bodyguard – as if he needed it – the rest of them followed him round like sheep. I didn't like this. Col was a mate, but he'd never back down from anything, and sometimes he put himself in stupid situations. Throw the lunatic fringe into the mix and you had a recipe for trouble.

I remember one gig in Berlin. There were a couple of bars across the road from where we were staying, and they were open till 4am, so after the gig was over that's where we went. I'm sitting in one of them, having a couple of beers, talking quietly with Paco, chilling out and enjoying myself, when Col – wanting to liven things up – starts chanting *Millwall! Millwall!* and all his lunatic friends do too. *Come on Igs! Join in!* No. And not just because I'm a West Ham fan, either. This is wrong. When the *Millwall* chants change to *Two world wars and one world cup* and *There's only one Winston Churchill* I've had enough. More than enough.

I just walked out. It was a quiet pub – there were people drinking down their local and punks who'd been to the gig and watched us perform – and now all of them were seeing this shit. A group of pissed-up blokes behaving like arseholes. I said to Paco *I can't handle this, mate. It's embarrassing.* And I walked. A couple of hours later Col and the others came back, and tried to tell me they were sorry, but I was still too angry to listen. I didn't want to be anywhere near them, so I went back across to the bar and had another couple of beers. Paco was still over there, so I sat down with him. I ended up chatting with some of the locals, which was far more my scene, and then this really good-looking German girl walked in, and – let's just say the night got much better from there.

I'd always known Conflict were a lot livelier, and a lot more ready to duck and dive, than Crass had ever been. Time was, that had given me a buzz. What they were doing now didn't. Maybe they felt they had a reputation to live up to, I don't know. But, too often, being around them wasn't a laugh any more, it was just ugly.

Like the time we played Manchester. After the gig we're loading the van, and the gear's all over the pavement. This local lad walks past, picking his way carefully through the equipment, apologising for getting in the way, and Col turns on him. *Do you like hospital food?* I can't believe what I'm hearing. The bloke can't either, because he looks at Col and goes *What?* Now Col's right in his face, and he's asking again *Do you like hospital food?*

The next thing you know we've got a situation, because although the lad gets on his toes and does one, a few minutes later he's back with eight or nine of his mates. They're lined up across the road, some of them are tooled up, and it's all ready to kick off. We just throw the gear in the van and fuck off quick, but as we're driving away I'm sitting looking at Col thinking *Why the fuck did you have to do a stupid thing like that? Why?*

Don't get me wrong. If there'd been trouble at the gig, if we'd had a load of BM skinheads storm the show, then fine, you get stuck in. No problem. And there's few people you'd rather have on your side then than Conflict, because they know how to fight and they'll always stand their ground. But to arbitrarily start something when there was no need, when we should have been chilling out and having a laugh and a beer – I didn't get it. Once you started picking on people for no reason at all, what was the difference between you and some right wing skinhead?

As far as I could see there was none, and I wanted no part of it. The last gig I did with Conflict was at the Greyhound in Fulham. We finished and I told them *I don't want to do this no more.* Because I didn't. I couldn't enjoy it. Col and I had been through a lot together, and we'd been really close, but that was all in the past.

If he wanted to look for trouble, he'd have to do it on his own.

Loss

The day Yazoo and I got married had been a proper pauper's wedding, done on the cheap with loads of friends there, and the whole thing was a lot of fun, just as I'd hoped. But as we celebrated down the Old Queen's Head, every now and then – if I laughed too hard, or bent down too quickly to take a shot at pool – I'd get a little twinge, a little niggle of pain, a reminder that me and my brother had finally gone our separate ways. We'd seen each other two or three times in ten years, and none of the meetings had ended well. I really didn't want another.

Back in the early days of Crass, not long after I'd come back from Bristol, David had visited Dial House to tell Pen I was throwing away my jolly good job. He didn't approve. Well that was fine. We didn't care. Which kind of threw him, but he stayed over for a few days, looking a bit lost and waiting for us to take what he'd said more seriously. Then he left, and Pen and I got on with the important things in life: rehearsing, and feeding the goats.

By the time my brother turned up again a few months later I was hanging around with the Deptford punks I'd met at the Roxy, so when I was heading over to see them one evening David came along. Being as I was meeting up with my London mates I wanted to look my best, so I borrowed a pair of Pen's Seditionaries, which had a zip all the way round the crotch from front to back and a bum-flap which hung down behind. Very cool. We ended up at a party in someone's flat on the Crossfields estate, and it was everything you'd expect. Loads of people getting out of it and misbehaving.

I ended up copping off with this girl called Mad, who was also wearing Seditionaries. We spent most of the party over in the corner of the room with our zips undone, oblivious to what was going on around us, hoping the bum-flaps hid what we were up to. Fat chance of that. Eventually we decided it might be best if we took our enthusiasm back to her flat, so I found my brother and told him I was off. He's not too happy about this, but I tell him he'll be fine and I'll see him in the morning, and away I go.

Mad and I are walking across the courtyard and there's this shout from the balcony behind me. *Williams!!* I turn round and my brother's pelting after me with a bread knife in his hand. He catches me up, flings me against a doorway and yells *I'm gonna fucking have you! What have you brought me to? Where am I?* I tell him *You're in Deptford.* I can't believe what's going on. Dave's a grown man. He's chosen to come along. It's not like we've fallen off the edge of the world or anything. Deptford is still on the map. There's buses into town. What's this all about?

All I want to do is get to Mad's and get back in her Seditionaries. Instead my brother's screaming at me for no reason I can understand, and waving a knife in my face. Then he tells me he's going to stab me. By now I've had enough of this bullshit. I went *Go on then. Do it.*

There's a moment's silence. I wonder, briefly, if I've made the wrong call. Then David throws down the knife, bursts into tears, and tells me *I'm sorry. I'm sorry.* Over and over again. *I'm sorry.* I tell him everything's ok. But even as I say it, I know I don't believe it.

I didn't see him again for nearly ten years. Then in the autumn of '87 David turned up at Dial House. Things in Bristol weren't going too well. He'd lost his job and his marriage to Rose was falling apart. So we took him in. I was away with Conflict quite a lot of the time, or off in London visiting Yazoo, so I gave him the use of my room and hoped he'd sort his head out.

Two months on and things were getting uncomfortable. Pen and Gee were asking me *How long's your brother staying for?* Because they'd had enough. It wasn't so much that he was smoking their tobacco and eating their food while putting nothing in the kitty – we'd all been skint some time, and all relied on the generosity of others, so even though we couldn't afford to keep him, we sympathised – it was his attitude. David was surly. Selfish. Bitter. He was taking everything and giving nothing in return. It couldn't go on.

I knew I was going to have a word. But I told myself I'd leave it till after Xmas and New Year. Partly because David was family, but also because I wasn't looking forward to it. I knew what I'd have to say would go down like a lead balloon, and I quietly hoped that – if I put it off for a week or two – my brother might move on of his own accord.

That didn't happen. I was back in Dial House over Xmas and I saw just how bad things were. But fuck it. New Year's Eve was my birthday and I wasn't letting anything spoil that. I told my brother I was off into London to meet up with Yazoo in Islington, I left him a £10 note so he'd have a bit of money in his pocket to see in the new year, and I walked up to Blake Hall and caught the Tube.

Later that evening I'm down the Old Queen's Head, having a few beers with my mates and some of the locals, when David walks in. There's no *Hallo* or *Thanks for the £10*. He just goes up to the bar and orders one pint after another till he's spent all his money. He's really pissed and now he's knocking everyone round him for drinks *Get us a beer, mate. I'm Steve Ignorant's brother.* This is really pissing people off, so I take him on one side and tell him to cool it, but it's a waste of breath. My brother's not listening. Five minutes later he's taking liberties again.

I can hear him right across the bar *Give us a fag, you wanker! Come on, you tight bastard!* He's picked up that's how we all talk to each other, but the point is we're all mates. David's just a drunk, annoying stranger who's tapping folk for beer and cigarettes and really getting on their tits. He's calling them *Cunt* and it's not banter, it's an insult, and any moment someone's going to lose their temper and thump him. All I want to do is enjoy my birthday. Instead I'm spending my time calming people down, apologising for my brother who either doesn't know or doesn't care that he's causing a scene. And there's no talking to him either. He's not having it.

All in all, he's a proper pain in the arse. When the pub shuts and everyone heads back to the squat for a party, I really don't want him to come. But he's my brother, and I can't leave him on his own on New Year's Eve, even if he is being a prick. With any luck he'll just pass out in a corner and the rest of us can get on with enjoying ourselves while he sleeps it off. For now though, keeping an eye on him is a right drag, and when one of the girls needs to go and get some cigarettes from the all-night garage, I say I'll go with her, just to get a break from David for fifteen minutes, give myself a chance to relax and get some fresh air.

It works. By the time I get back to the party I've chilled out completely. I walk back in, hear David say *You're a fucking actor, ain't ya?* and the next thing I know he's chinned me. I went down like a sack of shit on the floor and he proceeded to give me a severe kicking. I felt one of my ribs pop. *Dave* I told him

You've really fucking hurt me. David stopped for a moment. *Good* he said. And then he started kicking me again and he didn't stop till people jumped on him and pulled him away.

That pretty much finished the party. And my relationship with my brother too. I got up in the morning and found him still in the house, still drinking, and still up from the night before, and I took him across the road to a cafe and bought him breakfast. *Dave* I said, *this can't go on.* He didn't even try to argue. I was cutting him loose and there was nothing he could say to change it. And he knew that. I left him sitting there staring at nothing. Two days later he moved out of Dial House and was gone.

It's hard to feel much sympathy for someone who's broken your ribs. Especially on your birthday. But David was my brother, and I knew what had made him. I had a lucky streak and David didn't, that was at the heart of things. Granddad took to me, but he laid into David. I got Mr. Padfield and Mr. Stewart for teachers; my brother got beaten up for having sticky-out ears. Stan tolerated me; his brothers called David a long-haired poof and took the piss out of him if he dared to show his face. There was no rhyme or reason to what happened, but it made all the difference in the world to how our lives turned out.

I won't make excuses for David, and after what happened at the squat party I was happy to see the back of him. But sometimes I wonder – if our roles had been reversed, if I'd drawn the short straw, if I'd got the rejections and the beatings, would I have dealt with it any better than my brother?

And I really have no idea how to answer that.

Puppets

When I left Conflict I had no idea what I'd do next. All I knew was that I'd had enough. And when I've had enough of something, whether that's working in a supermarket or being in a band, then I've had enough, and that's all there is to it. It's time to move on. Something will turn up. Something always has. That's how I ended up doing a couple of gigs with Current 93.

I'd met David Tibet when I was down Annie Anxiety's squat in Vauxhall. He wrote for *Sounds* and was into Crass, he was a really interesting bloke, and he made this weird avant-garde music with a band called Current 93. I gave it a listen. It was certainly nothing like what I was doing with Conflict. That wasn't a problem. I was into broadening my ideas about what music could be, and I was intrigued by what Tibet was doing. We'd sit in the squat having a drink or two at the bar, talking about bands we both loved, or hated, and about where music was going, and then we'd head off to a pub – the Elephant And Castle, for example, which was a transvestite pub full of lorry-drivers with missing teeth, stubble and lipstick, and always a bit of a laugh – and carry on drinking.

I had a good time hanging out with Tibet, and when I left Conflict he asked me if I fancied singing with his band. I said *Yeah. I'll give it a go.* I called myself Stephen Intelligent, and I did two gigs with them. One was at the 100 Club, and the other was a huge two-day industrial noise festival in Hamburg. It was all very strange. Full of people with bleached blond hair, leather coats and sunglasses, looking like Herrenvolk. I was eyeing up the girls and getting nowhere. We came to do our set and I said *Right. No fart-arsing about. We get on, we hit 'em with it, and we're off.*

I do the song, finish, throw down the mic, and I'm gone. I'm off stage, pouring myself a beer, and I hear this unholy racket. The guitarist is still on stage, smashing away on his strings while Tibet squats down at the front of the stage screaming *Ring-a-ring-a-roses* at the audience. For the first time it occurs to me that maybe our ideas about live performance aren't quite the same. Thanks lads, it's been fun. But I think two gigs will do.

I decided I'd been singing in bands for too long, doing the same old same old, and I was fed up with it. It was time to take a break from music, time to go off in a completely new direction. So I sat down at Dial House and started writing a radio play.

I'd been reading a book by Henry Mayhew about life in 1850s London. What made it fascinating was that he'd gone out and interviewed ordinary people – market traders, labourers, beggars – let them tell their own story, in their own words, and described their lives in rich, glorious detail. It was like a snapshot of a different world. I couldn't put it down. And when I got to the interview with the Punch and Judy man, with its script of the show, it really came alive.

When I'd been growing up in Dagenham, the council used to put events on in the park during the school holidays. Nothing grand. Just one-man acts, like a magician, or a clown. But my favourite was the Punch and Judy show. I loved it, but it scared me too. And as I read and re-read the script in Mayhew's book, I could see how it worked and why, and realised I appreciated it just as much as an adult as I had as a kid. There was a radio play in this, I just knew it.

I started writing the outline for a script. And carving a Mr. Punch figure to inspire me, which I put on my desk. Then, because there were loads of kids coming over to Dial House – a lot of our friends and acquaintances had families by now – I thought it would be nice to make them some little puppets to play with. So I did. By the time I'd done that, I thought I might as well make the booth. And once I'd done that, well, why not actually do the show? I'd got all the gear.

It was the kiss of death for the radio play. I never finished the script because Punch and Judy was much more fun. The kids loved it just as much as I had when I was their age, and I got a real buzz out of doing it. Even as I finished that first show I was working out which bits had gone well and which hadn't, where the pace needed picking up, what got the laughs and why. This was a craft I could learn, something to get my teeth into. Stuff the music business! Punch's Opera was the way forward.

For the next two years I was Professor Ignorant, Punch and Judy man. I watched other Professors – all Punch and Judy people are Professors – and I learned, and I practised hard. What had drawn me to it in the first place was that Punch is a natural anarchist, a real working class hero. He stands up for himself against all authority, and he stands for nothing. And he always wins. He turns the tables on the hangman and hangs him in his own noose, and that's how the story ends.

The more I learned the more I understood just how much hard work and how many hours of practice went into a good show. The story, the slapstick, the wordplay, the comic timing – all of that may look effortless, but trust me, it isn't. And all of it's done by one bloke, sitting in a booth with a swazzle – which is what you talk through to make Punch's voice – in his mouth, with a series of glove puppets laid out in front of him. It's theatre stripped down to its bare bones, and when it's done well, it's amazing.

All Professors start with the same basic script, with the same elements. Then they put their own interpretation on it. But they remain faithful to the original. If you pick and choose bits of the story, it doesn't make sense. If you get all PC and take out the violence – in case seeing glove puppets knocked about upsets the children – Punch loses its power and becomes something twee. And if you make it too overtly political – I saw one show with Thatcher as Judy and Major as the hangman – you end up with *Spitting Image*.

On the 9th of May every year – which is the date Punch is first ever mentioned in Pepys' diary – something like thirty or forty of the best Professors set up in Covent Garden and put on a festival to celebrate Punch's birthday. For someone like me there was nowhere better to go, because there were dozens of variations on the Punch and Judy story to watch and to learn from. A couple of the shows I saw were amazing. There were Professors whose timing in the body count routine – where Punch is trying to count the bodies but Joey the Clown keeps moving them so Punch never gets the same number twice – was utterly breathtaking. Sublime. Something to marvel at and aspire to.

I went back to Dial House and I worked on my show. I set my booth up at parties and markets and festivals – one of the things I loved about Punch was that you could do it anywhere – and tried it out on audiences. And I got bloody good at it. Which was just as well, because the money from Crass had dried up, and no one at Dial House had a bean. So I signed up with an entertainment agency. They got me plenty of work, and paid me £70 a show, but some of the gigs they sent my way were pretty weird ...

One of the regular ones was at Heathrow Sheraton, every Sunday. I was supposed to entertain rich arab kids while their parents were having a drink. I did four shows a day, so you can

239

see it was a bit of an earner. But in all the time I did it, in all the weeks I went there and set up my booth, I never performed to anyone other than the bar staff. Not a single kid came. The bar staff would tell me to put my feet up. *There's no one here Steve, why do it? We'll cover for you, we'll tell them you did your stuff.* But I never missed a show. The way I saw it, the more I practised, the better I'd get, and at least here I was getting paid to practise. So I treated each show as a dress rehearsal. If a kid ever did come in, I'd blow his socks off.

The agency didn't just give me jobs playing to an empty room in Heathrow. They also used to fix me up with gigs in people's homes, entertaining their kids. I grew to hate these. You'd barely have your foot in the door before you'd be getting told exactly how you had to censor your show *Don't do the hanging scene, I don't want Tarquin scared.* The kids weren't really a problem, but dealing with pushy, protective parents who were used to telling the hired help what to do, that just did my nut in. One day I went to a particularly opulent place in Maida Vale. The moment I walked in the father was making sure I was put in my place, letting me know he'd been friends with Tommy Cooper and he wouldn't be putting up with any old rubbish from me. *Oh really?* I looked round. The kids were bored out of their tiny minds and the last thing they wanted was Punch and Judy. They'd had the clown, they'd had the magician, they'd had this, that, and the other. They were sick to death of cakes and they'd had it up to here with entertainment. I thought *Stuff this* and walked back out of the door. I rang the agency and said *That's it. I retire.*

I didn't though. I just stopped doing agency work, and cut back to the stuff I arranged myself, the itinerant work I preferred. Most of it was occasional, and one-off, but I went to the Aldeburgh Festival in Suffolk every year, and the Charles

After the black, into the blues. Me with my niece and nephew.

Summerhill School, Suffolk. My tipi poles on the van in the background.

Rochester Dickens
Festival. A break
between Punch
shows.

Aldburgh Festival.
Punch about to
clobber the copper.

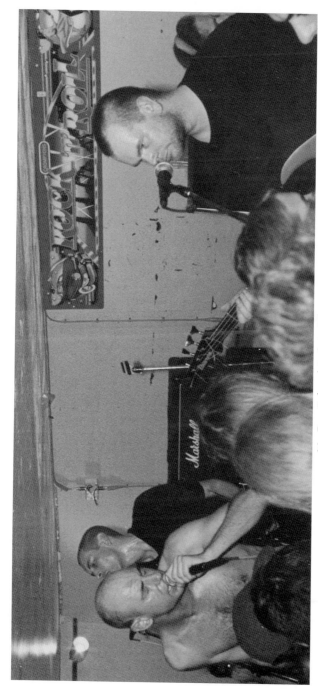

Me, Ben, Bob and Andy in Schwartzeneggar.

The American Dream.
Stratford Mercenaries.

Who would ever
have thought it?
Shepherds' Bush 2007

Soundchecking at the Empire. I'm sick with stage fright, Alice (typical teen) super cool.

What I do now. Launching 'Leo' in a lumpy sea. Flaxi (coxwain) in boat,
me furthest left and Clarkey (no.2 cox) at stern. Sea Palling 2008.

Steve (Spot) and me on the day we started this book.

Me, Dee and Alan: lifelong friends with hearts of gold. Sittingbourne 2009.

What's with the long face? The only Oscar I'll ever get, or want.

Iona: my soul mate.

Dickens festival in Rochester too. The one I missed out on was Punch's birthday festival, the one I'd been to see in Covent Garden. I got an audition to perform there, but I never did it, because by then I was following the lead of the Professor in Henry Mayhew's book, and doing the show wherever and whenever I fancied, taking it back to the streets, enjoying the reaction of people when they stumbled across it where they didn't expect it.

I went up to Leicester Square one winter and set my booth up there, right by the cinemas. It turned out to be a profitable pitch, and the show went down a storm. The homeless who were hanging out there loved it too – and why wouldn't they? Didn't they deserve some entertainment as much as anybody else, and more than that tosser in Maida Vale?

When I finished for the night I shared my money with them, in the spirit of Punch, and went home happy. That's the way to fucking do it.

Schwartzeneggar

I never really broke free of the idea of being in a band again. Not least, because I didn't want to. Even when I was earning my living from Punch and Judy, I was still writing lyrics, and when I got a phone call from Andy Tuck, the drummer in Thatcher On Acid, asking if I'd be interested in doing some vocals on their new album, I knew there was only one answer.

I went off down to Yeovil, recorded my vocals, and went for a beer with the band. They were nice blokes, and I already knew I liked Ben's Clash-style guitar playing because it gave me room to work in, so when they told me they were splitting up I saw an opportunity. And so did they. Schwartzeneggar was waiting to happen. But it was going to take them a while to sort themselves out, and in the meantime I ended up trying my hand as an actor.

A friend of mine was putting on a play, *Tooth of Crime* by Sam Shepard. It was going to run for four weeks at the Man in the Moon theatre down the King's Road, and he wanted me to play the lead role. I'd spent most of my adult life as a front man, and two years doing Punch and Judy, but I wasn't at all sure I could act. John cunningly took me down the pub to talk things over, knowing what would happen. Sure enough, after a few beers I was up for anything. *Acting? Yeah, I can do that!*

And so I could. I picked it up quickly, and I'm good at remembering lines. But my main memory of those four weeks is learning just how bloody hard actors work. Some nights were great, but there were others when just getting through the performance was a monumental effort. There'd be no audience reaction, or I'd be struggling to find the intensity and the delivery I'd mastered so easily the night before. Those nights, I'd get to the end of the show and hardly have the energy to move. Did I enjoy it? Yes, but I never for a moment thought it could be a new career. It was just another experience to soak up.

I was much better off with music, and when the play finished I threw myself into that. In pretty short order Schwartzeneggar started rehearsing, went into the studio and recorded a single, and did our first gig at what used to be the Pied Bull in Islington. We went down all right, as it goes, and I was feeling really positive about it all. Having Mark Pickstone playing keyboards gave the music a new angle; Andy, Ben and Bob were really tight; I was writing some of my best lyrics. There was a decent crowd, too. All the signs were good.

In comparison with Crass – who'd had to learn, and make contacts, as they went along – Schwartzeneggar hit the ground running. Thatcher On Acid had worked with Fugazi, which opened some doors for us, and John Loder was doing whatever he could to help too, so it didn't take long to set up more gigs and tours. I thought *This could really go somewhere*. A year and a half later, we split.

Bands break up – or stay together – for all sorts of reasons. Few of them have anything to do with music. Schwartzeneggar never really recovered from two early mistakes. One was our van. Because we had gigs lined up, and tours to do, we splashed out on a van. What we bought was a heap of junk which broke down so often it stopped being funny. If it wasn't the brakes, it'd be the clutch, or the exhaust, or some other mysterious fault no one could get to the bottom of. We'd go out on tour in Europe and have to hire a van in Holland because ours had broken down again. It cost us a bomb.

Our other mistake was to go back on the DIY circuit. We did

243

it because that was what we knew, but very quickly I remembered why I'd hated it before. All too often it was an exercise in endurance, nothing more. There was the gig in a cellar in Zurich where the pipe from the toilet ran behind the drummer's head so you'd hear every time someone flushed the bog, where we had socks over the mics because we were getting so much static off them, where there were pools of water on the floor. Or the one in Italy where we were expected to sleep on a bare concrete floor in the venue, which was an empty factory. I kicked up a fuss, and a couple of us got to go back to someone's house and sleep on the floor there, *on actual carpet*. The luxury of it.

I felt like I'd seen it all before, ten years earlier with Crass. But I was wrong. Nothing could ever have prepared me for one particular French gig.

We were playing in one squat, and staying in another. This was nothing unusual, and the tour – arranged by an organisation called Cochise, run by a guy called Eric – had been brilliant from start to finish, so we were looking forward to it. We turn up at the place we're going to stay, and this bloke comes out to meet us. He's covered in dirt. It's all up his arms, under his nails, and in his long, matted hair. He's so filthy he looks like he's covered in soot, like he's been up a chimney. So naturally we call him Sooty.

Sooty takes us to the venue. It stinks of piss and shit and old beer and stale cigarettes, it's littered with empty bottles from the night before, and it hasn't been cleaned since forever. There's a bare wire hanging down from the ceiling over the stage where someone's tapped into the mains, and the place is freezing. Sooty tells us *You can have the heating, or you can have the PA*. Well, we'd best have the PA then, please. So he kicks it into going, we get the gear in, do the soundcheck and get things as good as they're going to be, and then Sooty takes us back to his squat, so we can have something to eat.

Where he lives is an old shop, with a big plate glass window which looks out onto the street. They've knocked holes in the walls to connect it to the buildings on either side, and they're living in this strange subterranean world, with passages leading through walls, and everything lit by candles. There are kids everywhere. And everyone, and everything, is just like Sooty – absolutely, indescribably filthy.

Sooty asks us if we'd like some wine with our meal and I think maybe things are looking up. OK, so his personal hygiene isn't wonderful and he lives in a fucking bombsite, but at least there's going to be something to drink, and I could murder a good glass of wine. When you're on tour, it's the simple things – like a glass of wine and a hot meal – that lift your spirits after days of driving and help you feel human again. Then Sooty hands me a dirty old jam-jar, which has been used as a paint pot, and pours the wine into it. *Er, thanks.* I think I just lost my appetite. If they can't even find a clean jam-jar for the wine, what's the food come in? A bin? A look round the table tells me everyone's thinking the same. *Tell you what, mate. We'll just head back to the gig.*

All we're doing is swapping one shithole for another, but at least – now the doors are open and people are turning up – the venue's got atmosphere. As we get closer to stage-time it fills up nicely, and it's clear there's going to be a good-sized crowd. Now the anticipation and the adrenalin kick in, and it's time for my pre-gig shit. So I ask Sooty *Where's the toilets?* He takes me behind the bar, fills up a bucket with water, and gives it to me. There's an onion skin and a carrot top swirling around in the water. It's a bit of a jam-jar moment. I follow Sooty across the main hall and through the crowd, carrying this bucket, trying not to spill the water down my jeans, with people going *It's Steve Ignorant! Bonjour, Steve!* then noticing the bucket. I might as well have gone on stage and announced I was taking a shit.

Sooty takes me to the toilet, moves all the drug-takers out of the way, and opens the door. The stink is incredible. There's no lock, there's no light. Just a dark, dirty cubicle with two foot-plates and a hole in the ground. Well, fuck it. Any port in a storm. I pass Sooty the empty bucket that's in there, go in with my bucket, and jam it against the door to keep it shut. I look round. There's no paper. So I let myself out, go and find Sooty and tell him. *Yes,* he says, *we don't believe in using paper.* I went *Right, what do I do?* And the penny drops. That's what the bucket of water's for.

So, I make my way back through the crowd to the bog again, jam the door shut with the bucket, drop my trousers, and assume the position. I'm looking at the onion skin and the carrot top bobbing in the water in this filthy bucket, thinking to myself *Fifteen years in bands and I'm squatting over an open sewer. Bet Bowie never had these luxuries.*

There's one thing I'm certain of: no way is that water going round my backside ... so I undo my Doctor Martens one at a time, being careful to keep my balance so I don't tread in the piss-wet floor, take off my underpants, rip them up, and wipe myself with them instead. I sloosh the water down the hole, and fling the underpants over the courtyard wall. Job done. I walk back into the hall and Bob goes *Where's the bog, Steve?*

I smile, and pass him the empty bucket.

The gig, though, is a stormer. We're tight and fast and aggressive, and the crowd are really up for it. This is why we do what we do. This is why we put up with shit food, and sleeping on floors, and the exhaustion that comes with doing it for weeks on end. For the one hour a day when we're on stage and the audience go wild. When everything comes together.

246

All too soon it's over, and we've packed down the gear and everyone's gone home, and we're back at Sooty's. We're sitting drinking bottles of beer, which is fine by me – I never want to see those jam-jars again – and I need a piss. So I ask him, *Where's the toilet here then, mate?*

He said *We use the street.*

You don't have a toilet?!

No.

How long have you lived here?

Two, three years.

What? And you haven't plumbed in a toilet??

Well, we don't feel it's important.

But you've got families living here. Kids.

I can't believe it. Rejecting the consumer society is one thing; living like animals is something else. Because what Sooty and his friends do – every man, woman, and child in the squat – is go and shit outside in the street at night, like dogs. And every morning at dawn the street sweeping machines come by and it all gets cleared away. That's how they live, how they've lived for three years, and how they intend to keep on living. And I thought the jam-jars were bad.

I tell him *I'm not going to piss in the street!* Sooty shrugs. He doesn't see what the fuss is about, and he doesn't really care. He points over his shoulder to a little bathroom cubicle and says *There's a sink through there. Use that.* Fuck it, I will. I've given up trying to be polite by now. So I go through. I turn the tap on, and there's no water. I try the other tap, and get a tiny trickle. I start pissing, and all this stuff starts coming up out of the plughole. *Please, no! No! No!!* But yes. Some dirty fucker has shat down the plughole and now it's started coming back up. And everyone's going to think it was me.

Life on the road isn't always all it's cracked up to be. It's not all sex and drugs and rock and roll, whatever we tell you.

Sometimes, if you're lucky, you may just find yourself staying with people who believe in revolution through squalor, holding your breath and pushing someone else's shit down a plughole with a stick.

Belgium

It doesn't matter how good a band you are – and Schwart-zeneggar were bloody good – you need to have a bit of luck, and a few things need to go your way, if you're going to get anywhere. Tours take it out of you. When you're tired and hungry and your van keeps breaking down, and then you end up staying with someone like Sooty, life gets really hard.

That's why you have to enjoy the good times, the moments that remind you just why you're putting yourself through all this hardship. If you can't have a laugh, then you're done for. We stacked the odds against ourselves as soon as we bought the van, because from the first moment it broke down we were playing catch-up, spending what money we made on repairs. And it's hard to enjoy what you're doing when you can't get out of debt. But we could still have pulled through. The personalities in the band were our real problem.

Ben and Andy were good enough musicians, but they didn't enjoy being on the road. Andy really hated it. He was vegan, which didn't make life easy; he didn't drink or smoke, so he couldn't unwind; and he wanted to go to bed on time, which is next to impossible. He was a nice bloke, and you could have a laugh with him, but it was hard work. Ben just focused on the negative. A good gig would be glossed over; if we did a bad one he'd be talking about it for days. I remember one gig we did in Slovenia – there were only about forty people there, but it was a small venue and it was really jumping. We came off stage and

I said to Ben *That was a good one!* He just shrugged and went *Yeah. It was all right* in that flat, disinterested tone of voice that says enjoying what we do is just stupid. I didn't get it. And I still don't. Why not be enthusiastic? Why not enjoy it? Why not accept that – just occasionally – we were great?? How does being miserable help anyone???

I hate to think how it looked to an audience. We played Belfast once. I'd done a radio interview for the gig, and Crass had played there back in the day, so there was quite a bit of interest. We did the gig, and the boys weren't too impressed because the audience had been sitting on chairs through the set, instead of leaping around. But in the end everyone stood up and clapped, and I said *Come on, let's do them another one!* And Ben said *What for?*

Well, because they've spent their fucking dole cheques to come and see us and the least we can do is give them another song before we get our money and piss off. I can't believe Ben doesn't get that. Then Andy goes *I just want to go to bed.* We're meant to be a punk band, we've written songs we want people to hear, and now we're standing on stage arguing about doing an encore. What's this all about?

It was clear we were never going to see eye to eye, but I could have lived with that. It was the sneering, sniping negativity I couldn't handle. It all came to a head on another tour through Europe. Ben moaned from the minute he got up till the time he went to bed. He hated the van. He thought I looked like a knob on stage. He didn't want to do interviews because they were boring. His glass was half-empty and it was everybody's problem.

This went on for weeks. Then one night we did a strange little gig in Modena, in Italy. We came off stage, Ben started mouthing off, complaining about anything and everything, and I just snapped. Violence has never been my answer to anything

– I don't like fighting and I don't pick fights – but now a red mist descended and I went for Ben with a glass in my hand. I'd chased him out of the building before Andy got me in a ju-jitsu lock, and the others bundled Ben into the safety of the van. He sat there pulling faces at me, so when Andy let me go I flew at the van and tried to punch my way through the window, because what I wanted more than anything else right then was to beat the living shit out of Ben. It might just stop the little fucker moaning. I was pretty certain it would make me feel a whole lot better.

In the end I'd have settled for hitting him once, really hard. But no one would let me. So there and then, mid-tour, I quit. Schwartzeneggar was over. We sorted out the money that night and drove back to England in silence. It took a day and a half to get back. It took a year for me and Ben to start talking. We could be mates – we just couldn't be in the same band. I couldn't be on tour with someone who was so negative and cynical about everything all the time. To me, life's too short. You're going to have crap times anyway, so at least try to enjoy things when they're good.

It's a crying shame it ended the way it did, because we wrote some great songs. And I still think we could have gone further, if things had been different. It wouldn't have taken much, because sometimes it's the tiniest things that send you off down the wrong track and build into a major problem. Your van keeps breaking down, and costing you a fortune, and suddenly you're skint again when you hoped you'd have cash in your pocket, and instead of enjoying being in a band you're arguing about money. All the time. Getting on each other's tits. It's easy done.

And then you lose sight of why you're in a band in the first place. For the buzz of being on stage, watching an audience go wild to your music. For the laughs you have on the road, for the wonderful people you meet, become friends with, and see next time round. A bunch of you pile into a van and head off across Europe, not really knowing what the next few weeks will bring, what mad things will happen. It might be good, it might be a nightmare, but it's all an adventure. That's what keeps you coming back for more. And we had enough of those moments with Schwartzeneggar to give us a taste of how things might have been.

We were on our way to a gig in Belgium once, and we were lost. I don't know what it is about Belgium, but whenever you're driving through it the road signs disappear. One minute you're sailing through the flatlands on the A13, the next you're on a back road going past someone's farm, with no idea where you are. You get to where you're going in the end, but it's confusing.

Anyway, we're lost and we're going to be late. Everyone's moaning, and I think I'll give this a miss and have a bit of a daydream instead. So I close my eyes and slip into this erotic fantasy about some little punkette who'd been at the gig the night before. Suddenly I hear this droning noise, the same as the van engine. It's Mark Pickstone. I go *What's up?* Mark has this very deep, Northern voice, and he talks really slowly, like he's thinking about every single word. He says *I was just thinking.* And there's a long pause.

What were you thinking?
Oh, it's funny.
What were you thinking? What's funny?
Oh, you'll laugh when I tell you.
Right. Well why don't you tell me?
It made me chuckle.

All the time I'm having to strain to hear his voice because it's deep and rumbling and the van's loud, and I'm pissed off anyway because I just want to drift back off into this erotic day-dream I was enjoying when he woke me, but getting Mark to explain what he's on about is like pulling teeth, which isn't helping my mood at all.

I was just thinking …

What?! What?! What were you fucking thinking?!!

I was just thinking I wish I'd taken out the patent for all the sodium lights in Europe.

You woke me up for that? I'm back off to find that punkette.

We get to the gig, and we're late. There's no time for a sound-check. There's barely time to set up our stuff. The house guy's worrying about the lighting. The organisers are panicking about the doors *We have to let the audience in! We have to let the audience in!* The band bosh the gear out, I tell the lighting guy four blues, two whites, will do. And I tell the two promoters to chill out, it'll all be fine. Twenty minutes after we walk into the building, we're done, everybody's happy, and we can relax.

We go backstage for a fag and a beer. Five minutes later I decide I'll nip back through to the venue. I open the door and the place is full. It's full to bursting. People are jumping around and laughing, there's a fantastic atmosphere, it's totally rammed. I shut the door and go *Look at this lads!* In the dressing room, it's so quiet you could hear a pin drop. I open the door, there's a wall of noise and a sea of people. Shut it – five tired blokes in a silent room. Open it – half of Belgium having a party.

Seeing as we hadn't soundchecked, I said to Ben we'd better go up on stage and check the gear was all ok. So we do. The lighting guy sees us, thinks we're starting our set, and brings the lights up. Ta-dah! There's me and Ben onstage in front of 300 people. Who all go quiet. Everyone's looking at us. All expectant. Ben starts fiddling with his guitar, but all I've got to do is check the mic stand's the right height, which takes half of no time at all, so once I've done that I'm standing there feeling like a real spare part.

Over the shoulders of all this crowd, who are waiting and watching us, I can see the boys in the dressing room, so I wave them over, because we might as well start now. I see Andy put down his water, tut, mutter and moan and change into his shorts – he always played in shorts – grab a pair of sticks and come through. Mark ambles onto stage. Right, that's four of us. Where's Bob?

All the audience are looking at us, we're looking at them, everyone's waiting. Eventually Bob shuffles through from the dressing room with a pint and two carrier bags. He clambers on stage, dumps the bags on the floor, puts his pint on top of his amp, and empties the bags on to the stage. No hurry whatsoever. He bends down and starts sorting through the cables he's just tipped on to the floor. By now everyone's watching him. Even I'm watching him. It's mesmerising, like some sort of performance art. He untangles the cables, plugs into the amp, into his pedals, and into his bass. He throws the bass over his shoulder and tunes up. Minutes tick by. Finally he's satisfied everything's ok. He takes a sip of his pint, and turns round. I catch his eye. *You ready now, Bob?* He's fumbling through his pockets *Er ... no, mate. Not quite. Anyone got a plectrum?*

It was a great little gig, once Bob finally found his plectrum. One of our best. The crowd was bouncing, kids were getting on stage and diving off again, everyone was having fun. It was one of those days which made up for all the hours in the van and the miles on the road, for sleeping on floors and going hungry. Sometimes Schwartzeneggar really fucking rocked. And that's what it's all about in the end.

Dark

Sadly, though, there weren't enough nights like the Belgium gig. Certainly not enough to overcome the underlying tensions in the band. We drove back from Modena in silence, went our separate ways once we got to Stratford, and a few hours later I was back in Dial House, torn between relief I wasn't sleeping on floors any more, and anger and disappointment about what had happened.

I felt like every time I tried to do something, I ended up in the same old rut, stuck in the back of a grotty old van, trundling round Europe from one dodgy venue to another. Schwartzeneggar had been a good band, with competent musicians, but our records hadn't sold particularly well, and we'd not really been getting anywhere. True, we'd supported The Levellers at Brixton Academy, and the show had gone really well, but we hadn't been able to build on it. Instead we found ourselves back on the DIY circuit, which was – at best – exhausting. Music wasn't something I enjoyed any more. I was tired. I was bored. I was skint.

So I turned my back on the whole thing. I decided I was never, ever going to be involved in bands again. What was the point? Why go through all the effort of starting another band just to end up in a shithole in Europe, playing a venue where we had to put socks over the mics and sleep on the floor and hope we got enough money out of it to pay for the petrol to the next show? Why put myself through that? If being in a band meant falling out with my mates because of the pressure and the hunger and the lack of cash, I really couldn't be bothered with it. It was over.

Thing was, I didn't have a clue what I was going to do instead. I stayed at Dial House, and turned in on myself. I told myself I was being domestic, but really I was in limbo, marking time, wrapped in my own misery. I felt as though Pen and Gee were too busy with their own lives to give me much support: Pen was writing his book, so he was in London with Eve, or working in his shed; Gee was doing her artwork, and getting an exhibition together. A lot of the time I was in Dial House on my own, and that just gave me lots of time to beat myself up, which wasn't good. All I could see was my friends getting on with their lives, while I'd had another project come to nothing. My self-confidence plummeted.

I tried doing a bit of wood carving, but my heart wasn't in it. And what was the point in writing when I hadn't got a band? I'd always enjoyed being creative, but now it all went out of the window. I had no enthusiasm for anything, and the more miserable I got, the less I saw myself having a future. Crass was the biggest thing I'd ever done, and I'd never match it again. Trying was stupid. I was stupid. I was getting old and getting up on stage and looking like an idiot. That was why none of the bands I was in ever got anywhere, because I was an idiot. The glory days were dead and buried. I might as well accept it. And so on.

I thought I was being brutally honest, but really I was just kicking myself when I was down. I knew how to stick the boot in, sure enough, but I had no idea how to stop. Within a couple of months of coming back off tour, my world had completely fallen apart. I was depressed, properly depressed. And it scared the life out of me.

I had about two weeks solid where I couldn't stop crying. And I couldn't explain why. I couldn't see the point of anything. I hadn't the energy to write, or pick up the chisel, or even get out of bed. Then one day I was lying in bed, too depressed to move, and I thought *I've got to do something about this*. So I decided I'd make a mental list. Why I should bother getting up versus why I shouldn't. Maybe that would help.

It didn't. The reasons for not bothering far outweighed the reasons to get up and dust myself off and give it another go. And suddenly I realised I was considering ending my own life. I felt very cold and clear and detached about it, as if I'd simply arrived at a logical conclusion. If life was a problem, death might be the answer. It all made sense.

Fortunately I didn't make a serious attempt to follow this through. What I did do was get really really pissed. Then I fetched half-a-dozen sharp knives from the kitchen and took them to bed with me. I knew I didn't have the bottle to slit my own wrists, but I thought that maybe – with all those knives lying on the sheets around me – I might roll on one and bleed to death as I tossed and turned during the night. That way I wouldn't have to consciously choose to kill myself. If I was lucky it would just happen while I was drunk and asleep, and I'd know nothing about it.

I woke up in the morning and I hadn't so much as cut myself. I lay there crying, telling myself I'd been an arsehole again. I couldn't even get killing myself right. What hope was there for me?

I wouldn't wish depression on anyone. It's a horrible place to be. I got through it in the end, but I don't know how. There was no magic moment, no blinding revelation. I just hung on in there. One day I dragged myself out of the house and went down the local pub in North Weald, had a couple of pints in the daytime, and went home. That became a weekly event, then twice a week, then I was down the Queen's Head a lot, drinking and playing pool and having what felt a bit like a normal life. Hanging out with the locals, and being an everyday joe – which I hadn't done for years, because I'd always been touring and rehearsing and hanging out with musicians – gave me something else to think about. Ordinary, simple things like talking about boxing, or football, or looking at the barmaid's tits, helped me out of my depression.

I think that's all there is to it. There's no big trick. You just drag yourself through one day, and then the next, and slowly the crisis passes and one day you find yourself forgetting you feel shit. Just for five minutes, but it's a start. You inch your way back to sanity, little by little. You no longer want to fill your bed with knives. Life gets better. If that's where you are, hang on. Life gets better.

So I gradually got myself back on an even keel. I spent my days quietly at Dial House, or drinking with bricklayers and fork-lift drivers down the Queen's Head, living the sort of life I might have had if I'd stayed in Dagenham. I trundled along and kept myself to myself, slowly pulling my life back together. It took months. I wasn't depressed anymore, but things were still difficult, and I mostly dealt with the world by shutting it out. Except the world wouldn't let me.

British Telecom, who owned the farm Dial House was on, wanted to kick us out, turn the house and farm buildings into a restaurant, and build a housing complex and golf course. This was the start of what would become years of legal battles, fighting for the right to stay in our home. Gee was at the forefront of this – I certainly couldn't have been. She whipped up public support, got the North Weald Action Group together, and took BT on. I helped by going to meetings, and pushing leaflets through doors, and I lived – like we all did – with the fear of eviction. With all this going on, it felt like being in Crass again, with never a moment's peace, and in a strange way, it did me good.

I realised I could deal with it. A couple of months earlier, this kind of pressure would have sent me into a tailspin; now, although I hated it, I got out there and fought my corner. I'd spent too long feeling like the bloke who used to be Steve Ignorant, feeling miserable and living in the past, but I was starting to believe that could change.

I thought about what I might do next. I was occasionally writing bits and pieces down, which was a sign in itself how much better I was feeling, and although they rarely came to anything, I started thinking about getting back into music. Just as a session singer. That way I could be in a band, but it wouldn't be my band, and I wouldn't do Crass songs, or get caught up in organising everything, or do interviews. I'd just turn up to rehearsals, do the gig, get my money, and go home. It would be like a 9–5, just not in Tesco.

I was wondering about how to do this, whether I should go to auditions or what, telling myself I should get started but really just dithering and going for walks or heading down the pub, and fate stepped in. A guy from Slovenia, who'd put Schwartzeneggar on over there, came to visit. He asked if I was doing anything musically, and I told him of my plans to be some kind of guest vocalist. He looked at me.

Funny you should say that he said. *Gary from Dirt's got a new band together and he's looking for a vocalist …*

Moving On

I didn't want to rush back in to music and make the same mistakes I had before, so before I contacted Gary I thought long and hard about what I wanted. We met up in a pub in Stratford and had a few beers. I told him *I'm not interested in three-chord thrash anymore. I want to use brass, keyboards, and acoustic guitar. I want a new sound.* Gary took a sip of his pint *Yep* he said *I'm into that too.*

So we formed Stratford Mercenaries. Our first gig was a benefit down in London, and we did 'The Way Things Are', just myself and Gary on electric guitar, and it worked really well. Gary was playing around, getting feedback off the mic, and it was a million miles away from the usual punk four piece sound I'd got so bored with. Sid from Rubella Ballet told us he'd been so excited by what we were doing he wanted to jump on stage and join in! I'd loved it, Gary thought it was great, and already – after just one show – it seemed like things were moving in an interesting direction. Where should we go from here?

I knew. If we were going to do more gigs, I wanted them to be in America. I hadn't played there since I'd been over with Crass twenty years before, and I wanted to go back. And if we were going to bomb, if it was all going to go wrong, I'd rather it happened in LA than Huddersfield. Gary was well up for it, because he was seeing an American girl already, so he set up some dates, and we started rehearsing. We got Phil Barker, who was playing with the Buzzcocks, in on drums, and a guy called

Ed on bass. We only had six weeks till the tour, and we hadn't got a set, so we pulled in a couple of songs from here, a couple from there, threw some Crass songs in, and off we went.

It was a really good tour. We played New York, and Boston, and a couple more dates on the east coast, and then we flew over to LA and played a string of venues over there. We had 14 gigs in 18 days, and went down really well. I'd been worried that it would all be a bit of a circus, that people would come along expecting Crass, that I'd feel old and out of place, but I really enjoyed myself. The audience were young – I remember one cute punkette telling me *My dad was really into you when he was younger* and there he was, sitting in the station wagon across the street, waiting to take her home – and they were willing to give us a go, and once we'd finished playing, it was party time. This was what I'd missed. I was back out on the road and I was having a laugh and life was good again.

We even made a bit of money! Not much, but we came back with maybe £100 each in our pockets, having had a great time, with people telling us that if we came over for longer we'd do even better. It looked like we had something that worked. A few weeks later I was having a lie in at Dial House, enjoying the fact life was going so well, and Gee came in to tell me my uncle had phoned. Stan was dead.

Me and Mum and Stan had made it up over the years. I still had more in common with my friends than I did with them, but I'd dropped by two or three times a year and we'd got on fine. They liked getting postcards from places they'd never been to, and Stan had shown some interest in what I was up to. And now he'd had a massive heart attack in the middle of the night and Mum was on her own.

I went back to Dagenham to organise the funeral. My sister was having a rough time and couldn't do it, and David was nowhere to be seen, so that left me. I set up a table and phone in the corner of the living room at Whitebarn Lane, and made all the arrangements as quickly and efficiently as I could, so Mum could deal with grieving properly. It was weird being in the house without Stan there, and hard to think he wouldn't be sitting watching the telly, but for my mum her whole life was upside-down. She'd lost the love of her life. Every time I looked at her I saw a broken old woman, so after the funeral was over I stayed on, keeping an eye on her. I visited maybe three days a week, and if I wasn't there then I'd phone, because the hardest thing for her was the loneliness, rattling around in the house without Stan.

It was summer. The weather was fine and I thought a change of scene might do Mum good, so I invited her over to Dial House. It was a sunny day and we were sitting on the swinging bench in the garden, drinking tea and watching Gee's tai-chi class get ready, and this gorgeous girl with long blonde hair drifted past. I said to Mum *I'm going to have some of that!* and she hit me on the arm and told me *Behave yourself! She's far too young for you.* And then the girl came and sat down by us. I said *Hi. I'm Steve.* She said *I'm Jona. I do tai-chi.*

And it was love at first sight.

I knew I wanted to go out with Jona. So to try and get near her I joined the tai-chi group. I've never experienced such a boring martial art – if that's what it is – in my entire life. I stuck it for as long as I could, but it wasn't my bag at all. I was only doing it for one reason, but eventually I got to the point where even that wasn't enough. I couldn't handle the idea of wasting any more of my life on tai-chi, so I screwed up my courage, gave Jona a call, and asked her if she wanted to go for a drink. She said yes. And my life changed.

We saw each other a few more times, and then I was back out

on tour with Stratford Mercenaries. We had three or four dates in Europe and I brought her back a box of chocolates, or at least the two that were left in the box after the band got their mitts on them. In November we went off on our second US tour, which went fairly well, but wasn't as much fun as the first because all the time I was out there I was thinking about Jona. I got back to Dial House, met up with her again, and said *We should try living together. How about I move in with you?*

And so I did. The way I saw it, we were both old enough and ugly enough to deal with it, and if it didn't work then I'd just move out. That was easy. The hard thing was moving out of Dial House. I'd lived there almost all of my adult life, and it held so many incredible memories for me. On top of that the legal battle with BT was still going on, and I couldn't help feeling like I was running out on Pen and Gee. I was only moving two miles down the road, to Coopersale, but I felt I was saying goodbye to all those years we'd had together. It was an emotional time for us all.

I left at the end of January 1998 with all my worldly possessions: my carpet, two bin liners of clothes, and a sea-chest full of books. Pen came up to me with his eyes full of tears and thumped me on the chest. Neither of us had words for what we were feeling. I left Dial House with my eyes brimming and a lump in my throat. I was moving on. A new chapter in my life was beginning.

Vienna

Meanwhile, in Stratford Mercenaries, things weren't quite going to plan. The first US tour had been set up quickly, to see whether it worked or not, and because we'd had such a short time to rehearse we'd shelved our ideas for a new, more interesting sound, and gone out as a four piece band. No keys, no brass section, no acoustic guitar. The trouble was, that set the pattern for things to come. We came back and we were so busy rehearsing for the next tour, and going into the studio to record a single, that we didn't have the time – or the money – to bring more people into the band. I'd ask Gary *When are going to write? When are we going to add some brass?* But there'd always be something else that needed doing first.

I'd dreamed of a band that didn't do three-chord thrash, but that dream was slipping away. Even as early as the end of the second US tour, I was unhappy with the way things were going. I realised Gary could only play a certain style, and that Phil didn't like slow stuff, and that they were more comfortable sticking with what they knew than trying something different. If I'd been honest with myself, I'd have known that wasn't going to change. Eight or nine months in, and I could see which way the wind was blowing.

On top of that we were getting sucked back into the DIY circuit, because that was where Gary's contacts were, and that was the scene he knew. I had reservations about the fact we weren't writing enough songs and seemed to be relying on Crass numbers to get us the gigs, but I could deal with that, for a while at least. My big problem was that, after what happened with Schwartzeneggar, I'd promised myself I'd stay away from DIY, and now I wasn't. Gary was fine with it – he loved being on the road and being on tour and he'd have done it forever and asked nothing more. Ed was happy if there was a beer. Phil wasn't used to the way the circuit worked, and he really wasn't happy about going hungry and sleeping on floors. Neither was I. The older I got, the harder I found it to do. But there I was, doing it. Again.

It wasn't as if we made life easy for ourselves, either. When we went on tour in Europe in the spring of '98, we hired a van. It was driven by the South African woman who owned it, and it was only after we'd loaded it up at Gary's that she explained we'd have to push it to get it started. For the next three weeks we had to leap out and bump start it every time we stopped at a traffic light, and for all the talk of picking up a cheap battery somewhere, we never did. When we got a flat tyre in Belgium we discovered she'd welded a step on the back of the van which meant we couldn't get to the spare, and if we'd got to the spare it wouldn't have mattered anyway, because she hadn't got a jack. So we had to wait by the side of the road for the Belgian AA to do the repair that meant we could push the van so we could get it started so we could drive as far as the next time we stopped, when we'd have to repeat the whole process again.

We pushed that sodding van all the way round Europe. Until we got to Austria. The Austrian border guards took one look at our piece of crap van and said we could come in, but it couldn't. No ifs, no buts, no way. In fact, the van was so bad they were going to hit us with a substantial fine, and that wasn't up for discussion either. I was tired and hungry and pissed off, and my head went. I locked myself in the van and told them I was going nowhere. And so we had a stand-off for a couple of hours. After a while, the fine dropped to 200 schillings. A little later, they'd take 100. Eventually they agreed we could push the van a couple of hundred yards into Austria and get another van to come out from the venue and collect our gear. Then our van would definitely have to leave. Now please would I unlock the van and stop making a fuss and let them get on with their day?

So that's what we did. Our van turned round and headed into Slovakia and then back into Austria at another checkpoint where the guards weren't so strict, and we carried on to the gig. It was at a huge squat in Vienna, and we were running really late, but we needn't have worried. We rolled up at about 9pm to an all-day event with 25 bands, 12 of which still hadn't played. It was obvious we weren't going to play till 2 or 3am. It was also obvious everyone had been drinking since it started and was totally out of it. Why had we even bothered to come? It was pointless. No one would know if we played or not, whether we slurred the words or played a polka. And as for a soundcheck, forget it.

There was only one thing to do. Gary and I sat down and started drinking. We're having a lot of fun people watching, and then this really drunk girl stumbles over and collapses onto the other side of the sofa. She's got bits of metal all over her face, her eyes are boiling and rolling around, and she's clearly chock full of beer. Gary goes *My type of woman!* She sees me smoking and asks for a cigarette, which I give her. Then she leans over, throws up all these noodles onto the sofa, wipes her mouth with the back of her hand, and staggers back into the crowd. Gary is awestruck. *That is definitely my type of woman!* he tells me. *Definitely!*

We eventually do the gig at some ridiculous hour of the morning. Afterwards, when I'm getting in our van – which has finally made it into Austria – so we can go round to the promoter's house and sleep, Gary's in the front seat with two girls, one of whom is Noodles. He's clearly busy. We get to where we'll be staying and Stefan the promoter takes me to one side and asks me who the women are. I tell him I've no idea. Is it a problem? Stefan tells me *Yes*. He doesn't like uninvited guests, especially drunk ones. The last one who stayed got up in the middle of the night to go to the loo, came into Stefan's bedroom, thought the white plastic chair there was a toilet, and shat all over it. Then when Stefan switched on the light and shouted at him, he ran out into the winter night wearing only a vest, spent four hours hiding behind a motorbike, and almost froze to death. *So for that reason* says Stefan *I don't like strange people coming to my house, especially when they're drunk.* The words are barely out of his mouth and Noodles boots the door open and screams *Where's the ★★★★ing toilet?!* I didn't even have to say anything to Gary. He took Noodles back to the venue and slept with her there.

Next morning, we're sitting in the van. Phil's eating a bag of crisps, and Gary sticks his hand in to grab one. Phil looks at Gary, at the crisps, at Gary's hand. He thinks about last night and passes Gary the bag. *Have the lot, mate.* The thing about being on tour is you know each other's secrets. Phil would crap in a plastic bag rather than use the same toilet as the audience. Ed goes loopy after too much booze. And Gary never washes. We learnt that early on, when he made us cheese sandwiches after working on an engine and they had big oily fingerprints all over them. No one's going to fight him for the crisps.

Although touring with Stratford Mercenaries certainly had more laughs than life with Schwartzeneggar, we were still trawling round the DIY circuit, with all the problems it brought along. I'd had years of dealing with it – which was why I'd been so keen to get away – but for Phil it was an entirely new experience. And he hated it. I couldn't really blame him. Sleeping on floors was bad enough, but none of us had signed up for pushing the van. What Phil didn't see, though, was that every now and then you'd meet people on the scene – especially in Europe – who were saints. Wonderful people, who lived what they believed.

One of the gigs on the Noodles tour got cancelled, and no gig meant no money. Worse than that, it meant nowhere to stay. There wasn't the cash for a hotel because there never is. That's not the way the circuit works. Fortunately we weren't too far from Leipzig, and there was a squat there we'd played earlier in the tour, so we rang them and asked if they had any floor space going spare. And they said yes. So we turned up, really late, just looking for a place to sleep which wasn't the van, and they'd saved us some hot food and two crates of beer!

This was above and beyond our wildest expectations. So when they told us they had a little party going, and asked if we'd set up our backline and play, how could we say no after what they'd done? I was up for it, so was Gary, so we did our set to the twenty people there. We finish playing and this guy comes up to me. He says *We've had a collection and here's some money. It'll pay for the petrol to get you to the next gig.* I was nearly in tears. There was no need for them to do that. They were bloody stars. I went up to Phil and showed him, and he went *Don't suppose it'll cover our food costs though, will it?*

He just didn't get it. I know I moan about the DIY scene, but there's some great things happen in it. For me, though, the bad outweighs the good. And if I'd ever thought of forgetting that, our next tour would bang it home.

Japan

I was really looking forward to our third tour of the US. It was going to be a long tour – five weeks in total – and we were spending two of those gigging in Japan, which was somewhere I'd never been before. So I was excited. At the same time, the pressure was on, because we'd borrowed money from John Loder to finance the trip, and we knew we had to pay it back. We'd always done well in the States, but now we had to have our most successful tour yet.

It started well enough. We did three gigs on the East Coast, where we always did ok. Then we flew west. We had half-a-dozen gigs lined up through an English bloke who was living in Portland and made his living selling t-shirts and records at gigs. They were a disaster. We did one gig in someone's kitchen; another in someone's back yard. They were ridiculous places no one in their right minds would go. Even Gary – who lived for being on the road and took whatever happened on the chin – was furious. Had the gigs been set up simply for this bloke to sell records? It certainly felt like it. By the time we got to San Francisco we were all hugely pissed off. And then our promoter accused us of behaving like rockstars because we'd flown from New York to Portland.

I asked him if he'd expected us to drive, and he said *Well that would be the punk thing to do*. I couldn't believe it. What did he expect us to live on? How would we eat? Where would we stay? He was making money selling Crass t-shirts – and giving nothing back to the people in the band – but we were supposed to scrabble our way across the US, playing for petrol money every night and living on fresh air, just so he would approve? He had to be kidding. I told him *We've had to borrow this bloody money.*

Yeah he said *well the way you're just going to Japan …* As if it was just some whim. As if we'd dreamt it up as a wicked wheeze. We were musicians trying to make a living, that was all, and when we'd been sorting out the tour we'd asked this bloke in Portland if he could set some gigs up in Japan. He'd said he could, and now he was slagging us off for it. How did that work? I'd had enough of his bullshit and hypocrisy. I blew my lid. We all did. But he had the last word. *Wait till you get to Japan,* he warned us. *You'll be staying with Miyagi, and he's really hardcore.*

It was the only time he knew what he was talking about. We got to Japan and Miyagi was the DIY merchant from hell.

We were expecting him to meet us at Tokyo airport – that's what we'd been told would happen, though god knows how the arrangements were made because Miyagi spoke virtually no English – but he wasn't there. We'd just got off an eight hour flight from LA, we were tired and jet-lagged, everything was in Japanese, and we had no idea where to go. Fortunately, because Phil was in the Buzzcocks, a couple of girls from the fan club had come to meet him. They reckoned we were probably supposed to meet Miyagi at the central station, and they said they'd take us there. So we picked up our luggage and followed them.

One and a half hours later, after three changes on the Tube, we get to the central station, and there's Miyagi. He bows. We bow. He asks us what we want to do, and we say that if it's all right with him we'd like to go for a beer. It'll give us a chance to relax and chat and get to know each other. He says ok. So that's what we do. It's not quite like going to the pub – we sit round a table in a restaurant, and order bottles of beer from a waiter – but it gives us a chance to find our feet and get our bearings in a new place. Japan is like nowhere we've ever been before, and I'm hoping that the next couple of weeks will be an adventure every bit as exciting as my first visit to New York. I have no idea how wrong I'm going to be.

Five or six beers later we go back to Miyagi's. He's living with his wife in his grandmother's apartment, and we're going to be sleeping on the floor. It's the height of summer, so it's really humid, and we're crammed into this tiny place which is hopping with cat fleas. It's not exactly brilliant, but we get what kip we can. Next morning we get up, looking forward to our first gig, and Miyagi says *I have to tell you that yesterday you insulted my wife. All of you.*

This is news to me. We didn't even meet her. So I ask him *How?*

She cooked food for you, and you said you wanted to go for a beer.

Hold on, I think. That doesn't seem entirely fair.

Miyagi, you asked us what we wanted to do. You didn't mention anything about your wife cooking food. You asked us what we wanted to do, we said 'Go for a beer', you said all right. So we went for a beer.

Yes, but my wife had cooked food for you.

Well why didn't you tell us?

It's not for me to tell you.

But ... And what can I say? We're in the bloke's house. He's promoting our shows. We can't afford to fall out with him. *I'm sorry, Miyagi. We apologise.*

And that was how our stay in Japan went. Next day Phil upset Miyagi's wife. It was a mis-communication over tofu, I think. Something and nothing, but another big row, and once again we had to apologise. Whatever we did, you could guarantee it would be wrong. We weren't trying to insult either of them, but we obviously were. Every day there'd be something that me or Gary had to sort out and apologise for, and it was exhausting. We hadn't come over for this. In the end I said to Miyagi *Look, we don't know when we're doing something wrong, so if you see a problem starting, could you please just tell us, and stop it?*

And he said *No. You're in Japan now. It's for you to think Japanese.* And that was the end of that. He wouldn't tell us what we should do, he'd just be angry with us when we got things wrong. When we got things wrong we insulted him, and if we talked about that to each other then we insulted him again. He was completely unreasonable, and he wasn't interested in meeting us halfway. All we could do was get the gigs done and get out of there.

Our introduction to Japan could hardly have been worse. Then – luckily for us – we met an American guy who lived in Japan, and spoke the language. Miyagi had coloured our view of the place so completely we'd forgotten the generosity of the two girls at the airport, and begun thinking everyone was like him. Now we had someone who knew the culture tell us he was really odd. *On a power trip, man.*

At last we had someone to explain what was going on. And the news wasn't good. The gigs had been going really well, and we'd been looking forward to a decent chunk of cash at the end of the tour when we settled up with Myagi. We'd be able to pay back John, and maybe have a bit of cash left over for ourselves. Now we discovered that on the DIY circuit in Japan support bands don't get paid. Instead the headline band takes them out at the end of the night for a meal and some beers. Suddenly the penny dropped: every night, when Myagi had insisted we went to a restaurant to meet with the other bands, we'd been paying for their food, for their beer, for the lot. And he'd never told us. Japan was an expensive place. There wasn't going to be any money left.

We were in a restaurant at the time, with all that night's support bands. Gary put his shoes on and walked across the table and out of the door. I did the same. It's a big insult, and we knew it, but we were absolutely livid. We felt we'd been ripped off, lied to, and bullied all the way down the line. There was the mother of all rows with Myagi the next day. The American guy was there to translate, so we could be sure he knew just how angry we were, but it didn't change the fact we'd flown all the way over for nothing. It wasn't going to bring the money back. We did the last gig in Tokyo, and we left. And we never managed to pay John the money we owed.

When the DIY scene works well, it's brilliant. When people muck in and pull together and make things happen, there's nothing to beat it. But all too often it's nothing like that. And when it's bad, I think it's one of the worst things that could have happened to punk rock. When people get bands over to play in some shithole pub that holds fifteen people, where they know they aren't going to make any money, and then they won't even cover their costs, then I despise it. I've met too many promoters who won't pay a band cash. Instead they'll offer them a boxful of Italian hardcore records to take away and sell, or a bunch of books about some Polish miners' strike in 1912. Rubbish they haven't a hope of making money on, because if they could the promoter would have done it already.

There's always the good guys. The people in Leipzig. The promoter we did some gigs for round LA – immediately after the Japan fiasco – who made sure you got paid and was a breath of fresh air after what we'd just been through. But if you're a young band starting out and you get stuck on that circuit, then there's nowhere else to go. You're always living on a shoestring. If you stay on it you'll never make any money, and if you step off it you get accused of selling out. It's such hard work there's no chance to be creative, no hope of developing as a musician, no understanding that what you might want to do when you're 20 has changed by the time you're 35. It's boring and mundane, and you might as well work in an office 9–5. At least then you might get paid.

Stratford Mercenaries got asked to do a benefit in London. We were offered £50. I said we'd do it for £100, which would just about cover our costs. It was like getting blood out of a stone, but the promoter finally agreed. By now I was pissed off. Was I expected to spend my whole life putting my hand in my pocket just because I was performing for a good cause? What happened to having a laugh? How about we spent the money hiring a stretch limo for the night and turned up at the benefit in that? That would really mess with people's expectations. Gary was tempted, but we both knew the limo would get trashed. Safer to hire a battered old van as usual, and push it if need be.

So we did the benefit, and the place was packed. There was another band playing who had no money at all. They'd driven up from Cornwall, and they'd put every penny they had in their broken-down old van. They got paid £25. Their singer was almost in tears, because they were playing in Leeds the next day, and they hadn't the money to get there. So I told him to ask the promoter for another £10. He did. And the promoter said no.

I knew the guy, so I called him over. *Go on,* I said, *give them another £10.*

I can't do that, it's a benefit.

Yeah, but it wouldn't be a benefit if they hadn't played, and they've come all the way from Cornwall. Help them out.

Well, I've offered them some records they can sell.

And that was his bottom line. If they couldn't put records in the petrol tank, that wasn't his problem. This was everything I hated about DIY. Punk had been about something better than this.

I had a word with Gary. Stratford Mercenaries gave them the cash instead.

TB

Even when I'd been in Crass, with all the screaming and shouting at gigs, I'd sometimes strain my throat so much I'd cough up blood. So although it was happening again on the tour of the US and Japan, I wasn't too concerned. I just put it down to being the singer in a punk band, and presumed it would clear up when I got back home. But it didn't. I started losing weight, and feeling tired all the time. So I went to the doctor. He took some samples, sent them off, and came back with a diagnosis. I had TB.

I had no idea how serious this was. TB belonged in the past, to people of my Nan's generation or earlier, who called it consumption. It had nothing to do with punk. Even when the doc gave me a prescription for a six month course of antibiotics, and warned me to be sure I finished the course, that if I didn't I'd just make the bug stronger, I didn't really get it. As for the possible side effects, the bright orange urine, the mood swings, and the tunnel vision he talked about might affect other people, but I was sure I'd be fine. And – what was that? I mustn't drink?!? Hmmm. We'll see about that.

I took the prescription to the chemist in North Weald, who'd known me for years. He read through the prescription and shook his head. *Listen,* he said. *You go out tonight and have a big celebration, because you've got a long six months coming up.* And suddenly it hit me. This was real, it was serious, and it was happening to me.

The next six months were a heavy old time. We couldn't tour, because although I looked ok, I was constantly exhausted. Lying round doing nothing at all was sometimes enough to wear me out, so gigging was out of the question. Even on good days, life was hard. And what made it even harder was that a couple of weeks before I'd gone to the doctor, I'd got myself an English bull terrier pup.

We'd gone to a breeder in south London. It had been easy to find the house: it had a bull terrier sign on the wall, bull terrier gnomes in the garden, the door knocker was an English bull terrier, and when the bloke came to the door he looked like an English bull terrier too. I'd picked the smallest pup there was, and called her Oscar, but even a small bull terrier pup has energy to burn, and Oscar didn't stop. Because of the TB I was tired and exhausted anyway, and with the mood swings kicking in as well, taking her for a walk was sometimes more than I could handle. Jona would come home from work and find me sitting on the sofa in tears of frustration.

My emotions were all over the shop, but the antibiotics were doing their job, and I made bloody sure I took them. I wanted to be sure they worked, so I didn't drink either. It wasn't as if I went to the pub a lot, but when I did drag myself out there I drank non-alcoholic lager. Recovery was long and slow. Although I managed to get up on stage for a gig in London just before Christmas, it knocked the stuffing out of me. I looked ok, and I felt much better, but my energy levels were really low, and I got tired way more easily than I liked. It was frustrating. We only managed a handful of gigs through the following year, but eventually I was back to something like full health. By the start of 2000 I was ready to go out on tour again, and we lined up a string of dates in the US for the spring.

I was really looking forward to going. And then it all went wrong.

A couple of days before the tour I went out for a drink down the pub with my mates. At the end of the night I walked back along the railway track to Jona's, like I always did, jumped over the fence, slipped, and heard a loud *crack!* as I fell. When I tried to get up, I couldn't put any weight on my leg. I shouted for help, but no one came, so I gritted my teeth, crawled across the field, and hobbled home. Maybe it was just a sprain. Maybe it would be all right in the morning ...

It wasn't. I'd broken my ankle. Next afternoon I was down the hospital, getting my leg put in plaster. I couldn't believe it – I'd only just got my health back and now I was on crutches. And what about the tour? I phoned Gary. He came over and we talked things through. I wanted to do the tour, but I warned him I'd need looking after. *You'll have to buy my cigarettes for me, and get my beers, because I can't!* He was fine with that, bless him, so I did a three week tour of the US on crutches, and watched the world from the back of the van.

I can tell you now that doing a tour on crutches isn't easy. I'd been determined not to let my injury stop me gigging, but determination only gets you so far. Pretty quickly I got to the point where I realised what I was doing was stupid. How far was I going to take this martyrdom? Being in Stratford Mercenaries still had its fun moments, and it had taken me to the US and it got me to Japan, but we weren't making a living. We weren't writing new material, and we'd never brought in a brass section and keys. Much as I loved meeting people and being abroad, this wasn't building into the musical career I'd hoped for.

The crunch came in Chicago. The guy driving the van – Rob – was a nice young geezer, interested in music and literature. We'd talk about jazz, and Walt Whitman, or listen to some Joni Mitchell, and we had hours to do this, what with me being on crutches and stuck in the van. So we were chatting in Chicago, while the others explored the city or found a local bar, and he asked me *How long do you think you can do this for?* I really didn't know, but I knew I had to make a hard decision, one that I'd been avoiding for a while. I asked him what he'd do, in my position. He thought for a moment. *If I wasn't enjoying something I wouldn't do it.* And that was the nail in the coffin, right there.

So by the end of the first week of the tour, I knew what I was going to do. I just didn't tell anyone. The tour trundled on, but I was just ticking off the days. We still had some good times, though. After the Pittsburgh gig we went off to a karaoke bar, thinking it would be a bit of a laugh. It was serious stuff: there were over a hundred people there, singing Frank Sinatra and the like, and doing it really well. I decided I was going to have a go. I looked at the list of songs, and chose 'Alfie' by Cilla Black. That would sound great with my cracked old grainy voice!

My turn comes, and I limp over to the stage. Now, in the States, if you've broken your leg they give you the big wooden Long John Silver crutches. The little metal NHS ones with a hand grip and an upper arm support, like I had, are for people crippled from birth. Throw in the fact I was wearing kung-fu trousers, with a black sock over my plaster so it didn't look like I had a broken ankle, and the people in the karaoke bar didn't look at me and see an injured punk singer at all. In their minds, I'm Tiny Tim.

I sing the song, and at one point – for effect – I stand on my good leg and raise my arms and my crutches in the air. The place goes wild, clapping and cheering. What a brave little English cripple I am! The woman running the night was in tears. Gary and Phil just laughed till they cried. When we left, they gave me a recording of my song as a memento. I listened to it over and over. It didn't sound bad at all. At last I had proof I didn't just have to shout along to three-chord thrash. For me, that was one of the highlights of the tour.

After three weeks in the back of the van, driving round America, after all the effort and the discomfort and the struggling round venues on crutches, I came back home with just $20 to my name. It wasn't even enough for a night out down the pub. I was so furious I took it into the back garden at Coopersale and burnt it. Then I phoned Gary and told him I quit. We were supposed to do a gig at the Garage in London, and then go on to Europe, but I couldn't do it. Gary said *I had a feeling that was coming.* He tried to persuade me to change my mind, but he knew I wouldn't, and he understood why. So did Phil. There were no hard feelings. They did the tour anyway, as a three-piece with Gary on vocals, and when they came home I asked him how they'd done.

Igs, it was awful. You'd have been on the first bus home. One gig we were sitting round an oil drum fire in someone's back garden in the rain, drinking soup out of old baked bean tins.

If even Gary wasn't enjoying life on the road, I was well off out of it. It was time to settle down, and give normal life a try.

Coopersale

When I moved into Coopersale from Dial House, it took me two or three years to stop feeling homesick. That's the truth. It wasn't easy for Jona, but there wasn't anything I could do about it. Dial House had been such a huge part of my life, and I'd been involved in so much while I was there, that leaving was a real wrench. A lot of my spirit was there. It wasn't just the people I missed, it was the house itself. It was the hornbeam tree up the road, or the way the sunlight filtered through the willow tree and fell across my bed. It was the walks I'd go on, and lifting the latch to open the door when I got home. It was sitting at the kitchen table.

So moving took some getting used to. I'd spent all those years out in the middle of nowhere, and now I was living in a mid-terrace house, in a close, on a new estate. There was some woodland and a train line – the same one that ran past Dial House – across the road, but there wasn't the sense of space. I'd been used to having my own room, and no neighbours, just fields stretching out in all directions, and a massive garden where I could sit and carve wood if I felt like it. I loved Jona, and I was really happy, but it felt strange to meet Pen and Gee in Epping for a coffee and then go our separate ways. And Jona had a mortgage – did this mean that I'd sold out?

I'd moved, but I wasn't settled. Then one day I was over at Dial House, visiting. Normally I'd stay for hours, sitting chatting at the kitchen table, but on this particular day I left way earlier than I'd intended. I wanted to go home. Home to

Coopersale, and home to Jona. I'd finally got my head round it. All I'd had to do was give it time.

We lived a pretty frugal life, me and Jona. I relied on the cheques from Southern to be able to pay my way. I'd hand some of it over to her to cover my share of the mortgage, and I'd keep the rest. Even in a good year, it wasn't a lot of cash, but that didn't matter. Money was never something I'd had a lot of. I had a place to live, I'd bought a piano I could write tunes on, and I had a dog. When I hadn't got TB, or a broken leg, everything was fine.

I always kept in contact with Pen and Gee. If I wasn't on tour I'd pop round to Dial House, or go down to the jazz club in Stoke Newington. It was called the Vortex, and it was a nice little smoky place to go, upstairs in a rickety old building, with some great musicians. Most of the time I'd just hang out, but when Pen asked me if I wanted to do some spoken word, I gave it a go. I talked while the musicians improvised on some Coltrane track. It sounded pretty good. When I got asked to play a punk festival in Milton Keynes shortly after I'd left Stratford Mercenaries, I knew exactly what I wanted to do.

This time it wasn't just going to be three-chord thrash with guitar and bass and drums. I was getting a decent fee, so I could afford to pay a proper band. I got the brass section and the keyboard player from the Vortex in so we'd have a different sound. We rehearsed and it went well. We did the gig and I loved it. Even if I never did it again – and who was to say I wouldn't? – I knew now it could work. We came off stage and I was so happy I was in tears. After all those years of waiting, I'd finally done a show the way I wanted.

I settled into life in Coopersale. I wasn't in a band anymore, so I just took things easy. I walked the dog, or wandered over to Dial House, or Jona and I drove over to visit my mum. I'd show Jona all the places I'd hung out when I'd been growing up in Dagenham, and we often ended up walking the dog down by the Thames at Rainham, where everything still washed up on the shore. While Oscar hunted out tennis balls, I collected driftwood. I took it back home and made a few bits and pieces of furniture out of it, which brought in a few quid, but it was just a bit of a hobby, nothing more. Mainly I was just hanging out. Being happy. Looking for a new direction, but not too hard. The long-running battle with BT came to a head, and was found in our favour. The courts decided Pen and Gee could stay in Dial House, which was a great relief to us all. There were no more meetings to organise, no more campaigns to run. We could all relax at last.

I started going to a pub round the corner in Coopersale, called the Garnon Bushes. In next to no time I'd got to know the locals, and I was picking up casual work. I'd give pretty much anything a go. I did a couple of months as a plumber's mate, bending pipes and soldering, and then this guy called John asked if I'd give him a hand collecting photocopier machines, taking them to a place in Ashford to be cleaned up, and delivering them back to the firms. He could only pay £20 a day, which wasn't a lot, but he was a good old boy, and I liked him, so I gave it a go. We spent all day in the van, he was a courteous driver, he wasn't in a rush, and he was happy to have a couple of drinks when we got home. Before long I was doing a job or two a week with him.

Then one day we went out to Reading to deliver a machine. It was our first day in a new van with a tail lift, which meant we didn't have to lift the machines on and off, so it was going to be a breeze! We're driving down the M4 and the van starts drifting from lane to lane. John was lighting a fag – he smoked like a bloody chimney – and he didn't seem to have noticed.

You're drifting a bit, John.

Am I?

Next thing, he's drifting across all three lanes. We miss a Volvo with a family in it by inches. *What the fuck's going on??* He tells me he's seeing four of everything, and I tell him he'd best pull over. So he swings over onto the hard shoulder. We're flying down it, doing 85 mph. I'm not joking. I looked at the speedo, and I'll never forget it. Posts and trees are whizzing past my ear. *Bang!* The wing mirror goes. *Fucking hell!*

Now I'm shouting and screaming at him, because I don't want to die on the M4. Not for £20 a day. John pulls back out off the hard shoulder just before a junction, speeds down the slip road, straight across the roundabout at the bottom, back up the slip road and on to the M4 again. I'm thinking *I've got to knock him out.* I don't drive, so I'll just have to hit him, grab the wheel, and hope for the best. It's not much of a plan, but I'm considering it. Just then I see the colour come back into his face, and his eyes focus, and he slows down, starts driving normally again, and pulls over. *Sorry,* he says. *I'm diabetic. My blood sugar must have gone wrong. It's not a big deal.*

Not a big deal, John? That was terrifying! We nearly fucking died! Don't take it to heart. I don't normally do that.

We delivered the machine and I made him take me home, and I didn't once let him go over 60. Back in the Bushes I found out John was well-known for not taking his medication, because he didn't think he needed it. I never worked for him again.

Two or three years later I was in Belgium with Jona. We were going to drive to Holland, and I went to get in the car and I couldn't. It was a lovely sunny day, the birds were chirping in the trees, and suddenly I had this flashback to the day on the M4 and just burst into tears. Jona had to promise me she'd drive really slowly, and she'd tell me everything she was doing *I'm looking in the mirror, Steve. It's clear. I'm pulling out now, it's ok* and even then I didn't stop being scared till the journey was over. It's strange how things come back and bite you on the arse when you don't expect them.

Anyway, after finishing with John I got a bit of work helping out a bloke who was a gravedigger. Then I did some silver service, setting out tables for weddings, which was ok. The boss was a young Thatcherite with more money than sense, but the way I saw it, a job was a job. Then we went to Chingford.

Chingford screams of money, but it has no taste. We're at the house, and they've got the marquee and the big potted plants and the Rolls Royce sitting on the drive, and I'm setting out the table, measuring everything with a ruler so it's all in line and nice and square, and the bride-to-be walks in. She's a real Essex footballer's wife. And she's wearing a pink boob tube with *Punk Bitch* on it, in sequins. I could deal with working for Tories, I could handle menial work, but that boob tube was the straw that broke the camel's back. I'd *been* a punk. I walked.

Next I helped someone from the Bushes, selling bankrupt stock on the market, and then I got a job with a guy called No-no. He got the name because, when he disagreed with you, he'd go *No. No. No, no, no, it's like this*. Anyway, I was drinking in the pub and he said *You're a big strong boy, ain't ya? Fancy some work? £60 a day. Wear some old clothes.*

No-no had this rig, which looked like a mini oil rig. It drove a length of pipe down into the ground, then you'd attach another length of pipe to that, and so on, till you'd gone down-maybe 50 metres. Then you collected the soil samples, and sent them off to the contractor so they could see what the ground was like, whether it was sand or clay, stable or not. I did that for four months or so, in all weathers, and it was filthy, full-on work, with heavy machinery and heavy lengths of pipe. We started at seven in the morning and worked through till four in the afternoon, and then we went down the pub.

I'd have a couple of pints and head home. No-no would stay out drinking. He'd be out till ten at night, and he'd still be groggy first thing in the morning. I was thinking this had to be dangerous, being as we were working round fast-moving machinery, but I shouldn't have worried about No-no. I was the one who nearly got my fingers chopped off.

I wasn't concentrating, I was tired and I'd had too many drinks the night before, and I only just got my fingers out of the way before the pile driver slammed down. It would have taken them clean off, no question. I'd been a split second away from being maimed for life, I'd never have played piano again, and because I was working cash in hand, I had no insurance either. What was I thinking? No-no could find some other mug to take my place. This wasn't worth it. I'd rather be skint.

All these different jobs ran over four or five years. I wasn't having anything to do with music, I was just enjoying a quiet, steady life without getting stuck in a regular job, which suited me fine.

And then there was the year where it seemed I hardly ever had my suit off, because I was just going to one funeral after another. A good friend of mine had had enough and stood in front of an express train, some one else died of cancer, and another was found sitting in front of the telly, glass of beer in hand. In all I went to about nine funerals that year, including Deano's, a lovely young bloke from North Weald who was killed in an horrific car accident. This was just before Mothers' Day, and the following weekend me and Jona went to see Mum. She'd been having problems with her breathing for ages, but she wouldn't go to the doctor's. *He didn't look after Stan properly. And he's a darkie.* And she wouldn't see another doctor either.

Mum was very down. Even telling her I was off to a funeral the next day – and Mum loved a good funeral – didn't cheer her up. I'd seen her in moods before, of course, but this one was different. She didn't say much, just sat there listlessly stroking Oscar's ears. We asked if there was anything we could get her and she said she wouldn't mind a bit of fruit, so me and Jona went and got her a big bowlful. After about an hour we got up to leave and I said to Mum *Are you sure you're alright?* and Mum said *Yeah, I'm fine, I'm just in a funny mood, I'll be alright, Coronation Street's on later.* So with that we kissed her and left.

Driving home, watching the old familiar streets slide past, I had this strange feeling that Mum was on the way out, that she'd sort of given up, and I mentioned it to Jona, and she said she'd been thinking that too.

The next day I went to Deano's funeral, and went on to the Bushes for the wake. While I was there Jona rang me to tell me Mum was in hospital. Carol had popped round to see her and found her lying on the floor.

The following afternoon we drove down to Oldchurch to see Mum. I'd been assured that her condition wasn't life-threatening, but when I walked in the ward and saw her lying there, hooked up to a machine, not talking, not conscious, with a mask over her mouth, I knew that was it. My mum was dying.

The doctor was placating my niece and my sister, telling them that Mum wasn't in any pain, was in a comfortable condition, and afterwards I pulled him aside and quietly asked him if it was best for us to go home and wait for the phone call. He looked me right in the eyes, gently squeezed my shoulder for a moment and said *Yes.*

So Jona dropped us all off at Whitebarn Lane and then went on to Coopersale while the rest of us waited and talked about what to do if Mum was really, you know … etc. The next morning, there not having been a phone call, me and Carol headed for our respective homes, and I decided to go via Dagenham Dock station which was a longer journey but a bit more scenic, taking me past my childhood haunts. By the time I reached Coopersale I was busting for a piss – I mean my teeth were floating – and of course when I got in the phone was ringing. I picked it up and it was Auntie Dee in tears telling me that Mum had died about 9.30, just about the time I was at Dagenham Dock funnily enough, but embarrassingly, dreadfully, all I could think was *Hurry up and tell me so I can go and piss*.

And with the relief came the realisation and bewilderment, no tears, just a strange sense of *What am I meant to do in this situation?* I walked from room to room but couldn't settle to anything, Jona was at work and wouldn't be in for ages, so I thought *Fuck it* and went round the Bushes where I sat quietly with a lime juice and soda water and thought about everything and nothing.

It was a quiet funeral. Just family really, and a few of Mum's neighbours. For me, it was the closing of a door, not only because of Mum dying, but also because with her gone there'd be no reason for me to go to Dagenham again. And as I walked along Whitebarn Lane in front of the hearse, I quietly and privately said goodbye not only to my mum, but also these streets that I'd come out of.

We buried Mum with Stan at Rippleside, and a couple of days later we went back to No.3 and cleared her stuff out. I've never been back since. In a strange way it didn't really touch me, Mum's death, but then I'd made my peace with her long before, and I'd known it was coming, which somehow made it easier to accept. And she'd had a good, long life. It was the ones that were cut short I found harder to deal with.

In August 2005, Pen turned up on my doorstep and told me John Loder was dead. I went through to the kitchen and cried. I knew he'd had a brain tumour, and the last time I'd seen him – when he'd come over to Dial House earlier in the year – you could tell he wasn't well, but it was still a shock. And it seemed so wrong. John had been such an important part of my life – and of so many others – for so long, that it was hard to imagine life without him. He'd nurtured Crass, I'd bumped into him on Fugazi tours when I was in Schwartzeneggar, he'd helped Stratford Mercenaries. If you were working with John you knew he'd always support you, but he'd never seek control. He'd just stand back and let you get on with your music.

His funeral was at the crematorium in Golders Green. There were quite a few people there. It was our last chance to show John how much his loyalty to the bands on his label had meant to us. We were all waiting outside for the hearse to arrive, and then this little red delivery van that used to pick up the records from Southern came round the corner, with Ian MacKaye of Fugazi at the wheel. It screeched to a halt outside the crematorium, Ian opened the back doors, and there was John's coffin. He was doing things his way right to the end, and it raised a few smiles among the tears. Ian and myself and a few others carried the coffin in on our shoulders. It was bloody heavy. As we walked past Joy I told her *I think I know where our royalties went – this coffin's full of change*.

It was a good funeral, in so far as these things are. A fitting send-off. Afterwards, Pen and Gee came back to Coopersale and we went down the Bushes and drank a few bottles of wine. We chinwagged and talked about old times, swapping memories of John, how he'd been on those first visits we made to the studio, or how he'd sit at the side of the stage watching bands, with a big grin on his face. We laughed, and we cried, and we mourned him.

He'd loved music, and he changed our lives, and we were really going to miss him.

Shepherd's Bush

When Jona told me she wanted to move out of Coopersale, I didn't like the idea at all. *Move out of Essex, the best county in the world? No way! I'm Dagenham born and bred, I'm staying!* and so on. But once I got off my high horse and thought about it, I realised things had changed. What was there left for me here, really?

Mum was dead, I didn't see Carol much, my drinking buddies in Coopersale were just drinking buddies. My only real ties to Essex were Pen and Gee, and I'd keep in contact with them wherever I went. On top of that, London was encroaching, and we weren't in the country anymore. Houses were being built on what had been farmland; every now and then you'd see a burnt-out car. If moving was a big deal, it was because it scared me, but I'd moved before. If I could handle leaving Dial House I could look at a few houses. We might even find something good.

So we looked at a place in Lincolnshire. It was cheap, but too remote. We scouted round Cambridge. We didn't like it. Then we tried Norfolk. We came over Acle bridge, and the view was of marshland and windmills and the sails of boats gliding between the fields, and right there and then Jona and I fell in love all over again. We both knew we could live here.

It took us about a year to move. Someone bought the house in Coopersale, so we rented a place up here, in a little village called Hickling, and we looked for a home of our own. Jona was working, and I thought I might write books, or do some wood carving, or maybe work a few hours in a bar. A cottage came up in Sea Palling, and it was perfect, so at the start of 2007 we put an offer in, it got accepted, and we got ready to move.

In early March, while we were still in Hickling, a mate phoned saying he'd had a phone call from someone wanting to know if I'd be up for a gig. I wasn't keen. What sprang to mind was being wheeled out to do 'Owe Us', given a pint and a packet of fags and sent on my way. I hadn't performed since Milton Keynes, and I'd moved to Norfolk with no intention of doing anything musical. But eventually I was persuaded to give this bloke John Esplen a call.

He was planning an all-dayer at Brixton Academy with Conflict, the Damned, and all the usual suspects. I said I'd think about it, meaning I'd forget about it. A couple of hours later the phone rings again and it's John's colleague Chris trying to sell me the gig. Would I do something like I did at Milton Keynes? I said I'd give it some thought, wondering why I couldn't be left to live a quiet life away from it all, and went down the local pub.

There were these two Hickling blokes there, big old farmer types. Spinksy and Bealo. I must have been looking thoughtful, because they asked me what was up.

I've just had this phone call from a guy offering me a gig and I don't want to do it.

Why don't you do it?

What's it got to do with you?

Well, if you don't do it you're just going to sit round here moaning about it. Music's what you do, ain't it?

Yeah, but it's been years, and I could be crap.

Bealo looked at Spinksy.

Well, your music is crap, ain't it?

That evening, a couple of friends popped round, and Jona mentioned the gig. By then I'd decided I wasn't doing it. I told them the past was the past and I didn't want to trot out the same songs, yet again. Al and Sadie were outraged, and Sadie decided she'd put me right.

What's your favourite book, Steve?

Saturday Night and Sunday Morning.

How many times have you read it?

I don't know. Loads.

And you still enjoy it every time you read it?

Yeah.

Well, why isn't this the same?

It was a good point. I sat there thinking. If I was going to do this gig, I had to do something new. Something I hadn't done before. And then it hit me. I said *I'll do Feeding from start to finish, just like it is on the album. Unannounced. It'll blow everyone away.* We all thought this would be great, so I phoned Chris and agreed I'd do the gig. Then I told him what I had in mind. The line went quiet. After what felt like a very long time he said *I'll call you back in a little while.*

Forty minutes later he phones me back and says *You're not playing Brixton, you're doing two nights at Shepherd's Bush. Everyone's into it, everyone's agreed, everyone's up for it.*

And that's literally how it happened. Six months later we did the gig.

I got the band together. Two guitars, bass, drums, Sadie on vocals. Then I brought the brass section from the Vortex in, like I'd done at Milton Keynes. We weren't going to try to be Crass, we were going to do our take on *Feeding*, and celebrate it. In some ways, the germ of that idea came from a Stratford Mercenaries tour of the US, when we'd played LA and the promoter took us to a bar where 'Owe Us' was on the jukebox between tracks from Frank Sinatra and Tony Bennett. I'd put all three on. It was the first time I'd listened to 'Owe Us' in years, and I'd been surprised to rediscover just how good it was. Now I wanted other people to be reminded of that too.

We practised and we practised and we practised. Vom the drummer was fantastic. He learned how to drum just like Pen did, which let me know just where I was in a song. It was six months of hard work, but musically it was coming together. In just about every other way, things were tearing apart.

I was completely unprepared for the hornet's nest that the news of the gig stirred up. It seemed as though everyone who'd ever been in the scene had something to say. Loads of people were excited about the show, but there were also loud voices making clear they were against it. Stuff was being posted on websites and on the Crass forum accusing me of destroying everything Crass had ever been. It was a nightmare. I can take criticism, like anyone can, but I hadn't expected the spite and personal attacks that came my way from people who didn't even know me.

I don't do things lightly. I agonise over things, sometimes more than I should, because I don't want to hurt people. I want to keep everyone happy, and even though I know that can't be done, it doesn't stop me trying. The vitriol surrounding the Shepherd's Bush show reduced me to tears. My self-confidence took a kicking and I wasn't sleeping well. Some days I thought it would be best to just jack the whole thing in, because however much support the people round me gave, I felt very alone. I was the one who'd been in Crass, not them, and I felt I had this enormous responsibility not to let anyone down.

It caused trouble among the members of Crass, too. Pen wasn't happy about his material being used in a commercial venue, for example. But we could talk and meet and disagree, and talk again, and do it all as old friends, and that was something I could deal with. The debate was sometimes quite heated, but in the end Pen came round, which was incredibly important to me. I'd do the show now, and take the consequences.

There's probably nothing I can say that will ever change the minds of people who still believe that doing the gig was wrong. But what pissed me off was this idea that it was ok for someone else to perform Crass songs – Jeffrey Lewis, say, or some band in Manchester doing a cover – but me, who used to be in the band and was the lead vocalist and actually wrote some of the songs, I shouldn't. The fact we would be playing in a commercial venue kept getting thrown at me. Well, show me one that isn't. What we got was great sound, good lighting, wonderful visuals, and professional security. We missed out on socks over the mics and dodgy wiring. Where's the problem??

There are still idiots who expect me to be like I was when I recorded *Feeding*. Well, I'm not. And nor is the world. I'm 50 years old. And I'm not spending my days starving and sleeping on floors and grabbing leftover food in motorway services so other people can feel good about me. Not any more. When someone calls the Shepherd's Bush shows *Feeding of the Egos*, as if everyone involved was doing it for some kind of glory, then fuck them. They know nothing. I won't accept that. I wanted people to come along and get the same shot in the arm Crass gave them back in the day. I wanted people who'd been too young to see us have a chance to hear the songs. I wanted people to remember how we'd tried to change the world. And I wanted to show the members of Crass just how fucking good we'd been.

The people who said it was all about money ignored all that. When we got up on that stage we were determined to do the best show we could. We were taking it seriously, but we were going to have some fun too. Whatever happened, we'd give people something they'd remember.

And I think we pulled it off.

I remember looking out from the stage and seeing people with big fat grins on their faces. Everyone really really enjoying it. I'd been worried I might fuck this whole thing up, but now I knew I wasn't, and I wanted to smile back, but I was performing and trying to do it properly, so I couldn't. And that first night, when Alice sang the vocals on 'Big A Little A', on her birthday – her first performance ever, to 2000 people – it put a lump in my throat so big I could hardly sing. And suddenly the audience took it up and sang along with her, and all I wanted to do was shout at them *You beautiful bastards!*

After the show I went to have a pint in the bar, and there were people there I hadn't seen for ages. Bealo – who'd given me a kick up the arse when I went down the pub that first day – was there with a couple of people from Hickling, so I said *Hallo* to them and chatted for a while. But then I excused myself to catch up with everyone else. Or at least try. One of the first people I saw was Petesy who used to be in Stalag 17. They performed with Crass when we went to Belfast and I hadn't seen him since. I saw Sid and Zilla from Rubella Ballet. Colin Latter re-formed Flux especially for the show, which I was incredibly moved by. I wanted to go up and say *Thank you* to every single person who'd come along. People had come from all over, and I just couldn't thank them enough. The whole weekend was a great chance to catch up, to have a chin-wag and remember the good old days, to find out what people are doing and where their lives have taken them now.

On so many levels those two days were so moving and so emotional. And then on the Monday morning we got up, and it was all over. We'd been like a family, all the people who'd worked towards making the shows happen, and now we were heading our separate ways. Jona and I walked past the Empire to catch the Tube, and the letters proclaiming the gig were already down. Life was moving on and *The Feeding Of The 5000* was history. A few short hours later I was back in the pub in Hickling, with Bealo taking the piss out of me, buying him a pint and still getting walloped at pool.

It had been an intense six months. Some people had a genuine grievance with what I did, some just had a pop because that's all they ever do. But I think it was important to do those Shepherd's Bush shows, and when I look back at that weekend I'm proud of having done them. Absolutely proud.

Betrayal

On New Year's Eve, 2008, I was told something I simply couldn't believe. So I did what people tend to do when they're given bad news: I shot the messenger. I was drunk at the time and I went up the fucking wall. The person involved won't tell me what I said, and I can't remember, but there was one thing I was sure about: they had to be lying.

Then they showed me the proof.

One person – who'd never been a member of Crass – had registered himself as being the writer of all Crass' songs, and instructed his record company – who had no reason to suspect that what he'd told them was untrue – to collect whatever money was due.

John Loder had registered the members of Crass as writers of our songs, but since Southern was a record company first and foremost, rather than a publishing company, this wasn't really something that was actively pursued. While we got paid for record sales through Southern, other income – from live performance, or from digital download as technology moved on – was effectively up for grabs. So someone we knew decided to make it theirs.

It couldn't have been a mistake. This person had to fill in forms, and name the songs, and sign to say he wrote them. I know this because, since this all came to light, I've joined PRS and MCPS myself, to safeguard my income. I get less money now than I did when Crass just split the cash equally eight ways, but I prefer it because I know where I stand. And because now this can't happen again.

There's no innocent explanation. *Perhaps he did it to save the money for you?* Saving it for himself, more like. And if he was, then why didn't he tell us he was doing it? How come there's been no apology from him? How come he hasn't spoken to Allison at Southern? How come none of us in Crass have heard from him? Because there hasn't been a fucking peep.

The sad truth is that Colin, my supposed brother, and best mate, had been ripping us off. While he had his arm round my shoulder, telling me what great pals we were, he was taking money out of my fucking pocket. Even on the stairs backstage at Shepherd's Bush, when I was comforting him while he cried because he missed the old times, he knew he was getting the money for the Crass songs I'd just performed. And that deceit, that betrayal really hurts.

I'd always made excuses for Colin. Said he was a lovable rogue. But he lied to Crass, and he lied to Cherry Red, and he took other people's money and claimed it for his own. There's no excuse for that. You just don't do it. He really broke my heart. The clincher is that over the past two years, since all this came to light, I've heard nothing from him. I put myself in his shoes and I know if there was an honest explanation, one that would save thirty years of friendship, I'd have been straight on the phone.

It's not about the money. Cherry Red had collected it in good faith, and when they found out Col had lied, they paid every penny back. But Colin chose stealing from his mates over friendship, and the silence from him since this whole thing came to light has been deafening. I don't know how he'll ever hold his head up in public again. I know I'll never speak to him. I'll have nothing to do with him. You don't ever steal from your own.

Coda

Since those gigs in Shepherd's Bush, life has just trundled on. I live out here on the Norfolk coast with Jona, in a small village, where the pace of life is like Essex fifty years ago. On a clear night I can walk out into the garden and see a sky ablaze with stars. And I can always hear the sea. We've a lifeboat in the village, an independent one that's not funded by the RNLI or anybody else, but which relies entirely on donations. I met some of the crew down the pub not long after I moved here, and I learnt a lot about what they do. It set me thinking.

Every band I've been in has always done benefits, so after Shepherd's Bush I knew I'd give some of the money away. This time I decided I wanted it to go to something I knew, where I could directly see how it was used. So I donated £1000 to the lifeboat, and the crew spent it on new lifejackets. Then they took me out on the boat to show me what they did. We got to talking over a pint later, and they said *Why don't you join?*

It's not the world's biggest commitment – you give what time you can, and if that's fifteen minutes a week, that's fine. But I got more and more into it. After six months of learning chart work and what being in a boat means, I'm actually on the crew. A full-time member of the Sea Palling lifeboat crew. Every Thursday evening and every Sunday we go out on the sea and practise. We don't get paid. We're all volunteers, and we do it for the love of it. If there's a life to be saved, we'll be out there to save it. That's what we do, and I'm very proud to be part of it.

I never imagined I'd end up out on the North Sea as part of a lifeboat crew, but then my life's not really taken a conventional route, has it? I've always followed my nose, and I suppose I always will. If I need money I do washing-up at the local pub, or help out in the kitchens, and I'm happy with that. It's been a strange old journey to get here, but I like where I am.

In the world outside Sea Palling, Pen's been busy re-mastering all the old Crass material, bringing it into the digital age. Gee's been tweaking the artwork that went with it, too. It got so condensed on the CD format that half of it was missing and you couldn't read what was there. Now you can. I love the changes, but it's a matter of personal taste. Not all the old members of Crass agree, but you wouldn't expect us all to see things the same way, would you? We spent seven years together, over twenty-five years ago, living in each other's pockets, being part of something very very special. Our lives have changed since then. Our passion for what we did remains the same. We've all got opinions, and we're not afraid to voice them. But then we never were. We'll be arguing the toss about something for as long as we're lucky enough to draw breath. Which is as it should be.

We won't ever re-form. I used to wonder if maybe we might just get together for one huge celebration of what we were, but I know it'll never happen. I can't say I'll never get up on a stage again myself, though. I've a few plans, a couple of irons in the fire. And I've learnt never to say never.

I look back and I've been lucky. Sometimes I think my biggest skill has been to find myself in the right place at the right time. Where would I have been if Mr. Stewart hadn't encouraged me to read? Or if I hadn't wandered into Bristol Royal Infirmary, looking for a job? What if the Clash hadn't played Colston Hall? What would life have been like if I hadn't listened to Joe Strummer and gone away to start a band?

It's impossible to say. I might still be working as a plaster technician, or an ambulance driver, happily living in Bristol, married with a couple of kids. Instead punk happened. Up until then, I'd been curious and bored. Drifting. Punk gave me somewhere to go. Dial House gave me a home.

Right time, right place again.

I was off on the big adventure that was Crass, with Pen and Gee and the others. I called myself an anarchist then, but I think I was really an angry young man, inspired by the angry young men whose work I'd read, by Alan Sillitoe and Barry Hines, hoping to inspire others in turn. Part of the next generation of rebellion, passing the torch along.

And it never stops. I'm an angry middle-aged man now, and one day I'll most likely be angry and old. It's all still an adventure. Crass had its time and its place, and then that time was over and life rolled on. I've been lucky enough to go all over the world, come back more or less in one piece, and still be sitting on a swinging bench in the garden at just the right moment. I've had some fun. I've got to know some incredible people. I'm really happy. I wore black for years, but life was always full of colour.

And long may that go on.